THE ALGORITHMIC AGE OF PERSONALITY

AFRICAN HUMANITIES AND THE ARTS

Series Editors
Kenneth Harrow and Bob Cancel

The African Humanities and the Arts series mirrors the agenda of the African Studies Center at Michigan State University and its commitment to the study of Africa. The series examines all aspects of cultural research—including art, literature, film, and religion.

THE ALGORITHMIC AGE OF PERSONALITY

AFRICAN LITERATURE AND CANCEL CULTURE

James Yékú

MICHIGAN STATE UNIVERSITY PRESS | *East Lansing*

Michigan State University Press
East Lansing, Michigan 48823-5245

Library of Congress Cataloging-in-Publication Data
Names: Yeku, James, author.
Title: The algorithmic age of personality : African literature and cancel culture / James Yékú.
Description: East Lansing : Michigan State University Press, 2025. |
Series: African humanities and the arts | Includes bibliographical references and index.
Identifiers: LCCN 2024038535 | ISBN 9781611865332 (paperback) | ISBN 9781609177836 | ISBN 9781628955460
Subjects: LCSH: African literature—Social aspects. | African literature—Appreciation. | Authors, African—Public opinion. | Literature and society—Africa. | Cancel culture. | Social media.
Classification: LCC PL8010 .A486 2025 | DDC 809/.896—dc23/eng/20240926
LC record available at https://lccn.loc.gov/2024038535

Cover design by David Drummond

Visit Michigan State University Press at *www.msupress.org*

For Ken Harrow, who fought for many good things
and noble causes. And for this book.

Contents

Acknowledgments

In writing this book, I have depended mostly on the wisdom and generosity of many kind people. I am deeply grateful to them, especially to the late Ken Harrow. Ken believed in the project from the very beginning, supported it throughout peer review, and ensured a book on cancel culture was itself not canceled when the stakes became contested. It is probably the case that this was one of Ken's last fights on behalf of any manuscript and I hope this book is a befitting salute to his cherished memory. I am thankful to be able to dedicate the book to Ken's exemplary scholarship and even more selfless mentorship. I am also grateful to Rhonda Cobham-Sander and Ebenezer Obadare for their contributions. Whatever shape the book has finally taken is largely due to Rhonda, who very kindly agreed to read the entire manuscript at a point when it had no evident form. Thank you, Rhonda, for all you do and for seeing this book's potential very early and breathing some vitality into it. Ebenezer Obadare has been a constant interlocutor and mentor over the years. When, in 2019, I began documenting several African literature-centered controversies and cancel culture discussions online, I constantly turned to him to make sense of things together. My unending thanks to him. I also wish to express my profound gratitude to Stephanie Newell, Madhu Krishnan, and

Adeshina Afolayan who all read the manuscript at different stages, making very helpful suggestions that have greatly enhanced the argument of the book. Nathan Suhr-Sytsma, Dotun Ayobade, and Christine Matzke—who hosted me in Bayreuth in 2022 and has since become a trusted friend and guide—were also early readers of the first couple of chapters and their suggestions have enriched the book. My sincere appreciation to all three and to the poet at St. Louis, 'Gbenga Adeoba. 'Gbenga, I have nothing but gratitude to you for your friendship, encouragement, and generous help throughout the process of getting this book out.

I have been fortunate to have solid mentors, friends, and colleagues that have shaped my thinking over the years or supported my intellectual development: Adélékè Adéẹ̀kọ́, Jumoke Verisimmo, Jennifer Hart, Paul Ugor, Carli Coetzee, Jeanne-Marie Jackson, Omolade Adunbi, Akin Adesokan, Chielozona Eze, Shola Adenekan, Kwabena Opoku-Agyemang, Saheed Aderinto, Seun Abimbola, Cajetan Iheka, Sakiru Adebayo, Uche Umezurike, David Olali, Sola Olorunyomi, Rasaq Malik, Tope Oriola, Carmen McCain, and Connor Ryan. And special thanks to Remi Raji whom I met again in Berlin and who was most gracious in supporting the book. At the University of Kansas, I am grateful to the following colleagues: Peter Ojiambo, Amal El Haimeur, Nicole Hodges Persley, Brian Rosenblum, Tony Bolden, Peter Ukpokodu, Dorthy Pennington, Liz MacGonagle, Glenn Adams, and Shawn Alexander—who, aside from reading one of the chapters, has been particularly supportive of my work at KU. As a research fellow at the Center for Advanced Internet Studies (CAIS) in Bochum, Germany, I completed the first draft of the book's manuscript in the fall of 2022. I would like to thank Michael Baurmann, the former director of the center, as well as Esther Laufer and Andrea Porsfeld for inviting me to the CAIS fellowship. I am grateful for the lively discussions I had with other CAIS fellows, particularly Moritz Cordes, Innocent and Isioma Maureen Chiluwa, Sreekanth Reddy Mukku, and Katja Baumgärtner.

Participants and audiences at four major events provided invaluable feedback as I first presented the ideas in this book. First, at the Johannes Gutenberg University of Mainz in June 2023, I would like to thank Matthias Krings for inviting me to spend a month as a CEDITRAA international guest fellow at the Institute for Anthropology and African Studies where I was privileged to have been in conversation with colleagues at the institute, including Tom Simmert, Izuu Nwankwo (now at the University of Toronto), as well as James Ogone and Patrick Oloko, also visiting around the same time. I also presented a chapter of the manuscript in November 2023 at the Afrikakolloquium at Humboldt University of Berlin (HUB) and at a weekly African literature seminar at the start of the spring term in 2024. Both of these were facilitated by the very kind Susanne Gehrmann who hosted me at HUB as an Alexander von Humboldt (AvH) Foundation Fellow from 2023 to 2024. As research for this book was generously supported by them, I want to thank the AvH Foundation for providing me with an incredible opportunity to network and conduct research in Germany for one year, and Verena Wolf for guiding me through my fellowship year. Lastly, I would also like to express my sincerest gratitude to Rachel Taylor and Abigail Branford for inviting me to the African Studies Research Seminar at the University of Oxford in February 2024, where I gave a talk on the subject of the book and received some incredibly great feedback.

It should be noted that two chapters (three and five) are expanded versions of two essays published by the *Journal of African Cultural Studies* 29 no. 3 (2017) and *Digital Scholarship in the Humanities* 36, no. 1 (2021). I would like to thank the publishers of these two journals for the permission to reprint the work. I would also like to thank the editors and the anonymous readers whose suggestions enriched my arguments. A special thank you to the editors of the African Humanities and the Arts series at MSU Press, Bob Cancel and, again, Ken Harrow who were both supportive till the end. I also want to thank the two anonymous reviewers at MSU Press for the kindness and insight of their suggestions that have made this book stronger. I thank Caitlin Tyler-Richards, who enthusiastically took on the project at first, as well as Elizabeth Demers and Liz Deegan, who stepped in later to shepherd it to the end. I am also grateful to the editorial and production team, particularly Anastasia Wraight who was super helpful throughout her work with me.

Finally, special thanks to Johannes and Vanessa Brandes who became family in Berlin, and to Kemi Yékú who gave up everything to travel with me to the German capital. Not much gets done without the solid ground of your love and support, babe. Together with Ìwàlẹwà, Ẹwàolúwa, and Tìfẹ́olúwa who arrived during our sojourn abroad, you make home a world that is charged with the grandeur of God (apologies to Hopkins). Vielen Dank meine Frau, meine Liebe!

Introduction

The morning of March 14, 2023, was moderately chilly and breezy, and it met me around Mount Oread in Lawrence, where I was pondering a research trip to Germany. That same day, hundreds of miles away and some hours ahead of the local time in Kansas, the organizers of the African Book Festival in Berlin had just decided to withdraw an invitation to the Mauritanian writer and activist Mohamedou Ould Slahi, who had been initially invited to curate their annual Africa-focused literary event in the German capital. In their estimation, Slahi's cancelation and deplatforming was necessary to keep literature rather than any controversial individual at the center of the festival. But the organizers had, in fact, bowed to pressures from a section of the German press, led by a supposedly leftist media outfit TAZ, which called out Slahi's allegedly former ties to Al-Qaeda. In response to the dismissal of Ould Slahi, the Africa Multiple Cluster of Excellence, a scientific group at the University of Bayreuth, released a statement signed by some of its leading academics and global partners in which they condemned the writer's deplatforming by the festival organizers. In reference to a previous haranguing of Achille Mbembe by some German officials seeking to cancel his keynote address at the 2020 Ruhrtriennale festival due to purported anti-Semitic remarks, the Bayreuth cluster framed Slahi's treatment as yet another in a string of cultural and intellectual attacks on minority writers and scholars in Germany. Yet, in our algorithmic age, there are routine discourses of cancel culture and literary controversies that transcend the politicized barriers of a German-based festival on African literature.

At the height of a raging pandemic in 2020, for instance, I had the opportunity to make a virtual teaching presentation at a university in Canada, and a brief debate about Chimamanda Adichie's then-ongoing entanglements with the politics of free speech and cancel culture soon followed. During the Q&A session, a faculty member in the audience sought to know my approach to the continued relevance of Adichie's body of works, especially the viral TED talk, "The Danger of a Single Story,"[1] which, as I had explained in my talk, was often instrumental in classroom discussions on western stereotypes on Africa. This question was logical since the overarching framework of my talk that day was the centrality of digital media texts and social media aesthetics to my pedagogical approach to African cultural productions. But the questioner was rather specific. They inquired how I would set up a discussion on Adichie if I had transgender students seeking to cancel the feminist author from the classroom space because of the novelist's perceived equivocality and controversial stance on trans women. The question made me imagine the classroom dimensions of the Adichie debate in a similar way to how Chinua Achebe's criticism of Joseph Conrad in the late 1970s influenced future discussions of the novel *Heart of Darkness* and ensuing pedagogical decisions that consequently shaped the integration of pioneering postcolonial work, such as those of Edward Said, into undergraduate curricula. As I continued to reflect on that exchange in Canada, long after my talk, it became more obvious to me that the African literary landscape is witnessing an intensification of literary disputes and controversies. This controversial turn has been ongoing for many years and is now being amplified by the politics of big tech that privileges an infinite model of economic growth with its algorithmic cultures and commodification of literary information. Adichie's later impassioned tirade against a regime of self-censorship occasioned by cancel culture prompted my interest in the nature and function of literary controversies and outrage in the social media age, particularly how social media algorithms impact readers' reception and discussions of literary works.

Thus, this book is concerned with the problem of cancel culture and literary controversies in social media commentary discourses on African literary and cultural texts. Whether it is a 2023 South African TV miniseries such as *Unfollowed,* which aired on Showmax to provide cultural producers and entertainers with an avenue to articulate their cancel culture stories, or a Senegalese writer subjected to a cancel culture campaign because of his literary portrayal of homosexuality in a conservative Islamic society, African cultural productions and postcolonial culture industries are oftentimes constrained within a digital culture of offense and outrage.[2] Social media, with its commentary affordances, is often the contexts from which these strong emotions unfold. Cancel culture—a form of social penalty and rejection that is meant to deplatform, publicly shame, or withdraw cultural capital from popular figures or offenders—is increasingly connected, along with other controversial practices, to knowledge production and censorious political attacks, which in the context of African literature are, in fact, embedded in the institutional history of the African Literature Association itself.[3] Taking it as a toxic version of African American call-out culture that hinders social justice work, Black feminist Loretta Ross describes cancel culture as a situation in which "self-appointed guardians of political purity," believing they possess a higher moral standing or more sophisticated analyses, attempt to "expunge anyone with whom they do not perfectly agree."[4] Cancel culture's connection to call-out culture will be discussed further, but whether framed as canceling or calling out, this practice is ultimately an exercise of power and privilege, as Umut Özkırımlı describes in *Canceled: The Left Way Back from Woke*. Özkırımlı excoriates the individualism and narcissism of the radical identity politics of the social media era and its "performative outrage [that] does not advance the cause of social justice."[5]. The manifestations of cancel culture in the social frameworks of literary practices online offer insights into African literature that have scarcely been previously examined. Attentive, then, to reader practices in specifically digital environments, I am interested in this book in how controversies and cancel culture debates become manifested in social media conversations on African cultural productions and convey the social dimensions of aesthetic practices. My central argument is that we cannot think about African literary practices and their intimacies with digital modes of publishing and circulations without considering what role algorithms play in both alliance and in congealing a culture of outrage in literary conversations on African writing. Unlike other digital modes of publication and authorial curations of selves and texts, social media and blogging are the most prevalent tools of digital storytelling and cultural productions on the continent, but the design and algorithmic politics of these platforms are not sufficiently interrogated in the scholarship on African literary and cultural productions. Literary controversies and cancel culture discourses on literary prizes and festivals, as well as those on digital literary magazines in the African literary space, allow me to address this problem.

Therefore, in accordance with Frieda Ekotto and Kenneth Harrow's proposal "to reevaluate and to rearticulate new epistemologies in contemporary critical approaches," I pay close attention to the digital subjectivities and algorithmic configurations that animate the social worlds and conditions of African aesthetic forms.[6] I have organized the book into a series of different but interlacing arguments. The first is that digital culture, with its productive and circulatory mechanisms, motivates closer attention to writers' personalities as central to literary productions. The second is that African literature's current relationship to digital media publication should be understood as intensely mediated by algorithmic systems that shape reading practices on social media. These algorithms produce a culture of outrage that generates controversy, demonstrated by inflated ego tendencies that fit into the present censorious epoch of cancel culture. Accordingly, cancel culture manifests in intense debates about the ontology and social function of literature in Africa. Although the specific scope of my claims is within the framework of controversies, feuding, and scandals in and around Nigerian literary networks, particularly online but also in demotic offline spaces, there are considerable references to other areas around the African continent and its diasporic networks. There is, for instance, a similarly strong grounding in the literary networks and celebrity cultures of Kenya. Besides, I follow debates and reader responses closely in several other African digital and offline literary networks, such as those of Senegal, Uganda, Zimbabwe, and more, particularly those that allow for a fuller understanding of those two countries. Moreover, because of the transnational dimensions and publics of digital cultures, it would be difficult to call a work of this nature solely Nigerian or Kenyan as several controversies themselves take place either in reaction to or within the framework of other African literary cultures and their performance of digital celebrity. The focus on these two countries, also evident in Shola Adenekan's regional approach, is consistent with the actual uses of various digital platforms on the continent.

Kenya, Nigeria, and South Africa, for example, have some of the largest African TikTok communities of book lovers who create content to discuss or share book reviews and recommendations under the hashtag #BookTok. This makes it increasingly important to look at book culture and reading practices in these countries in relation to literary controversies within their digital spaces. Hence, I track these debates as they circulate across social media platforms, personal blogs, and other major online publications—a method that I hope becomes more pertinent to understanding the conditions under which African literature is produced today. In doing so, and building on other arguments I have made elsewhere, I hope to illustrate how digital publication informs literary production across a range of platforms, encouraging experimentation on social media and fan fiction forums, as well as rivalrous debates over literary prizes and social personae. Beyond my intimate engagement with the various literary networks analyzed, I examine how digital acts of cancelation differently shape offline reading practices, providing a framework for tracking the influence of digital debates on cultural productions. Overall, by focusing on a reception-oriented analysis of digital modes of publication, my goal is to underscore the ever more direct role of readers and the algorithmic systems they inhabit in shaping contemporary literary production and to open up new conversations in African literary studies. While connecting controversies in literary networks with pressing questions about African literature's role in the political, for example, I will develop these various arguments by addressing the longer histories of controversies in African—most particularly, but not limited to, Nigerian and Kenyan—literature. While highlighting throughout the significance of platform capitalism, algorithmic systems, and authorial brands to readerly practices, the work turns in the closing stages to how literary friendships displace rivalries to illustrate the power of community in online literary production.

To Cancel or Not to Cancel Chimamanda Adichie

The widespread online pushback from queer scholars, both on the continent and particularly in the Global North, to Adichie deserves some attention. It made me think more capaciously about the perspectives of the African literary segment of the trans community who published online commentaries and social media posts in response to Adichie. To be clear, the trans community is disadvantaged and society needs to be doing more to stand up for the rights of trans individuals and other marginalized groups. At the same time, the Adichie controversy also generates other important questions about the foreclosure of critical debates and free expression by some people in several minority communities, including some trans activists. The attempted cancelation of Adichie, therefore, prompts my exploration of literary controversies and scandals in an age of cancel culture. Amplified by social media, these controversies invite us to reconsider the role of African literature in fostering the ideals of tolerance and democratic freedoms.

Unlike the mostly print domains of previous literary controversies and scandals in African literature, the participatory web has emerged as the favored arena for staging the rhetorical spectacles of these forceful arguments and debates. More important than their reterritorialization, however, is the way these controversies are textured and shaped by the technical structures of the web platforms themselves. The role of digital media in the aesthetic expansion of African literature may be well-established, but how do African literary discourses circulate on digital media platforms that are algorithmically designed to monetize affective interactions? In tackling this question, my work is motivated by the fact of digital culture as proximate to extractive data relations, an area that scholars often overlook in discussions of African literature and social media platforms. Platform aesthetics and the literary networks and publics into which they assimilate African literature are as important as the culture of outrage, controversies, and scandals that conduce us to revisit previous debates on the politics of censorship, speech, as well as ethnic and sexual politics in postcolonial African literary criticism.

It might be helpful to return to Achebe and Conrad for an example here: if someone were to make the claim that Achebe, in his famous essay "An Image of Africa," sought to cancel Conrad because of what Achebe construed as the English novelist's racist condescension, that would be a *controversial* proposition.[7] It relies on a presentist reading of Achebe's sharp criticism of Conrad that is predicated on the contemporary rhetoric of social media cancel culture, the sometimes self-righteous, ideological campaign to hold erring public actors responsible for a moral breach of culturally acceptable norms. Although masked as a social logic of accountability, cancel culture—commonly deployed among both conservatives and, ironically, among so-called liberals—sometimes functions as a social practice whose many hypercritical impulses include the proscription of *unliked* speech because of a speaker's political views, a person's perceived moral failures excavated from their past, and the translation of assumed or actual social errors into conditions of public shame.[8] The German social theorist Theodor Adorno observes in *Minima Moralia* that "something once expressed, however absurd, fortuitous or wrong it may be, because it has been once said, so tyrannizes the sayer as his property that he can never have done with it" (2005, 138). Although Adorno is reflecting here on how individual speech and public conversations become harnessed to the assertion of competition and power, his observation is relevant to a social media age that conflates people's public speech and ideas with their identities, essentializing them in online dramas of moral censure and disputations.[9] To be sure, Achebe's condemnation of Conrad is far from this, and I will have more to say on both authors as I examine Achebe's popular essay on Conrad, foregrounding the imperative of upholding literary tradition and canonical integrity without submitting to the urge to cancel works with outdated racial and gendered depictions. In the meantime, the literary presentism of a hypothetical cancelation aside, controversies are generative, whether they are in the grids of literary feuds, the orbits of scandals involving strong literary personalities haggling over awards, prizes, the definition of the term "woman," or the ethnopolitical ciphers of a war narrative such as Achebe's historical memoir on Biafra.[10]

To have a full sense of algorithmic culture and its relevance to African literary scholarship, we do need to focalize literary controversies and feuds on social media, a space in which reader responses to literary texts affectively circulate as part of a vast digital literary network. Hence, the online space of African literature reveals a culture of outrage constituted by "vectors of personal and not-so-personal translations of the literary-aesthetic domain" that enable an understanding of the social (Quayson 2003, xv). I refer here to Ato Quayson's method of close reading that he terms "calibrations" in his correlation of literature to both society and the social. Quayson specifically describes calibrations as "a procedure of attempting to wrest something from the aesthetic domain for the analysis and better understanding of the social," since, as he argues, the social world is coded as "an articulated encapsulation of transformation, processes, and contradictions analogous to what we find in the literary domain" (xv). I build on his argument that literary culture configures the social and opens it up to readers, critics, or even nonexpert commentators, although my interest goes in the opposite direction: I read (African) literature through the social world—that is, as enabled by digital media and its machinic protocols of producing meaning, but generating offline resonances that exceed the simulacrum of the virtual. A consideration of how literary and artistic fields are driven by contradictions, struggles, and conflict, in the Bourdieusian sense, offers us one way to outline the contours of the algorithmic circulations that produce an affective landscape that fuels and is fueled by outrage and controversies. The entrenched vitriol we can track in the literary ecology of African social media—its scandals and cancel culture, its outrage economy and never-ending grievances—offers us an analytical prism for understanding the tense sociality of, and the everyday digital lives of, African literature in its entanglement with platform culture.[11]

In the frenetic world of digital media, we have passed the stage of needing to rehash old questions about the intersections of digital technologies and African expressive cultures. In fact, recent scholarship has established irrefutably that the African literary landscape has been significantly animated through digital media in the last decade. However, critics have paid less attention to the ways digital media platforms that maximize their profits by amassing active user minutes shape the discourse within these literary networks. This study, therefore, attempts a microhistory of contemporary African literatures through its analysis of some of their most controversial and vitriolic moments on social media platforms. Moving beyond the class politics of internet access, its focus is informed by the ubiquity of algorithms in the everyday lives of many African cultural producers.[12]

An algorithm is a set of instructions that facilitates the completion of a task. The debate between netizens from Ghana and Nigeria over which Jollof Rice is better is often a topic of playful controversy and banter on social media. But what often unifies both groups is the recognition of the distinctive recipes and taste of the West African rice dich garnished with tomato sauce. Even so, the recipes of both Jollof types constitute distinct algorithms, much like math equations and the codes of computer programs that work sequentially to produce an output. As a mathematical language that specifies the behavior and operations of data, social media algorithms regulate the platforms we inhabit and determine the order and aesthetic appearance of content. However, besides playful gastro-political banter on social media, algorithms have more insidious implications, given their connection to the systematic exclusion of minority communities as well as their reinforcement and deepening of racial and discriminatory biases in places like the United States. Safiya Umoja Noble's *Algorithms of Oppression*, Ruha Benjamin's *Race After Technology*, and André Brock's *Distributed Blackness* are exemplary works that have been written on a topic that is further rendered complex and visible by artificial intelligence tools that reproduce similar logics of internet-based prejudices.

The result of algorithms sorting content and structuring user experiences for their corporate owners is ultimately the maximization and optimization of engagement and attention. The ways in which such users engage with social media, in addition to the content they post, become lucrative sources for the production of capitalist value. As a result of today's technological zeitgeist, "authority is increasingly expressed algorithmically," as Frank Pasquale has noted, with tech companies relying on black-box systems to map social reality.[13] By scrutinizing the impact algorithms exert in the production of literary discourses, the homogenization of culture and the loss of difference, I aim to unpack the networked relations and logics of the literary field in Africa. As literary outrage and controversies in the reception of literary forms on Twitter, Facebook, and other user-generated media facilitate new connections between social practices and texts, "knowledge of the socio-historical context of a literary work or genre is not therefore an 'extra' to be kept in the margins of rhetorical analysis" (Moretti 2005, 8). Rather, attention to the social worlds of literature on digital media, in this case, augments the work of rhetorical analyses and literary interpretations. I am therefore interested in the socially vexing question of cancel culture and other forms of controversies—that are mostly, in my examples, based on gender identity, sexual orientation, and ethnic politics—and their specific connections to the unruly flows of African literary practices on the internet. I am attentive to the domains of disputations arising from the artistic productions of a new generation of cultural voices as well as the authorial performances of established writers who use social media to curate literary identities online. These controversies and arguments are vital because they allow those engaged in them to discuss African literature with its politics and aesthetic configurations, as well as the ways in which we define what counts as literature and the various systems of rewards that value and legitimize it.

When, in her 2014 blog piece on her platform *Brittle Paper*, Ainehi Edoro suggests that "controversies like these [ones involving Binyavanga Wainaina's 'irreverent tweets' about the AKO Caine Prize] stage opportunities for open and honest dialogue about the things that matter to us all in the community," her perceptive comments overlook the larger algorithmic conditions underpinning the social media culture of outrage into which the so-called *cainversation* and the community it activates was subsumed (Edoro 2014b). These controversies and feuds based on literary prizes and celebrity, involving writers like Wainaina and Elnathan John, later became heated to the point in 2016 where the latter called out Wainaina's hatred, retorting, "What makes @BinyavangaW think he runs African literature?"[14] The cultural politics of digital controversies on the AKO Caine Prize for African Writing (henceforth, the Caine Prize) have been cumulative over the years. The polemics that the prize, and other social media-based arguments about prizes, generated among online reading publics allow us to map the relationships between literary-aesthetic productions and the algorithmic mechanisms of social relations on digital media. Although he acknowledges that we live in "the age of the Twitter spat," William Fear, in the context of the British literary scene, argues that writers who once "got into fights with each other—when the personal was literary, and the literary was personal" are now increasingly reticent, shying away from a tradition of literary feuding now on the decline (2023). Nothing could be farther from the truth in the African literary space, in which a climate of literary beef, controversies, and spats continue to thrive and the literary environment remains very *personal*. As seen on social media, discourses on cancel culture, controversies, feuds, and scandals remain prominent to offer a prism for understanding the social, political, and moral economies of contemporary African literature, particularly in its articulation with digital media.

The role that social media plays in generating and circulating controversies in African literary discourses requires careful scrutiny. The expanded growth of African literature in the era of digital technologies is made possible not only by the democratized nature of speech on the participatory web but also by the literary disputes enabled by the technical capacities of social media platforms themselves. In thinking about the dissolution of boundaries between readers and writers, as well as the democratization of criticism that sometimes diminishes serious debates on literature, I go beyond the focus on social media-enabled literary experimentations and genres in the digital scholarship on African literature. My analyses pivot on literary controversies that are often elided in critical discussions as the logical outcome of a performative social media ecology. The unprecedented growth of African digital literatures has informed some key scholarly publications, including Adenekan's *African Literature in the Digital Age*, Akin Adesokan's *Everything Is Sampled*, and Susanna Sacks's *Networked Poetics*.[15] Although it could be more critical of the capitalist transformation of literary content to profitable data in online networks, Adenekan's ground-breaking book indexes the relationship between African literature and new media by exploring the class and sexual politics of online writings. Given how the internet functions as "a site of cultural performance and politics," Adenekan notes that "the online writing space shows the new way in which new Kenyan and Nigerian writers use literature to depict everyday political engagements" (2021, 19). Adesokan's book is more focused on Nigerian textual assemblages and their reconfigurations through digital media. With attention to the "possibilities for digital artistic effervescence beyond and within print" (2023, 33), he examines modalities of artistic praxes, including curation, composition, adaptation, remix, and platform, all of which overlap in their articulation of the technological transformations that refigure authorship and textuality. For Sacks, digital cultural productions, particularly poetic texts from Southern Africa constitute "algorithmic aesthetics," by which she means "the form literary production takes in response to digital selection pressures created and reinforced by technological sorting structures" (2024, 17). These three books, along with my earlier volume *Cultural*

Netizenship, which analyzes the platformization of African popular culture, are the only major published monographs in the field of African literary digital humanities, a fact that attests to the current state of research as evolving.[16] *The Algorithmic Age of Personality* addresses the significant question of how digital media and social media algorithms in particular are changing reading practices. Also, the specific ways in which both readers and writers consume and discuss literary texts are focalized in the ensuing analyses. In many ways, I am following up on the argument in my first book by examining the more insidious and cosmetic dimensions of the digital reception of literary and cultural productions on social media. If there is a bit of a romanticization of social media in *Cultural Netizenship*, this new work unsettles such utopian notions by focalizing the algorithmic conditions that contribute to make outrage and controversies a norm in discussions of African literature in digital environments. Through the optimization of user engagements and profits by social media platforms, we are confronted with extreme content and negative effects that are increasingly manifested in the ways readers encounter and discuss African literary subjects on social media. The centrality of algorithms to that encounter is the subject of a 2023 cluster of essays "Reading with Algorithms," published in *Post45*. These essays were introduced by Sacks and Sarah Brouillette, who describe how social media algorithms read and shape how we browse as digital subjects. Algorithms track reading practices, affect user behavior, and "structure daily interactions online," while determining "whose cultural productions are promoted. And, in doing so, they shift users' reading and production behaviors."[17] This algorithmic intervention in African literary practices often goes beyond reading practices to shaping social relations and configuring affect among writers and readers.

A culture of outrage stems from this algorithmic permutation of reader agency. Thus, as outrage elicits clicks, which in turn produce engagements that are capital for the corporate owners of social media, African literature becomes an affordance that can be recruited to understand larger questions about digital culture. I am not suggesting that humans lack agency over machinic systems or over their means of consuming content online, nor am I positing any binary relations between humans and algorithms that efface their complex intermingling. Rather, a coproductionist, dialectical relationship pervades the workings of algorithms trained by human actors on our data. These algorithms, in turn, shape and influence what activities humans perform. An instantiation of this may be found in the Twitter dialogue box that encourages users to read stories before retweeting them. Although these kinds of prompts are less frequently encountered in the Elon Musk Twitter era, the algorithms involved in that action seek to associate user experience to broader questions about epistemic flows and the nature of truth and reality online. But because people have power to subvert technical systems, this means that not every Twitter user submits to these machinic prompts and others like them on social media platforms. The fact that auxiliary data like Facebook likes, for example, have to be trained by humans to predict information about user behavior online is an essential indicator of human participation in computational environments.[18] As Nick Seaver writes in *Computing Taste*, algorithms are never simply unaccompanied machines; humans are central to their operations and the ways in which they produce and shape cultural taste and meanings. In other words, algorithmic systems are sociotechnical worlds populated by people who make choices and whose "motivations and ideas about the world actually change how algorithms work."[19] Besides, it is humans, with their agitations and coarse language that draws attention to them, that encode their own social worlds and values into technology. Any argument presented on the authority of human-made algorithms in this book is, therefore, largely contingent on the recognition that algorithms themselves have been generated by socio-technical actors with specific cultural values and ideologies that are coded into the design and function of systems they design.[20] Online outrage itself, therefore, becomes understood as partly determined by both a flawed human nature and algorithmic culture.

Hence, at a 2022 award ceremony, Adichie spoke about the fragility of truth and abjured any propensity for self-censorship that is contingent on the erasure of truth. She then added that when we "participate in the algorithm-driven outrage machine of social media, without looking first at primary sources, without looking at full context, without having a full understanding, we make truth fragile" (2022a). If we looked past the assumption here that primary sources are neutral and a full understanding (whatever that means) of a subject can indeed produce truth, there are other stakes to pursue here. Particularly, what Adichie means by "the algorithm-driven outrage machine of social media" might refer to her own experience of cancel culture on social media, but the expression also marks an important premise for this book, which is to understand the roles of algorithms in the production of controversies and censorious outrage in African literary and cultural discourses online. In my reading of literary controversies, what Brian Larkin describes as "an aesthetic of outrage" produced by transgressions of moral norms in Nollywood films takes on an intensified techno-social force that not only rests on the design of social media platforms but greatly structures our contemporary culture (2008,

172). As outlined in the next section, the algorithms that drive the production of outrage in online discussions of African literature enable an exploration of my thesis through a critical dialogue between contemporary African literary studies and aspects of British Romanticism. What I am calling the "algorithmic age of personality" both captures Adichie's anxieties about an outrage machine and the projected public persona partly generated by social media self-exhibitionist cultures.[21] But it also names the fact that algorithms are now very formative of African literary identities and subjectivities. These algorithms underpin and are readily applicable to understanding contentious and antagonistic social relations in contemporary African writing. However, it should not be forgotten that there were similar literary developments in earlier eras, such as African literature itself and the English Romantic period.

Bọ́lẹ̀kájà and the Algorithmic Age of Personality

Since the early 2000s, strong personalities such as Adichie, Wainaina, and Teju Cole have, in their capacities as famous writers and literary influencers, determined the social inflections and affordances of African writing through their Instagram and Twitter politics rather than only through their extraordinary artistic talents. The Romantic era furnishes us with a similar performance of personality politics and can be a starting point for a more historically inflected reference for the algorithmic age of personality. In *Romantic Feuds*, Kim Wheatley writes that literary disputations often signpost other more crucial cultural and social realities, which, in the Romantic era, propelled the rise of Romanticism itself (2016). It may help to segue briefly here to African literature, though, since we can think similarly of the role of literary magazines such as *Black Orpheus* and the literary and political debates they facilitated. The growth of African literature and the cultural awakening that came with it can be partly traced to these early ephemeral forms, just like online literary platforms and digital litmags invigorate African literature today. To understand the personality cults of the social media era, or its print antecedents, we could consider the founder of *Black Orpheus*, Ulli Beier. For some scholars, Beier presents an example of literary impersonations and several authorial identities that were contingent on (or that were enabled by) a politics of appropriation. This was further made possible by his strong personality in early, predigital Nigerian literature. Although his cultural advocacy and literary support for emerging literary traditions and indigenous forms and aesthetics are well-documented, Beier faces some criticism. As Maebh Long harshly piques, the German is also "responsible for writing fraud" into Nigerian literature to which he introduced counterfeit texts and fake literary names and problematic aliases that were supposed to transgress Western notions of identity and authorship (2020, 294). Long argues that while Beier excused his false identities as swelling the body of work arising from local communities, it is difficult "particularly in light of growing research on cultural appropriation and racial hoaxes, not to see Beier's pseudonymous excursions as predicated on the arrogant adoption of identities Beier felt entitled to possess" (294). Clearly, pioneering Nigerian writers such as Soyinka, Achebe, and Clark dominated early Nigerian literature. However, it's important to also recognize the significant contributions of literary outsiders like Beier, who played central roles despite his controversial authorial practices and personality politics being woven into the literary publications of that period. The same can be said of the digital age of Wainaina and Adichie. However, these cults of personality, along with the cultures of deprecations often entangled with their performance of literary celebrity, are not limited to the African literary scene.

Returning to Wheatley's treatment of Romantic-era literary journalism, her work explores how writers of the period, such as Robert Southey and Samuel Taylor Coleridge, sought to rise above what Coleridge himself described in his *Biographia Literaria* as the "age of personality, this age of literary and political gossiping."[22] It was a culture that bolstered the development of a new culture of literary and political controversies derived from personal attacks in the print periodicals of the era, particularly the *Edinburgh Review* and the *Quarterly Review*. The claim I am making is about "the connection between the prevalence of 'personalities' in Romantic-era print culture and the literariness of periodicals" (Wheatley 2016, 15). Similar to how Romantic-era books and their reviewers emphasized the identities and politics of their authors, literary content on social media also follows a similar pattern, with algorithms shaping our reading habits and social interactions. Hence, my description of our digital epoch as an algorithmic age of personality.

The various cases of intrusions by some of the era's magazines and periodicals into the sacred space of private life undermined the distinction between individual authors and personalities. Explaining a Romantic-era feud between John Scott, the editor of the *London Magazine*, and Jonathan Christie, Peter T. Murphy shows how terms such as *person* and *personalities* came to acquire a range of meanings and roles by the end of the period: "persons have a part that is theirs alone, and decency requires that we leave personalities to their owners. 'A personality,' in other words, does violence to persons by rudely exposing to public view privately held, personal things" (1992, 631–32). While the collapse of the boundaries between the private and the public anticipates similar patterns in online environments, the parallels between the digital era and the Romantic period extend to how, according to Richard Cronin, personality became paradoxically "at once the most widely deprecated resource of those engaged in political and literary controversy and the most valued characteristic of modern writing" (2010, 53). The inescapable egotism of the print culture during the era meant a performance of authorship that was contingent on personalities and their endemic trade of salacious attacks, similar to how personality and ego are often the pivots of social media commentary discourses.

Minus the frenzy of clicks and clickbait, the prevalence of personality and personal hostility transported in popular Romantic publications, like Blackwood's *Edinburgh Magazine*, could be understood as foreshadowing the current social media culture of personal attacks, feuds, and scandals. Similar tendencies were exhibited in African literary networks, controversies, and discourses of abuse, from a print era (e.g., *Transition*) to digital periods involving Krazitivity, an important digital literary network before the social media age. For instance, when Adichie first began to trend online in 2017 because of her comments on trans women, literary influencers and personalities often resorted to personal attacks, mixing up the condemnation of a behavior and vilification of a person, the merger of identity and discourses. The print culture example of controversies and insults from British Romanticism suggests ways for us to read outrage culture on social media in the realm of current African literary production as a field that stages personality struggles. As James F. English reminds us, "there is perhaps no device more perfectly suited than scandal [for example] to making things happen on the field of culture" (2005, 190). With respect to African literary forms, the issues that motivate and are motivated by scandals and controversies are particularly informative because they conjure up other issues such as the politics of social prestige and its appropriation in the writing community.

For instance, in the digital era and in what seemed like a pre-#MeToo moment, the scandal involving Nigerian poet Chijioke Amu-Nnadi, the 2002 winner of the Association of Nigerian Author Gabriel Okara Prize for Literature, enables an understanding of the connections between literature and social media as a cultural space of contestations over controversies and notions of accountability.

In a Facebook post about the 2014 Ake literary festival, the writer Miracle Adebayo offered details of being forcefully kissed by Amu-Nnadi. After another writer, Mary Ajayi, a 2015 Moremi Initiative Leadership Empowerment and Development Fellow, wrote in the blog post "Of Kisses, of Sexual Predator, of Chijioke Amu-Nnadi,"[23] the poet posted what seemed like a nonpology on Facebook. That post basically undermined Amu-Nnadi's accusers and their anguish and was met with condemnation and fierce debate about its sincerity from online commentators. The scandal and the controversies that trailed it illustrate the major themes of this book. These include personality struggles, contestations over sexual and ethnic politics, the state politicization of the literary festival tradition and the language of boycott or cancelation that follows it, and the role of algorithmic cultures in constraining the agency of online and offline literary networks of readers and writers.

Controversies, scandals, and outrage constitute complex nodes of analysis, which unpack pressing questions for us about the entanglements, for example, of literary prizes with social media practices of commentary. They are discursive imbrications of the online production and reception of African literary texts with their prizes, digital magazines, and platforms, and are driven by the strong personalities these spaces and networks amplify. For instance, in a 2022 tweet the writer Carl Terver wondered if "the Nigerian literary space [would] ever trend on Twitter when it's not Chimamanda, or beef," fostering the idea that Nigerian literature becomes visible on Twitter only when the platform becomes animated by controversial subject matters involving influential personalities and authors such as Adichie.[24] In other words, the production of literary and political controversies and "beef" are crucial to the visibility of online literary culture. In the absence of literary beef and rumors of conflict based on literary prizes or recognition, literary discourses from the continent may not accrue trending value or gain traction on Twitter. This directly reinforces how Twitter algorithms are designed to generate trends on a topic based on maximal user activities around it. How literary works and their writers are rendered in online discussions through the popular cultural idea of the "trendy" might suggest a reduction of their identities and works to trivialization, but the point is really how the notion of content moderation must be seen as central to the overly celebrated articulation of digital media with African literature. If "algorithms select hashtags for Twitter trending topics, highlight certain headlines atop Google search results, and determine which items appear prominently in Facebook News Feeds," then a new generation of African writers who circulate their works on these platforms have their subjectivities, storytelling, and public persona shaped in more significant ways by digital media than have extensively been explored (Nechushtai and Lewis 2019, 299). Again, rather than succumbing to the suggestion that algorithms and digital technologies wield an unrestrained and all-powerful Orwellian control over society, it helps to keep in mind how technology and social frameworks coproduce each other. Even without this fetishizing logic of technological determinism, cultural producers may find their production of literary value significantly impacted in ways they do not realize. To acknowledge this is to confront the largely celebratory gesture in African digital literary studies, which tacitly overlooks capitalist relations of data.

The discursive power of social media-enabled literary controversies recollects historical cultural feuds in anticolonial and postindependence small magazines such as *Présence Africaine* and *Transition*. For example, *Transition*, founded by Ugandan writer Rajat Neogy before the Makerere conference of 1962, was the most influential African literary journal of the period after political independence. It served as "the single most important intellectual meeting ground for African intellectuals and writers," providing a natural home for the Makerere Conference proceedings" (wa Ngũgĩ 2018, 3). Hence, while keeping in mind the different manifestations and public implications of a "feud" or "controversy," I need to stress that the new media context of my argument does not translate to a newness of feuds and controversies in African literature. Neither is it meant to imply that the combative and often muddy intellectual debates of the print era were seen as ethical and passable. They may have been more nuanced and substance-driven than what is found on social media today, but they were, in most cases, as ego-driven and antagonistic in their genealogical links to what circulates in the social universes of algorithmic systems.

References to current literal and literary combats, therefore, are reminiscent of previous cultural and intellectual battles in African scholarly discourses, such as the ones involving Wole Soyinka and Kenyan writer Ali Mazrui.[25] In the first pages of his 2006 memoir, *You Must Set Forth at Dawn*, Nigerian playwright and Nobel laureate Soyinka quotes a Yorùbá proverb that roughly translates as: "As one approaches an elder's status, one ceases to indulge in battles" (5–6). The specific kinds of battles Soyinka refers to may not be immediately obvious, but it is no secret that writers sometimes have intense and combative relations that play out publicly and activate debates among readers and, in the age of social media, fans and followers. Circulating in the context of digital media, these skirmishes shape literary fields. As literary controversies, outrage, and scandals proliferate on social media through the various opportunities of digital technologies, the agency of algorithms and data-centric systems fundamental to sustaining African literature in the digital age becomes legible.[26]

The literary and cultural arguments between famous writers like Soyinka and Mazrui date back to the 1990s, following the TV series *Wonders of the African World* by Henry Louis Gates Jr. It began with Mazrui's uncharitable critique of the series, which Soyinka, a mentor of Gates, was quick to defend. The warfare, as Mazrui would later describe it, covered issues as diverse as the role of Judeo-Christian and European values in Africa as well as the erasure of Arab and Islamic legacies in western colonialism of the continent. Soyinka mainly complained that the late Mazrui was evidently resolved to demonize Louis Gates Jr. and that he had also endangered Soyinka's life among Islamist fundamentalists in Northern Nigeria. The initial debates and arguments over Gates's TV series took place in *Transition* magazine but resurfaced online a decade later. The publics, medium, and nature of the intellectual conflict between Mazrui and Soyinka are obviously different from what obtains online, but I want to reproduce their written exchange at length so to establish the print genealogies of my current interest in African literature-based controversies and heated arguments on social media. An excerpt from Soyinka's letter to the Kenyan offers a sense of the salacious exchanges between both writers:

> You bring it on yourself, since you have never yet learnt to take the ego of Ali Mazrui out of straightforward, intellectual exchanges . . . Why does Mazrui distort, extrapolate, slander, indeed—lie, yes, lie—against the actual content of the series? We shall not bother with evaluation, of the attribution of ideological impulses—these remain fair terrain of exploration for the critic but are also, quite often predictably subjective. Why, above all, has Ali Mazrui turned this into a personal, relentless crusade—jihad, lest I be accused of eurocentricity!—a battle taken into town meetings, extended into radio interviews and insinuated into literary conferences? (2000)

In response to Soyinka's letter, Mazrui, who wrote at different points to answer what he saw as Soyinka's repeated attacks on his personality and his own TV series, also fires back:

> You ask of me, you demand of me "decorum in handling colleagues," yet you make this demand within the most indecorous diatribe to hit the Internet since the Gates debate began. Your recent unrestrained critique of me is full of false, dangerous, and libelous inaccuracies. You implicitly accuse me of being in support of the death-penalty fatwa issued by Imam Khomeini against Salman Rushdie when I am and have been an unrelenting opponent of capital punishment in all cases . . . In a letter addressed to you in 1992, and copied to Skip Gates, Kwame Anthony Appiah, and Henry Finder, I begged you to end the "fratricidal" warfare between us. I said that many younger African scholars and intellectuals were disturbed to see their elders in such brazen confrontations. I begged you to bury the hatchet. I attach a copy of that letter to this open memo as an appendix. Until the Gates TV series this last fall, I thought you had heeded my appeal. I had not seen any personal attacks on me in international publications since our debate in TRANSITION magazine in 1991–92. I thanked the Lord that two aging African intellectuals had indeed decided to bury the hatchet. (2000)

The ideological differences between both writers' letters play out through name-calling, personal attacks, and "indecorous diatribe," resembling controversies on the Internet today. But even though Mazrui suggests this episode "hit the Internet," the difference in style and degree of vituperation between these public engagements and today's social media culture of spats, feuds, and outrage needs to be stressed. On the other hand, though the Soyinka-Mazrui exchange took place mostly in the print space of *Transition*, print culture does not necessarily lessen the vituperative force of their controversy, and the internet dissemination of their "fratricidal warfare" only exacerbated the tensions. While controversies in internet commentaries are mostly produced in real time, and sometimes without being subjected to the thoughtfulness and time print interaction allows, print-based controversies sometimes exhibit the same heated language. As a matter of fact, although *Transition* initially began as a space "for thoughtful and creative contributions in all spheres," its editor later turned away from creative literature toward literary and political controversies (Benson 1986, 109). "In doing so, he seems to have been making a conscious decision gradually to relax his primary commitment to the pursuit of 'Poetry Prose Criticism' in order to develop a facet of the magazine that had been growing in prominence from the first few issues—its role as a platform for debate" (132). Whether print or digital, therefore, we need to account for a medium's capacity to foster specific kinds of intense debates and emulous relations.

The novelty of new media often becomes a pretext to obscure the virulence of older debates of African literature in long-standing media like print, but discourses of fights, controversies, and underground feuds have always underpinned postcolonial literary criticism in Africa. For example, the Nigerian trio of Chinweizu, Onwuchekwa Jemie, and Ihechukwu Madubuike famously described themselves the Bọ́lẹ̀kájà critics in their blatantly polemical book, *Toward the Decolonization of African Literature*, stating in what seemed like a manifesto, "We are Bolekaja critics, outraged touts for the passenger lorries of African literature" (1985, xiv). Bọ́lẹ̀kájà, the Yorùbá expression for "come down, let's fight!" captures the combative nature of cultural commentary and literary exchanges on social media—which is my focus—although its aesthetics and politics were produced in an anticolonial and decolonizing framework. In replacing Eurocentric epistemologies with indigenous critical paradigms, these critics called for a time "in the affairs of men and of nations, when it becomes necessary for them to engage in bolekaja criticism, for them to drag the stiflers of their life down to earth for a corrective tussle" (xiv). Bọ́lẹ̀kájà criticism, like the accountability rhetoric of call-out culture, was a corrective project that, in the frame of the online reading practices of digitally outraged touts, sometimes get entangled with algorithms of outrage. In a later section of the book (chapter 4), I will return to this idea of fights, wahala, and rọ̀fọ̀rọ́fọ̀ and their entanglements with algorithmic systems, bearing in mind that every theory of literary culture on social media must put at its center questions about the interpolating power of algorithms and the social fractures to which they contribute. In the meantime, the Fanonian "literature of combat," in the schema produced by social media outrage culture, reconstitutes itself not as a liberatory or nationalist negation of colonial narratives and distortions but as a struggle among strong personalities and intellectuals who seek to outdo one another in the attainment of literary influence and visibility (Fanon 1968). This combative gesture attaches itself to and is effected through Western literary prizes, media platforms located in the global north, and foreign systems of cultural valuation that undermines any radicalism that is inherent within it.

If the Soyinka-Mazrui controversial exchanges were particularly focused on both personalities, social media commentaries would take such occasions to a more conflictual and performative level that centers similarly on personal politics. On Facebook and Twitter, which, without doubt, support the literary visibility of new and established writers, intellectual and cultural exchanges are as much about personalities as they are about literary content. As will become evident throughout this book, commentary practices on social media serve as important dialogic locations for some of the materials I collect and analyze. I have argued elsewhere that "the expectation of a response" in oral and written texts, as Karin Barber frames it (2007, 138), can be found in social media commentary threads that may be read as discursive environments that engender the process of popular commentary as an epistemological practice (Yékú 2022a, 171). Commentaries serve as a productive ecology of knowing based on the more linguistic component of cultural netizenship—which I have described as the deployment of online visuality such as meme culture for cultural and political commentary on social media platforms. In a way, these platforms trigger a digital chorus, in the Greek classical sense, that communally participates in and freely comments upon the textual performances and mediatized productions of others online. But because user-based platforms also manifest as spaces of performative self-attention and a confessional medium of self-spectacle, they also make it possible for online discussions and commentaries to degenerate into individualized attacks on people and other participants in online arguments. This is what I mean by the algorithmic age of personality, which along with the core themes of cancel culture and social media algorithms, is progressively elaborated in this introduction and throughout the book.

Rọ̀fọ̀rọ́fọ̀ Fights and the Stickiness of Algorithms

Like Bọ́lẹ̀kájà, other Yorùbá vernacular expressions such as rọ̀fọ̀rọ́fọ̀ and wàhálà are useful categories that get to the heart of outrage culture in African literary disputes, as they almost naturally come to mind when people post online commentaries that stoke the flames of controversies on social media. Wàhálà and rọ̀fọ̀rọ́fọ̀ can name the frequent algorithm-derived appearance of troubles, social angsts, and indignation in online conversations and interactions. I should note that rather than any assumed focus on Yorùbá terminologies, and a mostly Nigerian illustrative archive, I grapple with incendiary subjects in the book, which are applicable in the online public spheres of several other African countries, particularly those with vibrant digital publics and communities. Depending on their contexts of use, these indigenous expressions have prior articulations in several cultural productions. For instance, *Wahala* is the title of the debut novel by British Nigerian writer Nikki May and is embodied by the disruptive presence of Isobel in the novel's exploration of female friendship with its tensions and intimacies (2022). The glamorous Isobel is a rich biracial woman who becomes the newest member of an Anglo-Nigerian cohort of four friends living in London. The novel explores the social lives of the four women, with Isobel centered at the troubling core of their interpersonal experiences and conflicts. Farther back in time, though, the album of Afrobeat legend Fela Anikulapo Kuti, titled *Roforofo Fight*, presents a meaning of the term that clarifies my recourse to social media spats as "Rọ̀fọ̀rọ́fọ̀." The song "Roforofo Fight" in the album thematizes the human tendency for conflicts and actual fights that often precede social shaming because they occur in a setting full of mud—in the case of Fela's fictional fight scene. This rhetorical combat, as Fela's lyrics indicate, accompanies a physical battle over words that sometimes start with: "You dey craze! I no craze! Get away Who are you? Go and shit." As this argument takes place between two people in an open place full of rọ̀fọ̀rọ́fọ̀ (mud), it attracts crowds who are invited to advise friends in the battle to discontinue fighting because of the muddy elements that eventually leave everyone soiled and shamed.

What does Fela's *Roforofo Fight* teach us about social media controversies and the algorithms that propel them? In many ways, social media arguments and attacks resemble controversies and rhetorical skirmishes that operate like a rọ̀fọ̀rọ́fọ̀ fight, and that is the argument I make throughout this book. It is a common experience that participants in many online controversies sometimes sling mud at one another, particularly when their interlocutors have oppositional ideas that are naturalized as undebatable. This is sometimes a feature of cancel culture. The adhesive power of mud might not be literally forceful, but at a metaphoric level, mud actually does stick. The imagery of being stuck in wet mud evokes a blockage that Sarah Ahmed, in her theory of emotions, associates with stickiness as designating an affective value. "Stickiness," she writes, "then is about what objects do to other objects—it involves a transference of affect—but it is a relation of 'doing' in which there is not a distinction between passive or active, even though the stickiness of one object might come before the stickiness of the other, such that the other seems to cling to it" (2015, 91). I am reading social media platforms here as a product of the stickiness of algorithms, which connects to the adhesive quality of mud in relation to the screen media that glues people to social media and its outrage economies, networks and personality conflicts. In *The Cultural Politics of Emotion*, Ahmed describes the accumulation of affective value as involving two processes—namely, the production of stickiness, and the surfacing from which it is effected as "a contact between *bodies, objects* and *signs*" (90). Sticky algorithms can then be explained as what affectively sticks users to digital objects and adheres them to the performativity of digitized experiences and the tensions it accumulates. Stickiness in algorithmic systems explains how the design of social media is intended to capture people's attention, get them stuck to media signs (and the politics and controversies embedded in them), and orient user experiences into profit for the corporate owners of the platforms. Stickiness online is also about holding things together, holding us captive to digital objects and the surfaces that produce affect. It is in this sense that cancel culture can be understood as a *mudslinging business* that benefits big tech while keeping everyday digital subjects stuck to screens and platforms. Specifically, the stickiness of algorithms, as the ways in which algorithms stick us to social media, entails a contact between bodies and the affectivity of digital publics and the outrage produced in online networks. The messy blockade of sticky mud, to stay with Fela's lyrics, can symbolize the ways many social media platforms work similarly to glue or adhere us to online content. This makes users become stuck to algorithmic environments that facilitate particular forms of subjectivities and hostile relations.

In a post to explain how Instagram's technology functions and how it impacts the experiences that people have across the app, Adam Mosseri, writing for Instagram, describes how multiple algorithms, rather than a singular "The Algorithm," essentially control different parts of the platform, including the app's feed posts, Explore, or Reels (2021). The Instagram algorithms harvest thousands of "signals"—that is users' information, posts and preferences—and utilize these to personalize content that stick people to the app. In other words, people become stuck like mud to Instagram content because the app's algorithms are created to both set in motion and optimize such a behavior. This strategy of creating content derives from the information Instagram collects about a post, information about the person who posted it, their activity, as well as their history of interacting with others. As Fela's music portrays, driving through (and fighting in) muddy puddles is a common sight on some Nigerian roads in which mud gets splashed on people and, in the process, creates a multiplying effect as it spreads out into its immediate space. Algorithms that are created for multi-level optimization of social media user engagements function similarly. Like splashed mud, these algorithms can generate multiple channels to encourage social media users to stay online, engage with different content, and, in the process, increase their user active minutes. Trends and hashtag campaigns eventually peter out, but when they are in full swing, the dopamine rush that makes people engage with their narratives and messages illuminates how the digital is designed to make people become stuck to platforms.

Like a rọ̀fọ̀rọ́fọ̀ fight in which mud sticks to both fighters, the crowd of onlookers, and those intervening to help their friends, users on social media become stuck or hooked to the platform based on the signals they produce. Although different in their affordances and design, Instagram's method for user engagement, for example, is similar to those of other platforms where an economy of algorithms also predicts user behavior and engagement based on the data collected on them. To illustrate, clicking on Twitter's trending topics, curated by the platform's algorithms, might prompt participation in a viral hashtag to cancel a writer. The focus of these platforms is mostly the same: the optimization of profit based on the technical curation of the information users supply online. Personalization of content, together with the promise of retaining intimate ties with friends, become code for the capture of profit from our literary data and communication rituals. As strong personalities and nonexpert literary voices become prominent in African literature based on the so-called democratization of the technologies of cultural commentary and spaces of literary production, controversies and literary feuds are also on the increase, nurtured by an algorithmic ecology that sticks people to social media platforms. At the same time, like mud in a rọ̀fọ̀rọ́fọ̀ fight, algorithms make it possible for the discourses of abuse and disputes on social media to infect many people and instigate more wàhálà that spreads beyond the participants themselves.

What is most crucial is how mudslinging ends up tarnishing and silencing literary talent, as well as critical debates on literary objects, while connected to a platform culture that is designed to extract profit from online wàhálàs. One way, therefore, to explain the operations of algorithmic power is to interrogate how the promise of online connection is used to conceal an insidious regime of capital that renders digital subjects vulnerable to platform capitalism. Platform capitalism is Nick Srnicek's term for the way companies like Google and Facebook operate as platforms invested in the massive collection of our data as their central business model (2020). As capitalism turns "to data as one way to maintain economic growth and vitality," the platform has emerged "as a new business model, capable of extracting and controlling immense amounts of data" (6). This mainly happens through the technical determinations of affect online. For instance, algorithms thrive on negative emotions and drive attention and engagements that are based on affective responses like outrage, which they also reward and amplify. Algorithms anticipate what users want based on detailed information about their preferences. With algorithms shaping things in the background, African cultural producers and their works are also being interpellated by popular digital practices, which, as recent online literary controversies signal, include cancel culture. Hence, my engagement with the ways in which social media platforms and their algorithms, as a source of tensions and outrage, contribute to the field. In the chapters that follow, therefore, I identify and analyze the ways in which aspects of contemporary African literature constitute a conflictual superstructure on the technical base of digital communication.

The capacity of social media to generate affect and produce feelings like sadness and anger is central to the argument I am making in this book. As Martha Nussbaum has demonstrated, a conceptual part of anger is "the idea of payback or retribution—in some form, however subtle" (2016, 15). While this is not always the case with anger—which is historically catalytic of social change when devoid of retribution—a culture of payback makes it normatively problematic and unproductive for social justice. On social media, the anger and outrage of cancel culture becomes easily absorbed into a retributive strategy of shaming with its payback impulses appropriated and amplified by engagement-seeking algorithms. Whether anger or another emotion, social media platforms feed on a range of human emotions. Introducing *Post*, a new social media envisioned as an alternative to Twitter, shortly after Elon Musk's takeover of the platform, Noah Badim asks potential users of his new but short-lived platform to remember when social media "didn't waste your time and make you angry or sad? When you could disagree with someone without being threatened or insulted? We want to bring that back with Post. . . . Many of today's ad-based platforms rely on capturing attention at any cost—sowing chaos in our society, amplifying the extremes, and muting the moderates" (2022). The controversies in online environment sometimes descend into affective publics, which Zizi Papacharissi defines as "public formations that are textually rendered into being through emotive expressions that spread virally through networked crowds" (2015, 15). Algorithms produce affective-emotional effects that shape the ways in which controversies and scandals circulate in online communities and networks. The emotional response to controversial stories—and the social media on which they circulate—often generate hundreds and thousands of impressions for the participants who engage with content and remain *stuck* to the platforms and conversations. These numbers eventually become translatable into a reward system that may include revenue, likes, and follows for users.

As social media algorithms amplify controversies, the nature of digital media to generate affects like outrage, conflict, pleasure, and envy comes to square up with affect's transversal nature as well as its capacity to inhabit and adjust to multiple domains from which it shapes bodies. In "The Autonomy of Affect," Brian Massumi argues the ability of affect "to produce an economic effect more swiftly and surely than economics itself means that affect is itself a real condition, an intrinsic variable of the late-capitalist system, as infrastructural as a factory" (1995, 106). As humans interact with technologies, affect is shown to be everywhere and manifests in the connections between the social and the digital. In the case of social media, it is evident in literary networks that sometimes yield to conflictual exchanges. Affective capitalism may thus be understood in the Marxian framework that, in this case, what we post or produce online is part of data relations that subsumes our digital labor to capital. People are not just the product of a supposedly free digital ecology. Their cultural and media productions, too, are rendered as commodities. Hence, the sole function of stickiness becomes obvious as it works to glue users to digital culture through algorithms in order to generate value from their affective labors. Indeed, labor in this online space is the source of all value, while the algorithmic engines that facilitate such digital labors are often the means of the alienation and disaffection from what people produce online. Algorithmic affect describes the ways in which the affective schemas of social media relations, sensations, emotions, and public feelings become legible through algorithmic machines. In this sense, algorithms serve as the technological anchors of affect in cyberspace, or, in Adi Kuntsman's memorable phrasing, of the "affective fabrics of digital cultures" (2012, 1). Being immersed in digital spaces and performing digital labor involves profound affectivity, especially when users are consuming viral content that encourages tribal and schismatic relations based on, in the case of literature, books and literary conversations. The emotional and personal dimensions of these conversations regarding the African literary commentariat warrants a careful mapping of the role of algorithms in the affective labors of online reading publics and their practices.

To invoke Raymond Williams's useful concept, algorithmic affect names the appearance of "structures of feeling" in social media encounters in which algorithms are now intrinsic to quotidian life and foreground affectivity and affective publics as major elements of user-generated media (1978). As people perform indignation through Facebook status updates, tweets, and addictive TikTok short videos, their digital labors are shaped by machine-learning systems that use what they learn about them to organize their online affect. Williams explains "structures of feeling" in *Marxism and Literature* as "a particular quality of social experience and relationship, historically distinct from other particular qualities, which gives the sense of a generation or a period" (131). Based on this oppositional model of discourses jostling for dominance within specific historical formations, it is my contention that there is something distinct about the social experience of digital culture that is generational and definitive of the cancel culture era and its politics of moral policing. We can hardly get a proper account of the particular sense of this current mediatized conjuncture without paying attention to the technologies and algorithms shaping culture, artistic object, and the human experience. With profit-driven algorithms supporting networks of outrage, experiences of ideological divisions, online harassment, misinformation, and cancel culture emerge from our machinic interactions in ways that define our period.

In *Cultural Netizenship*, I demonstrated how the essential nature of social media platforms is the capture of value from our activities online: "social media platforms are rife with hierarchies and hegemonic tensions, as capital is the primal logic of the social web's ontological claim to connective relations" (2022a, 3). The digital ecosystems we inhabit daily are created and curated by developers and programmers, whose sole interest is to make profit through the production and manipulation of user engagement. Again, take Twitter's Trending Topics as one mode of user engagement, for example. The widget is one of several ways the platform's editors curate and sustain user engagement, as a list of most popular topics people tweet about amplifies certain stories from a particular region and can increase people's reaction to it. With Adichie and the transphobia controversy, most people who followed literary topics would likely have seen it, either because they follow and know Adichie as a popular feminist author or they follow someone who does. If the topic was on the list of trending topics, as it indeed was, people are more likely to click on it and engage with the story. This is one of many ways the platform influences what users consume and how they behave. There are other ways this can happen, as in the case of the operations of Twitter algorithms which are explained in an online thread by the account user @nft_god.[27] When Twitter released part of its computer source code that decides how the platform recommends content in March of 2023, it became clear, for example, that having multiple hashtags that are made to accompany one's tweets limits the flow and popularity of those tweets, while earning likes have more impact than retweets and replies. At the same time, if a person follows more users than they have others follow them, their content gets deprioritized and is not ranked or boosted by the algorithms. In simple terms,

Twitter algorithms contribute to one's influence, visibility, and circulations on the microblogging platform, shaping how they are "read" and perceived by others.

Back to Adichie, beyond the ways in which the Trending Topic algorithms feature and emphasize the controversies of her claims, the writer is also a celebrity whose digital self-presentations also invite outrageous clapback to her perspective on the trans community. To reiterate a point made earlier differently, as we interact with others on social media, algorithms process information about us and use it to determine our tastes, activities, and habits. Hence, readers might see controversial topics online because they follow other readers who post them or because they have liked a post by another reader who is enmeshed in a literary argument. While we may not always be aware of this process online, algorithms aggregate, store, and analyze our private data, using these to organize our digital worlds. For instance, when Abiodun Bello, an accomplished and notoriously introvert poet, won the Association of Nigerian Authors prize for poetry in 2020 and announced his award on Twitter, his tweet hardly received any attention from anyone in the writing community. Among other possible reasons, Bello's user active minutes on Twitter and his number of followers, both significantly low, appear to have been responsible. In other words, he was short on the necessary amount of microdata that algorithms would have used to predict his behavior and suggest his tweets and other online activities to more people. Without a robust digital performance of authorship, the poet escapes the algorithmic manipulation of his literary identity online.

Aside from predicting user behavior, there are other implications of this algorithmic curation of user reality. As people interact online, a systemic capture and commodification of their private data is built into the design of the platforms that enable these interactions. For Nick Couldry and Ulises A. Mejias, our uses of social media platforms translate to relations of data reminiscent of colonialism (2019). Such data becomes the means of normalizing the exploitation of human beings. In their view, data relations are "ways of interacting with each other and with the world facilitated by digital tools. Through data relations, human life is not only annexed to capitalism but also becomes subject to continuous monitoring and surveillance" (xiii). In a previous work, "Digital African Literatures and the Coloniality of Data," I build on these ideas to examine the costs of participating in literary networks through digital and social media in Africa (2022b). It is crucial to this analysis how African digital subjects are interpellated as data-generative creative agents through the algorithmic systems of platforms that are produced elsewhere. Similarly, echoing Jodi Dean's notion of "communicative capitalism"

(2009), Kate Eichhorn observes that the value of social media platforms, despite their so-called democratization of communication, is predicated on the free digital labor of users and have the "ability to engage all of us in unpaid datagenerating activities" (2019, 134). Hence, communicative capitalism captures value from things that were once intangible, which may include people's outrage, nostalgia, and all kinds of desires they express online. While users do not pay money to use these platforms, the intangible costs of being on platforms like Facebook and Twitter consist of their attention, time, and the narratives and stories they create and circulate on the platforms.

As with the Twitter prompt example, this is not to suggest that social media users lack agency when it comes to their experiences online. To do this would be a reification of algorithmic culture, which is not my intention whatsoever. There are many instances where people recognize and consciously resist the algorithmic call to the normativity of digital surveillance and domination. Thus, despite "the power dynamics encoded into the design and use of social media, there is room for subversions" (Yékú 2022a, 16). This view is shared by many scholars, including Ignacio Siles who, in *Living with Algorithms*, similarly draws on global south social media processes to show how people subvert algorithmic systems and integrate them into their quotidian realities, using them to produce vibrant digital publics and counterpublics (2023). Within this framework, people may not yet have the capacity to own their own data, as is common in increasingly popular decentralized networks with self-hosting social media. But they can, at least, recognize how their attention is being mined through different strategies of engagement and thwart or resist that process. Sometimes, "doing nothing," as a mode of resistance, means disengaging from the attention economy for reflection outside social media and "to do something else in another framework" (Odell 2020, 179). Even then, the strategy of logging off social media does not hinder the flow of rage on the platform. Neither is it a monolith in all social media contexts across the world.

For instance, the near-apocalyptic frenzy to leave Twitter or do nothing on it after Elon Musk bought the platform in 2022 did not reproduce a similar energy for many in global south contexts who would rather stay on these platforms because social media functions differently for them. At the same time, we can still focus on what makes profit and divisive relations tolerable on the platform and how that reality shapes the nature of African literature as it circulates online. I have written previously about what market-driven streaming in Nollywood has to do with the politics of datafication and the algorithmic designs of the platforms themselves.

As I argued in a 2021 article, the Netflixization of Nollywood urges us indeed to ask questions about how the experience of viewing film on digital platforms subject audiences to data control, especially in relation to streaming platforms that micro-target ads at viewers (2021). Although Netflix does not harvest the kinds of data that might directly capture monetary value from the viewing practices of users, it collects data from our interactions with the platform to determine how we interact with Nollywood films. If the algorithmic base of streaming platforms informs the New Nollywood films people choose to watch and the process of consuming narrative pleasures, then we need to be paying more attention to the affordances of the digital and its mode of subjectivizing Nollywood's digital audiences (449). As the natural processes of context and attention are lost in the thousands and millions of stories people react to through shares and clicks on social media, the ròfọ̀rọ́fọ̀ and storm that gather serve the financial model of this platform, resulting in "nothing but a bounteous uptick in engagement" (Odell 2020, 160).

The collapse of context can be adduced as one of several factors responsible for cancel culture and the storm of controversies that sometimes follow social media stories. Drawing from Joshua Meyrowitz's important work on electronic media, *No Sense of Place* (1986), which explores how changes in media affect everyday experience and sense of identity, Alice E. Marwick and Danah Boyd explain how social media technologies collapse multiple audiences into single contexts:

> Like many social network sites, Twitter flattens multiple audiences into one—a phenomenon known as "context collapse." The requirement to present a verifiable, singular identity makes it impossible to differ self-presentation strategies, creating tension as diverse groups of people flock to social network sites . . . participants must contend with groups of people they do not normally bring together, such as acquaintances, friends, co-workers, and family. To navigate these tensions, social network site users adopt a variety of tactics, such as using multiple accounts, pseudonyms, and nicknames, and creating "fakesters" to obscure their real identities. (2011, 122)

The challenge of understanding how people navigate multiple imagined audiences convened around media artifacts, such as social media, becomes more complex in an age of machine-inspired ideological polarization. Here, context collapse becomes a real problem, one that is exacerbated by the initial 140–280 character limits of the microblogging platform. Context collapse, as in the lack of context to a tweet, "generally occurs when a surfeit of different audiences occupy the same space, and a piece of information intended for one audience finds its way to another—usually an uncharitable one—which then reads said information in the worst possible faith" (Warzel 2021). It can lead to harassment while encouraging vituperative callouts. Context collapse is possible because there is mostly a context prior to media forms. The narratives and stories that circulate on Facebook and Twitter begin in a nonmediatized ecology whose affects and perceptions are not always wholly transferable to digital conversations. Hence, context collapse is oftentimes a logic of the platforms. That said, there are many occasions in which Twitter users, for example, are able to express themselves in the most succinct language that aligns with the brevity of microblogging. But my point is less about the required number of characters or words than about the inability to articulate the entirety of the social and psychic conditions that inform what we publish online. Besides, the performativity of social media platforms often means textual performances of the selves online may suggest a controlled curation of identity that makes the context of communication plastic, shifting, and incomplete.

If user engagements on controversial topics serve the financial models of social media platforms, then our emotional and affective encounters in these ambivalent "networks of outrage and hope," as Manuel Castells calls them, are easily convertible into forms of commodification (2015). Social media exchanges not only make legible the capacities to affect and become affected, but they also enact the conditions for the intersections of affect and capitalism, what Tero Karppi et al. refer to as affective capitalism (2016). Affective capitalism, which appeals to our desires in its intense needs for social relationships, describes "a particular mode of capture where resonances between bodies—both human and nonhuman alike—enter systems of value and value production" (9). What is effected by the fractured worlds of this affective-capitalist system in the context of African literary conversations on social media is the focus of this study.

Methods and Chapter Outline

My goal in this book is to make sense of the connections between social media algorithms and the intense grids of personalized debates on transgender identities, ethnicity, and the politics of literary awards in the African literary community online. It is likely someone might wonder how the sociology of the algorithm that, in my reading, defines cancel culture in online discourses on African literature, will get people to read literature better. This is important, although whether people will read literature better or not is less important to me than whether they read it at all based on seemingly offensive speech acts by some African authors on social media. It is not my intention to convert anyone to reading literature neither am I overly concerned about the evaluation of aesthetic value. It is rather my aim to explore how algorithms shape our encounters with literary artefacts based on the digital subjectivities of writers and the readers who encounter their digital performance of authorship. I am not suggesting that aesthetic considerations are not at all germane; they are, and I do address them in a few sections. Yet, my hope is that the feuding, scandals, and controversies of the online world might be seen as hindering an evaluation of aesthetic value, as they sometimes distract from the close reading of texts and from questions of artistic quality. The specific relevance of a sociological model of resentment to African literary criticism that captures the many fissions of the social media archive of contemporary African writers is its attention to how African writers perform authorship in an algorithmically configured terrain that blurs the social boundaries between authors and readers.

I will elaborate the question of how cancel culture and online furors are also enmeshed in the reward mechanisms of social media, bringing potential gains to those supposedly fated to cancelation campaigns. But it should be clear by now that the politicization of cultural productions by social media algorithms is by no means limited to the online world. The media, institutional, and social conditions of African reading cultures activate the analytical dimensions of my argument and its emphasis on the algorithmic protocols of literary communication. Yet, an examination of the relationship between algorithms and literature is not meant to reveal the ways in which algorithmic models underpin methods of distant readings that augment the interpretive paradigms of traditional close reading. Rather than this approach of computational literary criticism, my interest is to explore the techno-social consequences of a platform culture that intensifies literary outrage and ròfọ̀rọ́fọ̀ culture.

While social media commentary discourses supply most of the materials for this book, I nonetheless draw on traditional methods of close readings and analyses of literary works themselves in several chapters. My methodology involves some kind of digital ethnography, a netnographic approach that has often involved a real-time immersion in the actual spaces of literary arguments and deprecations on social media, and a necessary participant observation of ongoing controversies surrounding literary celebrities. I follow several ideas on the vocal antipathies that issue from algorithms by examining readers' and writers' personal posts about African literature topics through tweets and Facebook status updates. Social media manifests as the primary source of knowledge in this book, as age-long Facebook posts and stories as well as thousands of tweets that are in the public domain are exhumed on many occasions for analyses.[28] In several instances of some chapters, I used the internet archive or the Wayback Machine to excavate blog posts and essays from websites with broken URLs. This is besides manually recovering publicly available tweets from several years back through a painstaking search on individual feeds and timeline. The digital obsolescence of some online spaces suggests an archive of African literary productions that is buried in web archives and is sometimes, in the case of the Krazitivity archive and other literary listservs, irrecoverable.

It is inconceivable that one writes a scholarly work on social media without relying on sources created and distributed though digital media, and here I am referring to digital literary magazines and online platforms of news and cultural commentary.

Also, what is important to my approach is Boyd's suggestion about internet data, specifically the view that the publicness of data does not mean we should publish it. As she writes, "just because it is accessible doesn't mean using it is ethical" (2010). Hence, I take seriously ethics of disclosure with regard to what is deemed usable for social media research. Whenever possible, I sought permissions to use the tweets and Facebook posts I analyze, but it is the status of the writers themselves that ultimately determines my use of their data. Their positions as writers who publicly exhibit traits of literary celebrity and perform authorship digitally transcend any possible preference for anonymity. Like their literary and critical works circulating freely in print, their social media posts constitute an accessible and open-source archive, already made public by their own privacy options and settings. The fact that such sources are public means that researchers don't have to be friends or followers of the subjects whose stories are featured in this kind of work before having access to them. People post narratives on these platforms and quickly move on to share the next story on their mind, but the proverbial digital idiom that the internet never forgets ensures that what we post online is preserved in some, often fragmentary form, and becomes, as in the case of this book, material for all kinds of intellectual musings.

Despite the ubiquity of social media platforms, many in literary studies have always viewed them suspiciously, with some initially choosing to ignore them or continuing to approach whatever literary knowledge might circulate on the platforms condescendingly. I anticipate that the findings of this study will promote a renewed awareness of African literature in the age of digital technologies and will reveal the value of extending understandings of African digital literatures to the literary feuds and scandals that cohere around them. As Scott Kushner writes, everyday digital media "present literary studies with the opportunity to interrogate the category of the literary; to examine anew what the category does to texts, the people who read them, and the people who study them; and to think about how it can reimagine the boundaries of its disciplinary operations" (2015). What digital media does to the reception of texts and the circulation of discourses around them is similarly crucial to my approach, as my work turns recent digital scholarship in African literature away from individual authors, new voices, social media-enabled literary productions, and genres to literary feuds and quarreling that occur in the social networks of writers and their readers.

In my first chapter, "Achebe, Adichie, and Conrad's *Heart of Darkness* in a Cancel Culture Age," I track the intersections of African literature and cancel culture, using online commentaries about Adichie's comments on trans women as a point of departure. My attention to online contestations over Adichie's public opinions on trans identities is informed by Brouillette's assertion that the careers of authors in postcolonial nations "are key paratexts for reception and reproduction" (2007, 3). Whether Adichie is well received online or whether readers continue to embrace her work now depends, in part, on the digital struggles around her personae and identity. The point Brouillette makes is consistent with other long-standing discussions of the literary text's relationship to social structures outside of the individual author. This connection between literary expressions and social agents is a major idea that my various examples speak to. My argument here, thus, builds on earlier works, such as Howard Becker's *Art Worlds*, that point to art as a collective praxis involving many social actors and entities having different aesthetic functioning and value (1982). In the context of digital publications, these include both the reader-writers who critique and redraw the boundaries of artistic meanings through direct participation in the social world of art, as well as the creators of the recommendation algorithms that shape artistic encounters in digital literary networks. In my exploration of the role of algorithms in the production of social media outrage in African literary and cultural discourses online, Adichie's experience with the trans community enunciates a pretext to read cancel culture in relation to Achebe's denunciation of Conrad (and his *Heart of Darkness*) in "An

Image of Africa." Rather than an anachronistic reading of cancel culture invoked through a focus on Adichie's cancelation experience online, I focus on whether Achebe's firm but gracious desire to have Conrad thrown out of the canon because of the latter's racism could be read in the light of today's cancel culture rhetoric.

In chapter two, "Literary Networks of Conflict and the Politics of the Digital Litmag," I discuss prominent digital literary magazines from Kenya and Nigeria and use them to demonstrate how social media also functions as networks of conflict that restate the value of offline literary networks. The chapter's discussion of how digital literary magazines exhibit the occasionally petulant logics of online networks and communities is metaphorized by the name of another online platform, South Africa's *Chimurenga Chronic*, whose wide-ranging publications cover African arts, culture, and politics. The Shona word "Chimurenga," which can be loosely interpreted as "fights" or "struggle," underlines the various fights and contestations between literary editors and editorial collectives examined in the chapter. While exploring connections between the politics of state propaganda and literary productions specifically in Nigeria and Kenya, I discuss the role of social media influencers as public intellectuals and the personality conflicts that often accumulate through their challenge to established models of literary expertise. The literary influencer focalizes the power of non-expert readers who politicize literary objects, creating a scenario in which what a text actually says and how it produces meanings sometimes become less relevant than the opinions of nonprofessional interpreters who circulate online as critics.

The subject of chapter three, "Achebe's *There Was a Country* and the Ethnopolitics of Bọ́lẹ̀kájà Readers" is the 2012 publication of Achebe's wartime memoir *There Was a Country* whose divisive reception in Nigeria was the subject of ethnopolitical controversies in both print and especially digital commentary locations, including social media. My aim here is to demonstrate how the ethnopolitical and literary controversies that greeted the publication of the book explicate the contested nature of digital literary publics in the reception of contemporary African writing. In Chapter Four, literary prizes are critically interrogated as sources of literary conflicts and wàhálà, with a focus on the controversial politics of the Caine Prize for African writing, and online debates about an elusive Nobel Prize for Ngũgĩ wa Thiong'o. Because cancel culture is connected to power relations as well as class and institutional politics, the most vocal African critics of the Caine Prize have hardly canceled it, even though its influence appears to be waning in recent years. One reason I adduce for this diminished status is how the Prize is mediated by the signs of empire, as Ronit Frenkel makes clear in her discussion of the Booker Prize and its inherent assumptions that nominated texts that stand any chance of winning these Western awards must fulfill Western stereotypes, what she terms the Booker Prize's "post-colonial pathos" (2008, 87). Pursuing the claim, therefore, that one cannot move the center for cultural freedoms, as Ngũgĩ argues, by obsessing about the authorizing and consecratory opportunities of the center, this chapter tracks the politics of social media commentaries on literary prizes. It identifies how online commentaries contradict the ideological agendas of decolonization. The digital geographies discussed in the chapter show that cultural prestige from awards and prizes are also fostered by digitization, despite what James English argues to be the denationalization of its global market and the "more radical deterritorialization of prestige, an uncoupling of cultural prizes, and even of symbolic fields as such, from particular cities, nations, even clearly defined regions" (2005, 282). Aside from questions of awards themselves and their detachments from specific regional and national contexts, my interest in the chapter is the digital reconstitution of discourses of prestige and awards as well as the conflicts they engender on social media. In the context of the "extra-textual or extra-literary politics" writers engage in to gain literary fame, as a former president of the Association of Nigerian Authors once claimed, literary controversies and prizes are linked to the achievement of fame (Abdullahi 2023). Social media becomes the ideal environment for the curation of literary celebrity and the prestige economies that derive from awards.

In chapter five, "Thighs Fell Apart, Online Fan Fiction and Literary Friendships," there is a shift from the critical sites of literary interpretation and reader commentaries to the more creative side of things, as I read the online fan fiction "Thighs Fell Apart" by Kiru Taye as a pertinent mode of literary participation. Fan fiction itself is any "writing that continues, interrupts, reimagines, or just riffs on stories and characters other people have already written about" (Jamison 2013, 17). With its transformative encounter with a canonical text in mind, my goal in the chapter is to demonstrate how an Achebe fanfic illuminates the power of fan-writing as an aspirational mode of social kinship that deconstructs a social media culture of outrage and controversies. Based on a fan's rewriting of Achebe's *Things Fall Apart* posted on the literary platform *Brittle Paper*, the chapter shows the possibilities of literary friendships and solidarity and counters the aesthetics of digital outrage that is common in the age of cancel culture. My analysis in this chapter redeems the earlier sections of the book, and explores how, beyond literary scandals, feuds, and controversies, fan writing offers one possibility of literary friendships and other forms of generative literary sociality online.

In my conclusion, I explore what Achebe teaches us about cancel culture. Through a focus on Okonkwo's banishment and, more crucially, his speech impairment, I reread *Things Fall Apart* through a framework that illustrates the novel's politics of redemption that is often absent in the ornamental and hasty expressions of rage online. My argument in the closing section returns to the cultural politics of Adichie's so-called anti-trans speech and what becomes obfuscated when democratic and cultural expressions are undermined by a censorious mob mentality.

CHAPTER 1

Achebe, Adichie, and Conrad's *Heart of Darkness* in a Cancel Culture Age

In his 2014 presidential address to the African Literature Association, Tejumola Olaniyan stated that provocative scholarship "on African writers and artists is more frequently produced by those who have only a peripheral and tangential connection with the broader field of African literature" (2016, 6). It is also the case that in the context of digital cultures, to which writers like Adichie have contributed significantly, mostly by incorporating social media and blogging into narrative aesthetics, it is not only *actors* external to the specific field of African literary studies that define "the paradigms by which African cultural production will be evaluated" (6). There are also *ideas* that initially appear to have only the remotest connections to the field, including cancel culture. What Elleke Boehmer identifies as the interesting "undertow and overtones of Achebe in Adichie" occurs not only in "the configurations of plot and character" in the latter's work, but also in the ways Achebe's call-out of Joseph Conrad and his *Heart of Darkness* prefigures Adichie's own struggle with cancel culture in the social media age (2009, 148). While the major focus of this chapter is an elaboration of cancel culture, it also relies on the literary-historical dimension I tracked in the introductory chapter. Bearing in mind Peter Benson's study of the relationship of literary magazines to intellectual and cultural movements in Africa, I have already mentioned how print magazines such as *Transition* became "caught up in controversy—aesthetic, social, political and personal" (1986, 94). With writers like Wole Soyinka, Ali Mazrui, and several others bringing a solid body of creativity and thought into contentious discussions of African letters and culture, some of their artistic and intellectual ruminations and questions centered on Pan-Africanism, African socialism, and the place of ethnic and racial minorities in postindependence Africa. In the pages that follow, however, I briefly survey the circumstances of the Adichie transphobia kerfuffle and then connect this to Achebe's discussion of Conrad's novel in "An Image of Africa." Additionally, I also examine here what I suspect is an uncritical conflation of cancel culture and the present wave of decolonizing and decolonial rhetoric in African studies.

With the advent of social media, African cultural producers and their works are also now being interpellated by popular digital practices that, as recent online conversations signal, include the phenomenon of cancel culture, "defined broadly as attempts to ostracize someone for violating social norms" (Norris 2020, 2). This pervasive culture alternately manifests as either a right-wing or "leftist" practice that silences anyone who holds opposing views. As part of a Manichean understanding of the politics of conservative and liberal polarization, cancel culture, even when it is merely perceived as a mythic idea by some commentators, intensifies identity politics in mostly Global North societies. Its manifestations can be observed in both ideological camps, according to Umut Özkırımlı: "The woke Left [those who embrace some form of radical identity politics] was a mirror image of the reactionary Right in its disdain for dissent, its bunker mentality, and Manichean simplicity" (2023, 3). Although Özkırımlı's use of the past tense elides the persistence of these tendencies in the present moment, a middle-ground option for those who view social shame as powerfully shaping cancel culture is to transcend this polarizing ideology or moral assumptions of cancelation as good (for social accountability) or bad (for free speech). In a 2021 podcast, Ezra Klein posits that the deeper question we need to ask, beyond the good and bad parts of cancel culture, is whether it is possible to have "a world in which we speak about each other more respectfully, in which we listen to each other more openly, and that becomes a foundation . . . for a fairer and more inclusive politics where more people get to shape how they are spoken about."[1] Achebe's reading of Conrad, which foregrounds the ways in which Africa is addressed and constructed in European literature, anticipates this point about how people "are spoken about" in cancel culture discourses. This aspect is worth discussing in African literary studies because of the several literary disputes that have historically and recently shaped writing communities in places like Nigeria, Kenya, and even South Africa—given the Apartheid and post-Apartheid politics that sometimes structures literary participation. Although I am unambiguous about the inherent presentism of my argument, I want to offer a rereading of Chinua Achebe's response to Conrad and his *Heart of Darkness* in an "An Image of Africa," particularly in an era where there persists a tendency to ostracize people and ideas from the public realm due to perceived moral transgressions.

At the risk of sounding anachronistic or overinterpreting Achebe, another way to formulate this claim is that his objections to the representational aesthetics and politics of Conrad in *Heart of Darkness* summon parallels between cancel culture and Achebe's questioning of Conrad's place in the literary canon. This proposition is essential. In his 2003 reflection on his meeting with Achebe to discuss *Heart of Darkness*, Black Atlantic writer Caryl Phillips notes that it is "difficult to dismiss this man [Conrad] and his short novel," before asking, "Are we to throw all racists out of the canon? Are we, as Achebe implies, to ignore the period in which novels are written and demand that the artist rise above the prejudices of his times?"[2] Undoubtedly, even if considered as a pre-digital iteration of contemporary cancel culture, the question of throwing "all racists out of the canon," as a conceptual underpinning of Achebe's formulation of the racism in Conrad's short novel, may be argued as initiating the conditions against which we may tackle cancel culture in relation to Adichie and other African writers.

Cancel Culture and Adichie's "Trans Noise"

In the last couple of years, African literary conversations have exhibited intensified entanglements with social media cancel culture—also understood colloquially as "a new set of moral attitudes and political commitments that tend to weaken our norms of open debate and toleration of differences in favor of ideological conformity" (*Harper's Magazine* 2020). This description of cancel culture is according to a controversial July 2020 letter signed by more than 150 notable public figures, including J. K. Rowling, Cornel West, Margaret Atwood, Salman Rushdie, and Noam Chomsky. In "A Letter on Justice and Open Debate," published by *Harper's Magazine*, these writers and intellectuals decried the ways in which cancel culture fosters a stifling atmosphere and underplays critical nuance in public debates. Proceeding from the "restriction of debate, whether by a repressive government or an intolerant society," cancel culture invariably makes everyone less capable of democratic participation—an expressive leverage that the social media platforms on which it originates and circulates ostensibly offer everyday people (2020). While cancel culture manifests differently in several parts of the world—and it is contentious whether practiced by a book-banning Florida Governor or a university press that drops an author for challenging any prevailing cultural norms—not everyone agrees with this letter. Even more remarkably, some online commentators take issue with the politics of those aligned with it. Depending on the interlocutor, therefore, the letter elicited a plethora of perspectives on the ideological disputations over what cancel culture itself signifies. For instance, positioning cancel culture as disruptive to a unitary vision of the Habermasian public sphere and locating its origins in what she calls "Black discursive accountability praxes," Meredith Clark argues that the signatories to the letter, as "self-appointed regents of open debate," fail to anticipate "an age in which there is no longer a dominant public sphere, but a fractal sequence of counterspheres and oppositional publics" (2020, 92). Apparent from this viewpoint, also shared by Loretta Ross, is the long history of cancel culture that goes back to its discursive manifestations in virtual locations such as Black Twitter. The emphasis on the Black vernacular dimensions of call-out culture is to make visible what was an often effective strategy for highlighting social inequities and harmful behaviors rooted in larger social systems of oppression. By this account, cancel culture becomes a necessary strategy of oppositional speech that refuses the persistence of oppressive discourses in the public domain. Pertinent here is what Nancy Fraser calls "subaltern counterpublics" to mean "parallel discursive arenas where members of subordinated social groups invent and circulate counterdiscourses to formulate oppositional interpretations of their identities, interests, and needs" (1990, 67). In this sense, and as Clark appears to suggest, we can view cancel culture mainly as a strategy of the less powerful, although it is constantly co-opted by dominant groups, making its meanings elastic and negotiable depending on who uses it. While cancel culture existed in different forms before the social media era, it has continued to evolve to include strategies of boycotting someone for expressing politically unpopular views, withdrawing of public support because of past or unacknowledged moral failings, or deplatforming people online because of political positions that go against the normative grain of a culture. Instead of canceling or calling-out people, Ross advocates for a "calling-in" culture that "engages in debates with words and actions of healing and restoration, and without the self-indulgence of drama."[3] I will close this book by examining what this redemptive strategy looks like, turning to how Achebe details a useful paradigm of reconciliatory politics through the agency of Okonkwo's character and his speech impairment.

In the meantime, critics of cancel culture push back against the movement's silencing of divergent opinions by citing works like John Stuart Mill's *On Liberty*, which presents a notion of liberalism that assumes the fallibility of all opinions and promotes freedom of speech and tolerance for dissenting views that may criticize or complement the prevailing opinion on any subject (1972). The fact that J. K. Rowling is listed among the signatories to the July 2020 letter immediately conjures up other dissenting responses, particularly in the light of the strong criticisms that have made the Harry Potter author one of the most canceled authors and cultural producers in recent years because of her support for natal women that some people online consider to be a mask for transphobia. Although Rowling's case is potentially relevant—if only because Adichie's endorsement of Rowling's essay on the subject as "a perfectly reasonable piece" came across to some online commentators as a symbolic act of violence against the trans community—the literary dimension to cancel culture that interests me for now is the African literary space (Allardice 2020).

On Adichie's part, controversies and feuds about her views on trans identities became more intense after a viral clip of an interview with Britain's *Channel 4 News* that included a question about trans women. When asked if being a trans woman makes one "any less of a real woman," Adichie responded: "When people talk about, 'Are trans women women?' my feeling is trans women are trans women. And I think if you have lived in the world as a man with the privileges the world accords to men and then you . . . switch gender, it is difficult for me to accept that then we can equate your experience with the experience of a woman who has lived from the beginning in the world as a woman."[4] It appears Adichie did not suggest that trans women have any male privileges as some commentaries implied online. Rather, she called attention to the sociological facts and elasticity of gender itself, even if not completely in the manner of feminist scholars who are now deemed gender-critical. The online outrage to Adichie's views was varied, with some commentators questioning whether a cisgender woman could objectively understand and articulate the experiences of trans women, while others in the majority were startled that the Nigerian writer would dare insinuate a difference between trans women and women.[5] To this contradictory spectrum that reifies the difference that the *Americanah* author alludes to, Adichie later responded in a Facebook post in which she clarifies her position: "we can oppose violence against trans women while also acknowledging differences . . . saying 'trans' and 'cis' acknowledges that there is a distinction between women born female and women who transition, without elevating one or the other, which was my point."[6] It, therefore, needs to be emphasized that the need to affirm that trans women are women, which was expected of Adichie, ontologically posits a difference, as it simultaneously avows that trans women are not women in the way natal women are. The importance of Adichie's Facebook explanation should not be missed, for it illuminates the power of immediacy that writing on social media affords. Given the outrage and controversies around the topic, the Facebook commentariat on the post included fans and followers from both camps of the debate that offered their own commentaries and counter-commentaries on the subject. In this framework, the identities of the many readers of Adichie's fiction become transformed into affective and unruly publics that complicate Adichie's performance of authorship on social media. Social media's unruly publics are symptomatic of a widespread aversion to forms of authority and are sometimes enablers of censorious practices online.

In mid-2021, when Adichie published "It Is Obscene: A True Reflection in Three Parts" on her personal website, many readers found it moving because of a certain poignancy in the writer's tone. In this article, Adichie highlights strained relations with two former students from her writing workshop in Lagos. Although Adichie does not mention the names of these students, they are presented as people that have personally attacked and publicly maligned Adichie as a transphobic writer. The trans argument debate is pertinent for analyses, as the controversy was specifically framed as a public feud "about feminism, gender identity, cancel culture, social media and anti-LGBTQ violence" between two Nigerian literary stars, namely, Adichie and the nonbinary author of *Freshwater* Akwaeke Emezi (Tsioulcas 2021). Although Adichie refutes this categorization, the perception of Adichie among many in the trans community, particularly from the standpoint of Emezi, is that her rhetoric against trans people obscures the possibility of actual physical harm and discursive violence in the name of critiquing cancel culture.[7] In particular, OluTimehin Kukoyi, the second writer Chimamanda Adichie appears to have referenced in her essay, reflects on "this virtual violence" of Adichie's online expressions of transphobia, asserting a refusal to be named and defined by the more established writer who, in her view, has indeed "endorsed lengthy public statements that are unmistakably transphobic to those of us who actually understand transphobia" (2021). Hence, Adichie's critics construct her as a feminist who uses her social and reputational capital and literary celebrity status to exclude the rights of transgender women in her advocacy work. In the viral essay in which Adichie movingly challenges this claim and labels these two former students as opportunistic, she refers to a 2017 interview in which she had observed "that a trans woman is a trans woman, (the larger point of which was to say that we should be able to acknowledge difference while being fully inclusive, that in fact the whole premise of inclusiveness is difference)" (2021). While Adichie rails against the frequently uncritical and inhumane use of social media and disavows any transphobic ideology, the call to cancel her remained active on Twitter since she had essentially become a TERF—a trans exclusionary radical feminist. This term is not without its politics of digital shaming and has specific valences and histories in different social contexts. Its uses in the UK, for example, are different from how it is mobilized in the framework of American critical registers in which it is just beginning to gain some traction. But the point in contention was not Adichie's merits as an award-winning novelist whose aesthetics are unquestionably solid. Rather, it was that she had to be canceled because her feminist politics questioned the gender identity of trans women. Hence, it might be helpful to reread Chantal Zabus on this subject. Zabus points to "a clash between African feminisms and transfeminisms" that sometimes plays out in digital arenas that "contribute to new identity formations such as datafied and digitized selves as a result of being 'out online'" (2021, 393). The arguments and conflicts that arise from these datafied subjectivities suggest a need to engage more with transgender literary productions, which are relevant to African literature as the appearance of disputations among some of the continent's creative writers and scholars also demonstrate. Beyond African literature, these controversies mirror debates among traditional feminists and trans activists whose goals and doctrines are often different.

The article from Adichie's website, as well as a 2022 freedom of speech Reith Lecture for the BBC, led to more arguments that questioned her moral legitimacy as a feminist endorsing a binary view of gender. After her Reith Lecture, one Twitter user went as far as labeling the writer a "transphobic monster" who dehumanizes trans people, while others pleaded with her followers not to read Adichie's work. These debates are important, both for making visible the role of social media in the controversies and for consolidating a growing queer sensibility that writers such as Emezi, one of Adichie's online interlocutors, increasingly represent in African writing. But Adichie herself might argue that the motivation of those who want her canceled is attention and praise, which is often garnered from organizing an attack on the reputation of another person. Adichie is unapologetic in her stance that her attackers on social media were partly motivated because they are "seeking attention and publicity to benefit themselves" (2021). Writing to decry cancel culture made Adichie susceptible to the diatribes of social media users who gain from her crisis and from whom she continues to face backlash for what is seen as her transphobia. When Nigerian poet Dami Ajayi published an online essay on the Adichie-Emezi ruckus by detailing an earlier incident where Adichie herself had responded condescendingly to a question of his, Ajayi's personal inbox became a space of threats and "a lot of abuses" from Adichie supporters.[8] Ajayi's experience signposts how people participate in literary controversies by generating their own content and inserting themselves into the space of the original disputation, which often becomes the source of other controversies. This reproductive nature of literary controversies as something that refracts the divisive politics of the platform also played out in the online debates involving the writer Onyeka Nwelue, who questioned Emezi's spirituality and provoked some criticisms online. In all of these scenarios, the divisive nature of social media platforms manifests as configuring literary networks and publics that are combative and hostile to one another. The virtual enactments of Adichie's private feuds with her former proteges on social media also point to the role platformization plays both in producing a new literary culture and amplifying controversies among writers. I will return in a later chapter to Adichie's controversial encounters with these proteges some of whom, like Elnathan John, she famously referred to as "her boys."

Cancel Culture and Decolonization

As I discuss in my introduction, the call to exclude Adichie from the classroom as an act of respect for trans students in my classroom is not a new one, and my stance did not fully endorse it. A writer's humanity and their works—fiction and personhood—are on two different scales. However, in an algorithmic age of personality, these two are conflated more intensely than in a previous era, such as the Romantic era or post-Nazi Europe, when some scholars and public intellectuals supported the violence of the Holocaust. I did propose an alternative to any transgender students who may be concerned about engaging with Adichie. Several of Achebe's critical essays would be a good fit, but a more contemporary work to Adichie's TED Talk is Binyavanga Wainaina's *How to Write about Africa* (2011), which performs a similar task of de-essentializing Africa and dismantling persistent tropes of stereotypes.

In any case, although I believe strongly in the open exchange of all ideas, it is not primarily my task to defend Adichie in the classroom. Even if they are difficult topics and odious ideas, people can approach them freely and responsibly, while keeping in mind that free speech is sometimes socially constructed and can be made to serve power interests along any ideological lines.

Either way, although the two often overlap, the aesthetic merit of Adichie's writings, rather than her gender politics, should determine whether she would be included on a syllabus. A writer's morality is not coterminous with the inherent value or strength of their arguments and ideas. Perhaps more importantly, my point in response to the question is that in order to cancel Adichie, we would have to look further back and cancel Immanuel Kant, Georg Wilhelm Friedrich Hegel, and Hannah Arendt, all Western philosophers whose records on race and gender are somewhat problematic. I had in mind, for example, readings of Kant's work by feminists and Black scholars that uncover a pattern of sexism and racism that many would find morally offensive were they expressed today. It should be noted that I am merely revisiting some of the ideas of these philosophers in a manner consistent with the methodological approach to reexamine Achebe's ideas on Conrad and read them in the light of cancel culture.

While different Kantian philosophers might offer divergent thoughts on the idea that Kant's writings promote the growth of racist ideas, specific expressions in his published and unpublished work demonstrate chauvinistic trends that center racial hierarchies underpinned by a troubling sense of Eurocentric superiority. Kant, for example, constructs Africans as having "by nature no feeling that rises above the ridiculous," aside from his complete dismissal of Blacks as "lacking any finer feeling, and thus retaining perhaps the lowest spot in this hierarchy of racially or nationally based tastes" (Armstrong 1996, 224). His problematic positions also include the claim about the "unnaturalness of a female philosopher, 'who might as well have a beard'" (Huseyinzadegan 2018, 1).[9] His sexism is consistent with a provincialist conception of race that undermines his cosmopolitan philosophies and animates imperialist hierarchies. Hence, Walter Mignolo writes of Kant's cosmopolitanism as presupposing "that it could only be thought out from one particular geopolitical location: that of the heart of Europe, of the most civilized nations" as the frame of reference (2000, 735). Consequently, Paula Uimonen notes that contrary to his cosmopolitan claims, "Kant's work should thus be appraised in the context of scientific and moral claims that sought to assert the positional superiority of Europeans vis-à-vis non-European peoples and cultures" (2020, 85).

In the age of cancel culture, the falling of monuments continues to gain traction because of the widespread resistance to systemic racism in the aftermath of the 2020 George Floyd murder in the United States. The intellectual contributions of influential European philosophers are being reassessed based on identity politics masquerading as cancel culture. Yet, the argument is not to cancel Kant and retain Kwasi Wiredu; rather, it is that at a point, there was often a naïve marriage of the so-called imperative to decolonize and the zeal to cancel some philosophers—one in which those performing the act of canceling might insist on canceling every European thinker irrespective of the universal legitimacy of the thinker's ideas. As the philosopher Olúfẹ́mi Táíwò has cautioned, we need to stop calling something colonial simply because it has a European connection when it actually antedates colonialism as a natural human phenomenon that is common to indigenous populations everywhere. To want to decolonize such a phenomenon misrecognizes our own epistemic agency. This is not the approach I favor, and there are several Black scholars and theorists whose work support my own perspective. For example, in his *The Racial Contract*, Charles Mills tackles the works of Enlightenment thinkers like Hobbes, Locke, Rousseau, and Kant (sometimes called the social contractarians) engaging with their postulation of a nonideal "social contract" that, though foundational to liberal democracy, excluded Blacks and other nonwhite people. Although social contract tradition has been central to Western political theory, its logic of exclusion was made possible by the racism and sexism of its best theorists. However, rather than dismiss or cancel these European thinkers and present them as philosophers whose work should no longer be read today, Mills uses their work to demonstrate "the inner logic of *racial* domination and how it structures the polities of the West and elsewhere" (2014, 6). Hence, continued pedagogical and scholarly engagements with these thinkers becomes a way to lay bare the contradictions of the Enlightenment. Again, the ironic complicity of some Enlightenment thinkers in oppressive conditions such as slavery may be indefensible, but the strength of their argument is another matter entirely. The challenge is to uphold diverse literary and intellectual traditions without resorting to canceling works that promote sexual and racial ideologies that most people today find offensive.

Other routine subjects for some decolonial cancel culture advocates include Hegel's dialectical philosophy and its insidious racism, as well as those of many other European philosophers and cultural producers whose body of works intellectually justified the harmful logics of race. I will conclude this section by posing a question that routinely comes to mind each time I am confronted with the subject of challenging the racial underpinnings of Euro-Western epistemological dominance among decolonizing cancel culture advocates: should we no longer read Arendt because some scholars have accused her of racial prejudices, especially regarding her writings about people of African descent? Put differently, should we topple the monumental works and ideas of European thinkers who, in their time, produced a body of works that systematically established the foundations of European racism, while also opening avenues through their intellectual reflections to finally contemplate its evil? The language of cancel culture, which tends to withdraw support from individuals for saying or doing offensive things, might press an affirmative response in this case. But as long as it fails to promote rational and an open exchange of ideas, it undercuts its own project. If there is anything the Israel-Palestine conflict made clear in 2023, and the year that followed, it is that the threat to open exchange and the unrestricted criticism of injustices is mediated by powerful interests and people of different ideological affiliations become selective in what is critiqued.

Yet, besides the fact that an open exchange of ideas is not undifferentiated, there are two things that are worth stressing here: one is that reason, or the rationality of so-called public debates in liberal democracy, is not necessarily antithetical to expressions of emotions such as anger or rage. Anger, and indeed other emotions, can be *rationally* and intelligently articulated in public debates.[10] The second issue is to recall that decolonial critiques of reason itself convey it as a colonial mode of discursive oppression and epistemic erasure. To paraphrase Emmanuel Chukwudi Eze, reason is subjected to the logics of color in colonial modernity, with the racialization of so-called rational discourses, for example, central to the project of several Enlightenment thinkers (1997). Eze's assessment of the "colour of reason" is duplicated in Ngũgĩ wa Thiong'o's critique of Kant and Hegel, with the Kenyan writer arguing that Enlightenment reason proceeded not from a truly cosmopolitan epistemic model but from these philosophers' narrow and non-globalectical experiences of the world. For example, Kant, who never left Königsberg, "could only have based his knowledge on explorer narratives. . . . Many of these philosophers used each other as sources and proofs of their own observations; prejudice thus reinforcing prejudice till it became an accepted truth, an authoritative norm" (wa Thiong'o 2012, 32–33).[11]

In the specific instances of Arendt, her *The Origins of Totalitarianism*, an important text of postcolonial theory, was already tackling the question of racial ideology, which was central around the same time to Fanon's theory of decolonization.

For instance, in Arendt's estimation, the scramble for Africa and African colonial possessions "became the most fertile soil for the flowering of what later was to become the Nazi elite. Here they had seen with their own eyes how peoples could be converted into races and how, simply by taking the initiative in this process, one might push one's own people into the position of the master race" (1951, 206). Therefore, European fascist politics was the reterritorialization of norms of African imperialist domination into the heart of Europe itself. Despite her penetrative analyses of the evil of fascism and racist ideologies, Arendt has been called out (not in the fashion of cancel culture, though) for "her easy dismissal of African history, African literatures, African languages" as well as her readiness to ascribe academic inferiority to Black students (Norton 1995, 248). Anne Norton argues that Arendt's constructions of Africa and African Americans "represent so dramatic a departure from the scholarly and civil character of her work as a whole that one might read them as an aberration. . . . That course might do justice to Arendt as a private woman, but it would continue the unjust effects of her public writings" (1995, 248). While Norton refuses to question Arendt's private ethics, she nonetheless questions the approbation that is staged through the silence demanded by a veneration for Arendt's stature in the theoretical canon. Again, in the age of cancel culture, the dialectical tension is between the veneration of good or sound intellectual thought and the hasty dismissal of the unethical scholar from public debates—whether in print avenues or on the internet.

For those with this mindset, decolonization amounts to canceling Shakespeare and replacing him with only Soyinka. In some cases, any non-Yorùbá person that studies Soyinka becomes constructed as an impostor who should cling to only Shakespeare in Global North institutions, but an ethical decolonization shuns this vague shallowness that purports to epistemically free the Yorùbá mind from the West and includes both Shakespeare and Soyinka without encouraging any hierarchies between them. While the fact that some European scholars still worryingly see both writers as incompatible and unequal is something to acknowledge, both of them indeed participate in a similar world of significations from which they articulate the human condition, even if they write in different historical periods and cultural contexts. At the same time, that those seeking to cancel Shakespeare and replace him with Soyinka hardly engage with Soyinka's body of works undermines the decolonization they parrot. This is the point Táíwò persuasively outlines to demonstrate "how much is obscured by the call to 'decolonise' anything and everything" in his argument that a lack of critical engagement with African cultural materials by decolonizing scholars undermines their theoretical project (2022, 15). Whether it "is 'African music,' 'African Philosophy,' 'African literature' or something else, the place of colonialism in its genealogy must be considered and demonstrated to show why it is a candidate for decolonizing," Táíwò writes (16). The best example of this idea in Táíwò's body of work is the concept of modernity, which he has repeatedly argued was not facilitated by European colonialism in Africa. In other words, if something, say modernity, cannot be shown to have a solid origin in, or a close relationship with, colonialism, there is no basis to decolonize it, even if it has connections to European intellectual tradition. Like Táíwò, I am therefore unpersuaded by the tendency that saturates the current wave of decolonization (and cancel culture warfare) that is occasionally characterized by an unremitting and sometimes violent opposition to locate a colonial hangover in every process, practice, or institution, particularly when the rage is by people who confuse the logic of an insidious settler-colonial legacy with the traditional exploitative type of European colonialism. Although neither type, it has to be said, was benign.[12]

My brief excursion into the intellectual world of the European thinkers in a reflection on cancel culture is to argue that the epistemic framework that arises from colonial modernity is vulnerable to ambivalence and a certain messiness, partly captured in Arendt's treatise on the human condition itself. Writers of different cultural and racial backgrounds have all sought to make these legible in their creative outputs. A shift from solely Eurocentric ways of knowing to more pluriversal and truly universal systems of knowing is necessary as long as it, in its refusal to privilege any epistemic hierarchies, encounters reason and rationality as inherently human. The choice of an individual or European thinker that is routinely presented for cancelation online is sometimes dependent on a smug moralism that characterizes both the liberal and conservative iterations of cancel culture. More importantly, for those who imagine canceling Arendt and other European thinkers as an exercise in epistemic freedom and decolonial politics, the reasoning, as mentioned earlier on Mills, is contingent on European narratives of Enlightenment and progress that, they believe, have historically silenced other knowledge frameworks. The absence of inclusive paradigms and the enduring naturalization of mostly Western thought have motivated these renewed gestures of cancel culture and the overthrow of historical monuments and intellectual ideas. But it cannot be forgotten that Western culture—and I am not monolithizing it—both erected monuments to its supposed greatness and brought forth revolutionaries to tear down those monuments, and both possibilities have to remain in view. There is a need for continued resistance to any traces of the historical politics of canonization that favor hierarchical thought systems that marginalize ways of knowing from the Global South—even when the Global South itself is not homogenous. But asserting the epistemic freedom of non-European societies also means acknowledging that writers and intellectuals from postcolonial countries have the right to invoke, for instance, ideas on free speech, democratic deliberation, and human experiences (including those of the Enlightenment) from anywhere.

It goes without saying that cancel culture and decolonization are not necessarily coterminous. While being mindful of the ambivalence that Europe concurrently produced monuments of greatness as well as radical agents that toppled them, what is probably at stake is the need to diversify inherited European intellectual systems or to decenter European habits of thought embedded in our attempts to address questions of political modernity, as Dipesh Chakrabarty has argued. In his *Provincializing Europe* (2008), he argues that the task should not be a project of rejecting or discarding European thought as an exercise of postcolonial retribution. On the contrary, "European thought is at once both indispensable and inadequate in helping us to think through the experiences of political modernity in non-Western nations, and provincializing Europe becomes the task of exploring how this thought—which is now everybody's heritage and which affect us all—may be renewed from and for the margins" (16). We can think with Europe's so-called universal ideas, which themselves are translated differently in various places, without downplaying the epistemological logics of our own intellectual traditions. This approach is similar to Dilek Huseyinzadegan's feminist appropriations of canonical figures such as Kant. In reading Kant, Huseyinzadegan employs a methodology of "constructive complicity," based on Spivak's arguments in *A Critique of Postcolonial Reason*, presenting an ambiguous Kantian system that makes "Kant truly useful for feminist, antiracist, anti-colonial theorizing" (2018, 15). To be constructively complicit means we mobilize decolonial and postcolonial approaches that tackle the entire gamut of oppressive thought systems, while avowing the paradigms of other philosophical traditions and their cultural protocols of knowing.

In the context of African literary studies, the fundamental issue is to decolonize the mind, as Ngũgĩ argues, by upending any prevailing structures of coloniality that intertwine with the politics of language to displace African agency (1986). The Ghanaian philosopher Kwasi Wiredu similarly frames this imperative as an epistemological practice, which he describes as "conceptual decolonization" to name the necessary epistemic elimination of modes of conceptualization from our thoughts that came to us from colonization and remain active in our thinking and rituals of thought (2002). But we cannot forget that even this approach (Wiredu's or Ngũgĩ's) that favors a "thoroughgoing decolonization," that signals a necessary linguistic turn, as Adélékè Adéẹ̀kọ́ also recently suggests, is not universally accepted among African scholars.[13] While Ngũgĩ argues that English signifies the continued legacy of colonialism in Africa and re-mains oppressive and exclusionary in official contexts and cultural productions, scholars like Bio-dun Jeyifo prefer a strategic ambivalence. Jeyifo's approach champions "a radical departure from the orthodoxies of postcolonial African cultural and linguistic nationalism" and an acceptance of the sociolinguistic value of English in the continent (2018, 133). While Ngũgĩ does continue to write his critical works in English, Jeyifo celebrates Ngũgĩ's revolutionary recourse to Kikuyu but disagrees that all languages are equal, as many African languages are oral and do not have a well-developed writing system. For him, English has a functional status in Africa and has served important official discourses, including significant documents of political philosophy and constitution-making like the South African Constitution and the Arusha Declaration, both in English. For his part, and writing in a 1965 edition of *Transition*, Achebe hardly imagines writing in English as producing "signs of sterility" that beg to be decolonized. What he sees is a new voice coming out of Africa and speaking of African experience in a world-wide language:

> So my answer to the question, Can an African ever learn English well enough to be able to use it effectively in creative writing? is certainly yes. If on the other hand you ask: Can he ever learn to use it like a native speaker? I should say, I hope not. . . . The African writer should aim to use English in a way that brings out his message best without altering the language to the extent that its value as a medium of international exchange will be lost. He should aim at fashioning out an English which is at once universal and able to carry his peculiar experience. (29)

Linguistic nationalism aside, decolonization itself becomes merely a metaphor when decolonizing discourses are adopted or even coopted by superficial culture warriors on social media to designate all forms of social justice goals that obscure the necessary engagements with African cultural and linguistic materials (Tuck and Yang 2012). If, as Fanon maintains, decolonization is the total transformation of persistent colonial structures and their epistemic systems or a historical process and program of complete disorder that "sets out to change the world," then we are indeed far off from such a radical systemic transformation of *any* residual, colonial framework (1968, 36). This critical reconfiguration of the system might be possible in settler-colonial contexts that are not prevalent in Africa. Decolonization in this radical sense cannot be rendered "accountable to settlers, or settler futurity," but to "Indigenous sovereignty and futurity" (Tuck and Yang 2012, 35). But instead of a decolonial framework that has the potential to replace a totalizing discourse with an essentialist one that seeks to cancel all European thought systems, the focus lies in addressing the absence of diversity and inclusion in the intellectual canon, without undoubtedly the reification of Global North epistemologies. Not to have Europe as center means avoiding "the bad habit of regarding that slice of the globe [Europe and the West] as the whole thing," as Achebe, in his collection of essays *Morning Yet on Creation Day*, cautions in regard to African writers who uncritically export the orthodoxies of "colonialist criticisms" into their work (1976, 32). With the dispossessive and extractive logic of European colonialism most foregrounded in the realm of knowledge, it makes sense that decolonization and decolonial rhetoric sometimes emerge in discussions of cancel culture. But these cannot become a pretext for an uncritical overthrow of all existing ways of knowing connected to Europe. Rather than reject or completely negate European thought systems and the various literary forms that organically served the extractive visions of Empire, pluralistic epistemological cultures are more meaningful, one that neither seeks to cancel the literary classics of Western civilization in the name of inclusion nor locates Europe as any hegemonic center. Besides, the genealogies of an epistemological position should never become more pertinent than its universality in illuminating the human condition.

Canceling *Heart of Darkness*

While it appears in "An Image of Africa" that Achebe essentially calls for *Heart of Darkness* to be canceled from the literary canon, the essay can also be viewed as enacting a desire for open and rational debate that looks beyond the mostly positive views of Conrad to the initial absence of debates about his project in *Heart of Darkness*. Conrad's work is an excellent modernist meditation on how a discursively invented Western civilization mobilized its cultural archive to legitimize colonial structures and interpellate the subjects of Empire. At the time he was writing, the racism of many European literary classics was in full throttle, with disciplines such as English manifesting a long history of providing aesthetic rationalization for colonial exploitation. Hence, the University of Chicago's English Department, writing in solidarity with the Black Lives Matter protest, recognized in 2020 how "admissions might be another opportunity to materialize a commitment to Black people, Black thought, and Black Studies" (Snorton 2020). This move, though viewed as controversial by some, marks one way the discipline has made progress in anticolonialist and antiracist work in the last few decades.

Heart of Darkness undercuts the post-Enlightenment optimism over the triumph of science and reason and portrays Empire's capitalistic dispossessions and conquest of other people's lands. My goal, as I close this chapter, is not to reprise the numerous postcolonial critiques of Conrad; instead, it is to rearticulate Achebe's position about the controversial place of a great novel in the Western Canon in relation to cancel culture. "An Image of Africa" is a significant work of postcolonial theory, as Achebe was one of the earliest scholars to contest the unchallenged belief that Conrad's *Heart of Darkness* was an important anticolonialist text that is worthy of canonical status. Achebe objects to the notion that *Heart of Darkness* is "a great work of art" because of its racist and dehumanizing representations of Africa (1977, 788). First delivered at the University of Massachusetts as a lecture in February 1975, an amended version of the text was published as an essay in the *Massachusetts Review* (1977) and thereafter in Achebe's *Hopes and Impediments* (1989).

Unlike previous psychological readings of the text that focused on how Marlow's journey into a geographic "heart of darkness" symbolizes a movement into a conjuncture that reflects the darkened psychic interior of European civilization, Achebe's acerbic reading deepened a necessary postcolonial critique of Conrad's modernist classic.[14] *Heart of Darkness* begins with passengers aboard a steamer on the River Thames, with Charlie Marlow, one of the passengers, telling other seafarers about his experiences in Africa on what is often allegorically read as the Congo River. His narrative, which operates within the larger story Conrad's narrator is telling, begins in Europe, in the "sepulchral city" where an unnamed company that runs a colonial enterprise in an unnamed Central African territory (assumedly, the Congo) has appointed him captain of a steamer (Conrad and Page 1995, 28). He sets out for Africa, optimistic about what he will find. When Marlow arrives at his destination, he is exposed to the exploitation and evils of colonialism along with the violence and dehumanization it imposes on the local population. Specifically, Marlow encounters the brutality in the Company's stations and the exploitation of the region's inhabitants, who are cruelly treated and forced into the Company's service. Other parts of Conrad's work reveal Marlow's other journeys, including his mission to the Inner Station to find Kurtz, an ivory-collecting expert and colonial administrator who may have become mad and lost his way in the Congo. Marlow believes Kurtz has become depraved, having "taken a high seat amongst the devils of the land" (57). Marlow's recollection furnishes the reader with different tales of the indigenous people presented in less than humane terms, as Conrad's so-called anticolonial text deploys exotic and dehumanizing language.

There are, of course, pointers in *Heart of Darkness* itself that support interpretations of the text as a work rebuking the civilizing mission in Africa and exposing the evils of Western imperialism, "countless examples throughout the text that point to Conrad's recognition of the illegitimacy of this trading mission and the brutalizing effect it is having on the Africans" (Phillips 2003).This view of *Heart of Darkness* as excoriating colonial power while stereotyping African people can be seen in the work itself, right from the beginning when Marlow begins his story: "The conquest of the earth, which mostly means the taking it away from those who have a different complexion or slightly flatter noses than ourselves, is not a pretty thing when you look into it too much. What redeems it is the idea only" (Conrad and Page 1995, 7). Despite this early suggestion of its anticolonial vision, European imperialism itself, as a less than pretty location of profound evil, correlates with metaphoric readings of the title that stage the heart of darkness in both Europe and the Congo. But while Conrad depicts this vision of European colonialism as a sordid sea of violence that exploits and violates Africa, the possibility that there is something redeemable about "the idea" behind imperialism undercuts his "good" anticolonial gestures and possibly warrants the many postcolonial critiques of the text. If the redemptive force of colonialism is the focus in Marlow's line earlier, then ambivalence undergirds Conrad's engagement with the ambiguities and contradictions of the European civilizing mission. However, we have to question this notion that the "idea" was indeed redemptive at the end of the narrative since Marlowe can be seen lying to Kurtz's Intended about her lover's death. Rather than a redemption, a fundamental falsehood underpins both the excursion into the Congo and its closing moments—which some decolonizing scholars would argue never really ended.

Hence, Conrad's devotion to the idea of the civilizing mission is also complicated by the narrative irony around Kurtz, who, despite killing some natives, having sex with others, or stealing ivory through his highly efficient but brutal methods, transforms into one of the "natives," as he is becoming more brutal than the so-called brutes. Therefore, Marlow is unable to convey the darkness of Kurtz's true nature and of his death to the Intended. To excuse Kurtz's role as an effect of Conrad's narratorial presentation is to misrecognize how the novella is both based on an impressionist style that is seductively immersive and "enhances empathy, through something like hypnosis" and a subjective enactment of an African non-place "that circumvents readerly resistance" (Matz 2017, 134). Therefore, critics' identification with Marlow and Conrad is structured by this induced "hypnotic stupor in his readers [that is underhandedly organized] through a bombardment of emotive words and other forms of trickery" (Achebe 1977, 784).

In an essay written around the same time as Achebe's, Frances Singh admits that Conrad appears to be invested in lashing out against colonialism, although he also undermines his intentions (1978). Singh writes that "Marlow's ethnocentricity leads him to side with the colonizers against the Africans and that this approach is shared by Conrad" (52). This ambivalence manifests as a form of rhetorical violence in the novella's unflattering language and includes expressions that render graphic the linguistic contradictions of colonial atrocity. The argument can be made that Singh's observation is one example of what Stephen Ross identifies as critiques that "often depend on either collapsing the difference between Conrad and his narrators/characters or seeing contradictions as signs of bad faith rather than ambiguous—at times ambivalent—efforts to come to terms with a profoundly contradictory phenomenon" (2004, 187). In a radical departure from postcolonial interpretations of *Heart of Darkness*, Ross argues that Conrad's work could be read as confronting an inchoate post-imperialist formation or an emerging new global order, refusing the primacy of race and imperialism privileged the most in critical interpretations. While we should also seek to read Conrad's work both in the spirit of anti–cancel culture and for its complex engagements with the perplexing contradictions of modernity, the disturbing images of Conrad's language and the form of his narrative provide sufficient reasons for Achebe and Singh to detect racist ideologies that warrant the novella's exclusion from serious work of literature (Ross 2004, 187). This detection of the work's racist aspects is essential, but it hardly warrants excluding it from the canon. The messiness of human nature is itself proof that we cannot have only a clean slate of books, whether European or African. Nonetheless, my interest in Conrad is a close reading of Achebe's interpretation of the text to ground my argument that Achebe appeared to be calling for *Heart of Darkness* to be canceled from the literary canon because Conrad, as he argues, is a "thoroughgoing racist."[15] As Achebe himself writes, quoting copiously from the novella:

> *Heart of Darkness* projects the image of Africa as "the other world," the antithesis of Europe and therefore of civilization, a place where man's vaunted intelligence and refinement are finally mocked by triumphant bestiality. The book opens on the River Thames, tranquil, resting peacefully "at the decline of day after ages of good service done to the race that peopled its banks." But the actual story takes place on the River Congo, the very antithesis of the Thames. The River Congo is quite decidedly not a River Emeritus. It has rendered no service and enjoys no old-age pension. We are told that "going up that river was like travelling back to the earliest beginnings of the world." . . . What actually worries Conrad is the lurking hint of kinship, of common ancestry. (1977, 783)

It is possible that Achebe, in fact, fails to grasp the central argument of the novella entirely, namely, Conrad's attempt to deconstruct and unsettle the colonial and European notions of superiority that inform European civilization. In this reading, civilized Europe is structurally connected to the heart of darkness, which Kurtz has purportedly discovered in Africa. Kurtz, therefore, embodies both the interior darkness of European colonialism and the human condition itself. The redemptive idea is the capacity to read barbarism not in the Other but in the human heart itself; Marlowe discovers this when looking within himself and finding Kurtz but is unable to translate that to Kurtz's Intended. For a man who started out claiming to hate falsehood, he resorts to it in an attempt to deny it. The same argument can be made about the Thames, although it emerges in Achebe's analyses as the ideal ecological space by which Conrad presents a barbaric image of the Congo. In juxtaposing the formulations of both rivers in the short novel, Achebe recognizes the dialectical struggle in which the River Congo, as "the very antithesis of the Thames," lacks any agential capacity and merely facilitates retrogressive or prehistoric possibilities. The paradigm Achebe describes is similar to what Achille Mbembe later describes as a conception of Africa as a site of absolute otherness that renders the continent as "an idea, a concept, has historically served, and continues to serve, as a critical argument for the West's desperate desire to assert its difference from the rest of the world" (2001, 2). Hence, for Achebe, Western psychology through historiographical accounts and literary languages set "Africa up as a foil to Europe," such that the continent is "a place of negations at once remote and vaguely familiar in comparison with which Europe's own state of spiritual grace will be manifest" (1977, 783). Unlike Achebe's reading, if we saw the Thames as symbolically connected to the Congo rather than as negations of each other, it becomes obvious that the novella is true to the nineteenth century to early twentieth–century view about the nature of human as brutish, hence Conrad's indictment of humanity using a racist model that imagined colonialism as a civilizing mission. Does this reading undermine the fact that Conrad's work is potentially a racist work that might be canceled from today's classroom? Hardly, for the racist elements of the novella are uncontestable.

Achebe's goal in the essay is to expose both the politics of Conrad's narrative and the ethical infelicities of a supposedly great work of art that questions the very humanity of Black people and their shared ancestry with the architects of the evils of Empire. The racist stereotypes he addresses gain in intensity, as evident in this passage, which Achebe designates as the "most interesting and revealing passage" (1977, 784) in *Heart of Darkness*:

> But suddenly, as we struggled round a bend, there would be a glimpse of rush walls, of peaked grass-roofs, a burst of yells, a whirl of black limbs, a mass of hands clapping, of feet stamping, of bodies swaying, of eyes rolling, under the droop of heavy and motionless foliage. The steamer toiled along slowly on the edge of a black and incomprehensible frenzy. The prehistoric man was cursing us, praying to us, welcoming us—who could tell? We were cut off from the comprehension of our surroundings; we glided past like phantoms, wondering and secretly appalled, as sane men would be before an enthusiastic outbreak in a madhouse. We could not understand because we were too far and could not remember because we were travelling in the night of first ages, of those ages that are gone, leaving hardly a sign—and no memories . . . The earth seemed unearthly. We are accustomed to look upon the shackled form of a conquered monster, but there—there you could look at a thing monstrous and free. It was unearthly, and the men were—No, they were not inhuman. Well, you know, that was the worst of it—this suspicion of their not being inhuman. It would come slowly to one. They howled and leaped, and spun, and made horrid faces; but what thrilled you was just the thought of their humanity—like yours—the thought of your remote kinship with this wild and passionate uproar. Ugly. (Conrad and Page 1995, 41–42)

This passage—specifically the point on the ugliness that stems from the thought that a remote kinship exists between the European and the African—is the basis for an earlier argument about the flawed humanity that is being interrogated through the racism and violence of European colonialism. Deploying the horrid racial discourses of the era to interrogate the human experience may not be controversial then, but it certainly is today. Presented astutely in one of Conrad's most striking passages in the text, this descriptive schema of the indigenous people of the unmapped Congo offers a sense of Marlow's journey as he and the other Europeans penetrate "deeper and deeper into the heart of darkness," into the soul of a Congo plundered and ravished by an uninvited, thrusting phallus (Conrad and Page 1995, 41). This excerpt frames the Congo inhabitants as "prehistoric" bodies that emerge from the dark and constructs them as caricatured humans who, perhaps, are praying to and welcoming the White visitors that are obviously to be venerated by "the crowd of savages" (70). While the possibility of a shared humanity of the people encountered may be, according to Achebe, what fascinates Marlow the most, equating this humanity with ugliness and devilishness, as Conrad's prose unimaginatively does, is troubling for Achebe. Although Achebe too may be seen to conflate Conrad and Marlow—"since Conrad does not establish any distance between himself and the moral and psychological malaise of his narrator" and "neglects to hint . . . at an alternative frame of reference"—this argument is persuasive (Achebe 1977, 787). He claims that Marlow, dreading the possibility of any remote kinship, is appalled that the "ugly" people he meets in the jungles of Africa are indeed humans who have agential and creative power like any European. Since Conrad's description is neither absolute nor objective, the point needs to be reiterated that the narrative acknowledges a fear of an inherent capacity for violent forces, which is then projected onto the unknown Other and which Marlowe discovers in Kurtz. Edward Said is generally less dismissive than Achebe, summing up this problem with *Heart of Darkness* in *Culture and Imperialism*:

> Conrad's tragic limitation is that even though he could see clearly that on one level imperialism was essentially pure dominance and land-grabbing, he could not then conclude that imperialism had to end so that "natives" could lead lives free from European domination. As a creature of his time, Conrad could not grant the natives their freedom, despite his severe critique of the imperialism that enslaved them. (1993, 26)

Rather than read Said as advocating an improvement for a novel that set out to critique colonialism but became deeply emblematic of it, the question of African agency and its affirmation in Conrad's narrative space is indeed a tragic limitation. Unlike Said, for whom *Heart of Darkness* was a foundational anticolonial text, Achebe meticulously demonstrates "the fact that white racism against Africa is such a normal way of thinking" and that Conrad was a racist who was fascinated with an ugly Africa (1977, 788). In line with my argument earlier, it is possible to read that ugliness as uncovering the ugliness of the European heart. For Achebe, any anti-imperialist propositions in the *Heart of Darkness*, founded upon the breakdown of the European (or Kurtz's) mind, merely deploys Africa and its inhabitants as mere props. The notion of Africa as the geographical backdrop of European psychic disintegration arrogantly "eliminates the African as human factor" and is, therefore, even more perverse (788). The major problem, as Achebe argues, is the dehumanization of Africa and Africans, which an enduring racist mode of objectification prompts the Conradian exclusion of African subjectivity and social agency that is visible in Achebe's own novels. We may argue, though, that even Achebe's *Things Fall Apart* fails terribly in evoking the subjectivity of Mr. Jones and Mr. Smith since they, as cardboard characters who appear more stock than real, hardly represent Europeans.

The question, as Achebe argues, "is whether a novel which celebrates this dehumanization, which depersonalizes a portion of the human race, can be called a great work of art." Achebe's answer is emphatic: "No, it cannot" (788). Invoking the intellectual class that supported Nazi atrocities in Germany and how they have "generally and rightly been condemned for their perversions," he declares that the time "is long overdue for taking a hard look at the work of creative artists who apply their talents, alas often considerable as in the case of Conrad, to set people against people" (789). Aside from the fact that, based on David Denby's understanding, Achebe wants *Heart of Darkness* "thrown out of the Western canon," the logic of Achebe's argumentation stipulates the cancelation or elimination of Conrad from the great books of Western literary classics (1996, 425).

But the great books tradition, we have to bear in mind, was beset with problems, including parochialism. It does need to be said, too, that canons themselves have not always been timeless, fixed, and universal. The idea of a single and fixed Western canon discounts how canons are invented, diverse, and protean. Canons evoke colonialist discourses and set up their constitutive texts along hierarchical lines. Accounts of the Western canon imagine it as either texts of a supposedly high culture, the corpus of works at the height of cultural achievement in the West, or as the body of literary works dominated by dead, white European males that excludes voices from historically marginalized social groups. As Dean Kolbas argues, the "institutional processes of canon formation" like schools, which together with sociological explanations of canons "tend to discount or neglect the distinctive, *aesthetic* aspects of canonical works of art, invites us to think of an alternative account of the historical constraints and material conditions of literary canonization" (2001, 2). As an ethnocentric and evolving construction, therefore, the Western canon from which Achebe, following Denby, seems to expel Conrad makes the possibility of elimination an uncertain premise. Based on this, the claim may then be made that being "thrown out of the Western canon" is not really a form of censorship or even cancelation. To be clear, the suggestion of excluding a work from the canon is not isomorphic to canceling it.

Nevertheless, we cannot disregard the fact that Achebe's engagements with Conrad's racism betray an incipient logic that is exacerbated in social media call-out culture. It is possible to argue that both Achebe and current critics of Adichie are, in some sense, trying to hold accountable those whose positions make them immune to rational persuasion. This is hardly the case since Conrad did not seem impervious to persuasion (as his latter works and attitude suggest), and Adichie also appears to be quite persuasible based on social media posts that sometime clarify or restate her positions. By today's standards and the consciousness of race and resistance to re-inscriptions of colonial epistemologies, Conrad's text would be easily canceled, even if that might occlude necessary debates about the politics and ambiguities of canon formation, which texts such as Conrad's may engender. For some readers who parade a superficial decolonial logic, it would be apt to cancel a "book which parades in the most vulgar fashion prejudices and insults from which a section of mankind has suffered untold agonies and atrocities in the past and continues to do so in many ways and many places today" (Achebe 1977, 790). Achebe's perplexity, evident in whether *Heart of Darkness* can truly be called an aesthetic masterpiece on the basis of the novella's contradictory narrative aesthetics and dehumanizing tropes, means he is basically thinking of eliminating the novel from the canon. We might as well employ the language of today's social media culture to describe Achebe's characterization of Conrad's work as "an offensive and totally deplorable book" whose dehumanizing politics cannot be accepted in the current epoch (790).

In his response to Phillips's question about the fairness of expecting an artist to transcend the prejudices of his Victorian-era constructions of race, Achebe was indeed blunt: "Conrad didn't like black people. Great artists manage to be bigger than their times. In the case of Conrad you can actually show that there were people at the same time as him, and before him, who were not racists with regard to Africa" (Phillips 2003). But for Said, for whom Conrad's vision of Africa as primitive and savage would constitute a hegemonic discourse in the mode of Orientalism, we are still confronted with similar attitudes and views that repeat the imperialistic propensities of the Polish-British writer, "lest we think patronizingly of Conrad as a creature of his own time" (Said 1993, xviii). Again, it is not lost on me that I am reading Achebe through the prism of a different culture and temporality. But the fact that *Heart of Darkness* and other literary and philosophical classics by dead, white European male authors are routinely targeted for cancelation because of a perceived racism means Achebe's critiques, in the framework of Conrad, deserve scrutiny from the standpoint of cancel culture. One can hold this point and yet offer a nuanced argument that acknowledges another obvious fact: Achebe's dismissive evaluation of *Heart of Darkness* does not necessarily bear any traces of the social shaming and rhetorical violence that characterize today's cancel culture and its toxic predilections. Both men are long dead, and Conrad was already dead when Achebe originally published his critique. At the same time, a commitment to understanding Achebe's logic could produce useful "reasons for *also* describing the dead in other terms, their own terms," as Richard Rorty argues in *The Historiography of Philosophy*, and for the reproduction of "the intellectual scene in which the dead lived their lives" (1984, 266). Understanding Achebe's time, therefore, leads us to his sense of the African writer's role at a time when the humanity of the African was constantly questioned by colonial knowledge systems and racist epistemologies.

Achebe's critique of Conrad may actually illuminate what has changed about the current moment, especially the shift in the terrain of conversation from print ecologies to digital platforms on which debates are driven more by algorithms than actual arguments. Hence, Anne Applebaum argues that the formal and informal administrative bodies "that judge the fate of people who have broken social codes are very much part of a swirling, emotive public conversation, one governed not by the rules of the courtroom or logic or the Enlightenment but by social-media algorithms that encourage anger and emotion, and by the economy of likes and shares that pushes people to feel—and to perform—outrage" (2021). As technology enables new kinds of behavior, including novel expressions of literary sensibilities and attitudes among readers, algorithms and the affordances of the social web prompt cancel culture as a mode of social shame and public pillorying to achieve political ends. For scholars such as Clark, though, what is fundamentally at play in online cancel culture is the social media's utility as an oppositional arena of disciplining power through the protocols of Black vernacular discourses (2020). It is in this realm that we may locate Achebe's urge to eliminate Conrad from the canon. Where the disciplinarian stands when disciplining is something to consider, though, particularly given the case of Conrad, who positioned himself hegemonically to construct an image of Africa. An even more salient question may be whether disciplinarians should, in fact, be standing in positions of aesthetic and political judgment.

While it has become clear that Achebe did not, in fact, succeed in evicting or canceling Conrad from the literary canon, cancel culture presents us with language to reread Achebe's famously avowed doubt about the status of Conrad and his *Heart of Darkness* in the English literary canon. Achebe referred to Conrad as a bloody racist and insinuated that *Heart of Darkness* should be thrown out altogether from the reading list. Writing in a different time and using different language, he essentially expressed the same desire for cancelation to which writers like Adichie and Rowling, as well as other public figures, deemed to have breached social and moral norms, are increasingly subjected. Whether Achebe is justified in his reading of Conrad is less pertinent than the possibility of reevaluating the stakes of his critiques in the framework of today's culture. But a critic like Denby, who describes Achebe's intervention as "an act of rhetorical violence," represents several objections to Achebe himself (1996, 417). An even more scathing assessment of Achebe's view of Conrad is to be found in Cedric Watts's argument (1983). Watts suggests that Achebe is "difficult to please," and his judgments are inconsistent and discriminatory (202). As Watts writes, when "the tale offers views" that Achebe "regards as illiberal, he condemns them; and when the tale is humane and liberal, he redefines such liberalism as racialist illiberalism" (202). Whether Watts rightly captures Achebe's reading is also contestable, but his argument anticipates, over three decades ago, the selective and parochial impulses also to be found in today's cancel culture. This also provokes returning to Achebe's misgivings about Conrad, particularly because it also offers us a mode of shaming and calling out a racist work that does not foreclose the need for debates and speech.

Cancel culture imposes on our sensibilities a performative gesture that constrains thought and speech, and for that it can become a rhetorical affront produced by a misrecognition of the kind of human messiness and vulnerabilities that is inherent in all humans, the kind Marlow is confronted with in the image of Kurtz in the Congo. Again, the world of vindictive cancelation is not the world Achebe favors. His reading of Conrad and *Heart of Darkness* offers us an analytical prism through which to consider the subject in African literature. In short, Conrad's novel is ambiguous and racist, and that needs to be acknowledged and pointed out. But it is also an early critique of colonialism and people need to engage with it to reveal how its ambiguities connect to the politics of canonization. We may look to the example of Otoniya Okot Bitek, whose 2022 poetry collection *A Is for Acholi* performs this kind of critical engagement through a poetics of resistance rendered in powerful verses.

Bitek excavates Conrad's *Heart of Darkness* by rewriting his racist language and experiments with an abstract form and strategies of misquoting that enable her to reconstruct Conrad's novel. In a strategic challenge to Conrad's authority, Bitek employs a cryptic erasure and dismantling of the novel's rhetorical violence, recalibrating the systems of meanings that undermine the agency of the natives. In a sense, Bitek's strategy of poetic erasure is also an act of (textual) cancelation that aims to rehumanize the Congo and its indigenous people depicted as savages in *Heart of Darkness*. In reconfiguring the syntactic associations of expressions such as "dark human shapes" and "the apparition of a woman," Bitek appears to "cancel" Conrad in her poetry collection and re-infuses his language with a fresh and renewed power of articulation that is congenial to human dignity (2022, 64–65). The result of such an approach that simultaneously deconstructs and repurposes Conrad's narrative power and mangles his plot is a testamentary aesthetic that demonstrates poetry's capacity to recover agency and defy racist ideologies. Reading Bitek in this manner, I have to admit, is possible because of Adichie's social media rọ̀fọ̀rọ́fọ̀, my original pretext for returning to Achebe and Conrad. But Otoniya herself reanimates and extends a common tradition of African writing, namely, an intertextual fascination with and a critical engagement of Conrad and his popular work. Her poetry collection serves as a counter-text to a key work of postcolonial scholarship, modeling for us how to engage with dominant literary and intellectual cultures in the social media age.

Because of their aesthetic merits and their narrative portrayals of human experiences, the influence of the works of Achebe and, indeed, Adichie remain sedimented in African literary studies, whatever our views on their personal politics. In her own response to those who sought to deplatform her online, Adichie describes literature as "the messy stories of our humanity" and criticizes "social-media-savvy people who are choking on sanctimony and lacking in compassion, who can fluidly pontificate on Twitter about kindness but are unable to actually show kindness" (2021). But when Adichie concludes that the "assumption of good faith is dead" or that we "are now angels jostling to out-angel one another" on the basis of some obscene moral puritanism, she herself is reactionarily deploying her privilege against people who hold less power and privilege than she does. While those who insist on their rights as human beings should never have to see their positions constructed as obscene or puritanical, the trans social media users who advocate canceling others they perceive as critical risk undermining the very principles of liberalism that have normalized trans identities.

CHAPTER 2

Literary Networks of Conflict and the Politics of the Digital Litmag

As part of an experimental space for Nigerian creative writing on social media, I started a Facebook group called Muse on Fire with Nigerian poet Abiodun Bello in 2009. Around the same time, a new generation of writers from the continent, as Shola Adenekan has demonstrated in his book, were using social media as a test ground for their literary craft. Several Facebook literary networks, such as the now-deleted Muse on Fire, may have been replaced by small digital magazines that rely on blogging affordances to publish the works of young African writers, but these new locations of culture are not neutral spaces for creative experimentation and come with their own flaws. While the current literary scene in Africa cannot be adequately mapped without attention to various digital literary magazines and periodicals that expand literary culture and conversations, the politicization of digital literary magazines also makes them the perfect avenue for vituperative conversations and censorious relations between readers and writers in expanding, though often faceless, literary networks. Cancel culture, as the most recent iteration of patterns of controversy in African literary discourses, needs to be understood as laying bare the contradictions of online literary networks, especially the logic that assumes digital platforms, magazines, and journals are naturally predisposed to foster networks and coalitions.

Because of what Adenekan argues to be the vibrant digital cultures of both countries, this chapter discusses prominent digital litmags from Kenya and Nigeria and uses them to track the connections between the politics of state propaganda and literary productions. It also examines, where applicable, how controversies online often precede calls to cancel a writer. I will conclude by connecting some of the conversations discussed to the irruption of state politics and propaganda in the activities of literary magazines, exploring how "genocidal" regimes in both Nigeria and Kenya become imbricated with literary festivals through the entanglements of state actors and writers.[1] As I have maintained previously, literary controversies and feuds in the African literary landscape are not new. They hark back to the popular debates over Pan-Africanism and Negritude in print spaces such as *Transition*, *Black Orpheus*, and *Présence Africaine* in the twentieth century. These magazines functioned as what Chris Ouma and Madhu Krishnan frame as ecologies of decolonization that as cultural production during the "febrile moment of decolonisation could not be contained or articulated through any single genre, and more specifically could not be dominated by received genres of modern cultural production" (2021, 198). *Transition*, *Black Orpheus*, and other midcentury magazines "were partly the legacies of anti-colonialism and statist Pan-Africanism" and became central to the formation of Pan-African publics, networks, and communities of interests, which are increasingly reanimated in (digital) litmags such as *Jalada*, *Saraba*, and *Brittle Paper*. Like their digital descendants, these little print magazines were often terrains of controversies, heated exchanges, and debates. *Transition*, in particular, has been characterized as "a bit academic, a bit controversial, and a bit bohemian" and its first issue described as having "a tone of naive cultural alienation," which deeply offended the sensibilities of some readers (Benson 1986, 110).

The fact that literary productions and their modes of circulation are capable of provoking offence may not be new to the African literary space. However, this idea is ultimately generative for scholarly interrogation, especially in a social media ecology where algorithms and other technical elements of the medium significantly shape what interactions people see online, how they read texts, and respond to them. In this manner, algorithmic recommendations are increasingly central to literary culture, homogenizing and curating practices of reading online while shaping the flows of desires and affect. My goal, therefore, is both to explore how controversies and disputes play out strictly in the context of digital literary magazines, and to examine the discursive functions of these occasionally hostile debates within their digital environment. In the age of the social or participatory web, similar feuds appear to be more ubiquitous and increasingly connected, in some cases, to cancel culture, especially since more African literary actors are being called out for cancelation. This is evident in the call to cancel Adichie, a writer who has prominence as a literary and cultural celebrity and is thus easily targeted for cancelation. But in terms of subject matter, unlike the allegations of racism that anchored Achebe's evisceration of Conrad, various forms of sexuality and gender violence underpin the rhetorical furor around the Adichie case (transgender identities), the attacks on *Brittle Paper* (rape), and the cancelation of *Enkare Review* (pedophilia). The intersectional politics of class, sexuality, and gender shape these contestations around cancel culture and censorship, as well as the politics of the state—to be discussed shortly—which looms obscenely over the *Brittle Paper* case.

Canceling *Enkare Review* and *Brittle Paper*

The expanded ecology of contemporary African literary productions through the culture of digital literary magazines includes journals and magazines such as *Doek! Literary Magazine*, *Isele Magazine*, and *Lolwe*. In July 2021, the *New York Times* ran a story by their East African correspondent, Abdi Latif Dahir, about the ways in which digital magazines, as locations of culture, are shaping Africa's literary scene by enabling digital amplifications of new voices from the continent.[2] These digital litmags mostly publish fiction, poetry, cultural, and literary criticism, with some producing print issues and anthologies occasionally. They represent a new era of literary publishing in Africa that creates literary value through the incorporation of digital affordances, which intimately connect to the performative articulation of new relations of authorship and readership on social media. That said, without thought to sustainability as a major element of these digital literary magazines and the various labors of cultural interpretation they enable, we are simultaneously confronted sometimes with the loss of data and huge archives of stories. For example, *Enkare Review*, *Praxis Magazine*, and Krazitivity are some recent online publications and networks that have become defunct—with the fact of their digital obsolescence emerging as a common feature of African digital literatures and mirroring some of the infrastructural limitations of print publishing institutions on the continent. In any case, these digital literary magazines end up becoming digital ephemera, although they never set out to be transient spaces of literary conversations.

Also conspicuously absent in Dahir's article was any mention of *Enkare Review*, whose former editor, Troy Onyango, is foregrounded in the cover of the *Times* story as the founder and editor-in-chief of *Lolwe*. The exclusion of *Enkare Review* is perhaps due to the fact of its cancelation on Twitter. Founded in July 2016 by a collective of writers "based on the continent [mostly in Kenya] and un-ironically earnest in a shared vision for African creative production," *Enkare Review* presents one prime example of how digital media both facilitates new literary circulations and propels networks of feuds and conflicts that sometimes instigate the demise of otherwise vibrant digital publications (Mogami 2018).

Following Stephanie Newell's notion of "paracolonial networks," which designates her sense of cultural flows among local mimics in colonial Ghana (2001), Stephanie Bosch Santana has coined the term "paravirtual networks" to mark the emergence of offline literary networks such as the Story Club of Lilongwe in Malawi prompted by the disappearance of digital platforms (2019). Like the "Story Club—networks that are made possible by a shrinking digital world," paravirtual networks "operate in ways that exceed the digital's affordances" and are "likely to become more and more common" (396). The idea of "a shrinking digital world" might be a tad overstated, though; if anything, the digital exhibits an expanding digital network of cultural productions and important literary labors that suggest they have come to stay as the main space of the literary. That said, literary feuds and controversies similarly demonstrate the abiding connections between offline politics and literary networks of conflicts. By "literary networks of conflicts," I am drawing on Jodi Dean's arguments that the notion of the public sphere is specifically tied to the nation (2003). In her reading of social media publics, this fact forecloses online networks as affective public spaces for rational debates and consensus. In her estimation, the internet should be seen as "a space of conflicting networks and networks of conflict so deep and fundamental that even to speak of consensus or convergence seems an act of naïveté at best, violence at worst" (106). Dean's overarching thesis is that the communicative capitalism that underpins social media's so-called participatory culture renders all kinds of speech against a dominant political formation as noise since little is actually transformed offline by people's agitations online. The January 6th invasion of the U.S. Capitol and the rise of right-wing groups that recruit and strategize online refutes Dean's argument of online activity as mere noise. Her position is also dismissive of actual political conditions in many parts of the world, such as developing countries where the fact of the internet's communicative capitalism is hardly directly translatable to noise but rather coexists with possibilities of concrete social action. The circulation of feuds, controversies, and other discourses of outrage, however, support the existence of literary networks of conflicts, with cancel culture being a logical outcome.

Returning to *Enkare Review*, the publication, as Nathan Suhr-Sytsma explains in his genealogical account of online magazines, "was a relative newcomer among a crop of successful African-run digital litmags that include *Saraba*, *Bakwa*, *Jalada*, as well as *PalaPala*, which, though now defunct, is according to Dzekashu MacViban 'the most important platform for Cameroonian writing and analysis'" (2021, 246). Although there was already a 2018 dispute between the magazine's editorial collective and then-editor Onyango, who was called out on social media by the editorial team for hijacking the literary space, the team lost access to the publication's website. *Enkare Review*'s diminished position, reflected in Dahir's omission in the *Times* article, has some connections to the politics of cancel culture as a practice of ostracization and public shaming. In 2019, *Enkare* published a short story by the Nigerian writer Jekwu Anyaegbuna, which contains punchy sexual details of children's bodies presented in erotic encounters with adults. Based on this glamorization of pedophilia and the moral ambiguities of the story's subject matter, *Enkare* became the target of widespread condemnation by social media users, especially those in the LGBTQ community, who described the magazine's publication as romanticizing pedophilia and problematically correlating it with nonheteronormative identities.

The conflict surrounding *Enkare Review* was so intense that when another literary platform, *Brittle Paper*, published what its editors called "the Brittle Paper Position," their stance became the subject of another pushback by the scholar Keguro Macharia. *Brittle Paper* had written that the literary space in Africa "is one still developing, through the hard work of individuals, the hard work of collectives and groups, through collaborations, through social media as a networking tool. We are unhappy that circumstances did not let our colleagues at *Enkare Review*, an institution occupying an important cultural space, to work." Macharia's response to the statement was the charge of a "developmental imaginary" that infantilizes the members of the Enkare collective as "undeveloped." In "find[ing] it dangerous when a critique about power relations is framed as a problem of (delayed) development," Macharia was disproportionately engrossed in only a section of the statement, indeed its opening clause, and appeared to disregard the overarching solidarity of the *Brittle Paper* statement (Obi-Young 2018).

Similarly, another Kenyan writer, Shailja Patel, as one of the prominent voices that called out *Enkare Review* for this short story, wrote in a tweet that the magazine "publish[es] a story that celebrates the rape of children. That equates child rapists to LGBTQIA people. [And] When called out, you defend the indefensible."[3] Despite the usually expected solidarity among the founders and editors of digital litmags, *Brittle Paper*'s Otosirieze Obi-Young, distancing a magazine he was editing then from this controversial publication, also released a statement, noting that the "short story and the efforts made to promote it—by *Enkare Review* and Jekwu Anyaegbuna—constitute both an active endangering of children and an emotional oppression of LGBTQ+ people" (2019). Such censorship and erasure of potentially taboo subjects and difficult topics gets to the heart of cancel culture and shuts down any possibilities of conversations. One might interpret the exclusion of *Enkare Review* from the *New York Times* story as a discursive erasure that extends this censorious tendency and strategically delinks Onyango's current project from a past editorial task, which, though it predates Anyaegbuna's pedophilia story, is not without its slanders and tensions. Also, the controversial short story, which arguably sealed the fate of *Enkare Review*, needs to be read as a concrete reflection of how the literary spaces facilitated by social and digital media center around personalities.

Hence, in a statement by the *Enkare Review* editorial collective, Onyango's action was constructed as privileging the politics of personae, with a single individual exercising dominance over the network. The short history of digital literary productions in Africa has to be seen then as predicated on struggles and contestations between individuals and networks. Although the collective warns readers to be "wary of an internet call-out culture because of the spirit it is sometimes done in," their earlier attack on Onyango essentially laid the foundation for the cancel culture that was later meted out to them in response to the pedophilia story (Enkare Review Collective Team 2018). The travails of *Enkare Review* enable us to focalize other moments of cancel culture in the framework of African literature online, as I now turn the rest of my analysis to Edoro's *Brittle Paper*, as well the literary disputes and feuds involving another Kenyan literary magazine, *Kwani?*.

Brittle Paper, "an Afrocentric space of literary circulations," as I have argued elsewhere, "has consolidated its status as the most formidable literary portal into creative writing on the continent" (Yékú 2020, 4). *Brittle Paper* describes itself as "an online literary magazine for readers of African Literature," adding that it is

"Africa's premier online literary brand inspiring readers to explore and celebrate African literary experiences in all its diversity." The magazine aims to "cultivate a fun and informative platform for readers who love literature from Africa" and "inspire, entertain, and empower readers through an optimistic, diverse, and immersive experience of literature."[4] Digital platforms like *Brittle Paper* foreground the visibility and agency of new writers and voices from the continent, even if a playful cultivation of readership is often made there to derive from literary forms such as gossip. But because tech companies monetize the literary and cultural data people produce, *Brittle Paper*, rather than corporate social media, reveals the ways in which the ownership of digital platforms is implicated in the digital circulation of African literary genres and publics, underscoring the necessity of digital environments built and owned by Africans. Despite its contributions to African literature on the internet, the platform, as well as its owner and editor, were targeted for cancelation because of allegations involving a state government in Nigeria. In her capacity as editor of *Brittle Paper*, Edoro decided to pull down a story about the Twitter outrage against the response of Nigerian writer and wife of the former Kaduna State Governor Hadiza El-Rufai to an offensive statement on gang-raping women made by her son. *Brittle Paper*'s then deputy editor Obi-Young had initially published this story on the platform's front page but had employed what Edoro claimed, in her online defense of her action, was "inflammatory, even melodramatic" language and tone.[5] Here is an excerpt from the article as cited in the statement by *Brittle Paper*'s Ainehi Edoro:

> Interestingly, four hours after backlash began to her response, an article appeared on *ThisDay* titled "Endearing Qualities of Kaduna First Lady, Hadiza El Rufai." It is exactly as shabbily-written as you would expect of a hastily assembled, face-washing gimmick. But it is not as unintelligent as the one on OperaNews.
>
> There must be a name for this feminism whose reply to "Tell your mother I'm passing her to my friends tonight" is "I didn't see any threats of rape." A feminism that agrees to raise men to be better but says "All is fair in love and war" when their ethnic-bigoted men-children threaten violence on women's bodies.
>
> Shame. Shame. Shame. Shame. Do better.[6]

Obi-Young, on the other hand, argued in his own statement that he had been "made to leave because of my report on Hadiza El Rufai's comments on her son's gang-rape threat."[7] The context of their argument was Nigerian politics and the dysfunctionality of governance that Bello El-Rufai sought to defend, hence the widespread print coverage of this controversy in Nigerian newspapers. Obi-Young, in his online statement, calls out both Bello El-Rufai and his mother, Hadiza Isma El-Rufai, who is also the author of the 2018 novel *An Abundance of Scorpions*, which details the travails of a Muslim woman who overcomes tragic loss amidst a consuming patriarchal culture. Therefore, unpublishing this article was interpreted as a symbolic support for the political class, a tacit approval of sexual assault, which, according to Obi-Young's statement on the controversy, amounts to being censored or canceled (2020). It is ironic that supporters of Obi-Young resorted to canceling or censoring *Brittle Paper* because of an alleged censorship, but that's one of the many ironies of a cultural phenomenon that wishes to silence dissenting perspectives.

The Obi-Young episode demonstrates a crucial value of literary controversies that draw on the rhetoric of cancel culture. Specifically, it underscores how the censure of writers and literary institutions is often narrowly seen as the only means of addressing legitimate grievances and how these controversies stimulate the creation of other digital literary magazines. The pattern is evident in both Onyango's creation of *Lolwe* after the *Enkare Review* debacle and in Obi-Young's creation of *Open Country Magazine*—a self-described "truly multiplatform space for cultural storytelling" that he founded in reaction to industry backlash, in African literature, against young writers who criticize rape culture.[8] With Obi-Young's departure from *Brittle Paper*, animated calls emerged to cancel an African literature platform that had ostensibly forced out a deputy editor for daring to write about state actors believed, as consistent with the position of the social media critic Ikhide Ikheloa, to have financial ties to the literary scene.[9] I will return shortly to the implications of Ikheloa's claims in the context of state politics and the role of the social media public intellectual in Nigeria, but since he is connected to several of the controversies being discussed—from those involving *Enkare Review* and *Brittle Paper* to this chapter's major thesis on the links between online literary networks of outrage and offline state politics—I will now proceed to offer some remarks about him.

African Literature and the Social Media Influencer

The understanding that African literature is currently caught in an algorithmic age of personality is not only a consequence of the debates and disputes that cohere around particular names, rather than or in addition to their literary networks and communities and the power of their ideas. It is also exemplified in the digital labors of online actors such as Ikheloa, the quintessential controversial figure of African literary conversations on the internet. To his credit, at a point when formal academic critics were stuck with Achebe and Adichie, Ikheloa was responding to new literary texts being produced by the Caine Prize generation of writers, even if his style is the persistent attribution of an imprecise and troubling messianism to social media as the savior of African aesthetic practices. In other words, for Ikheloa, it is as if social media will save African literature from an ill-defined condition.

A former chief of staff-ombudsman at the Montgomery County Board of Education in Maryland, Ikheloa is not a literary critic in the conventional sense of a scholar formally trained in the rigors and interpretive protocols of literary history and theory. Yet his works have, in the last decade, motivated some pertinent conversations in the field. Hence, the scholar Alexander Fyfe urges a rethinking of any elitist dismissal of Ikheloa's online criticism of African literature.[10] Without a meaningful engagement with the kind of online scholarship Ikheloa represents, Fyfe argues, we undermine "the continued development and reshaping of African literary studies as a more ethical field of study," which opens up the space of literary evaluation to untrained outsider voices (2021, 157). In other words, this engagement with popular commentaries on African literature found on social media and blogging spaces is essential to the continued development and reshaping of African literary studies as an elastic field that rightly acknowledges the rhetorical and performative stakes of nonexpert perspectives on African literature. What explains Ikheloa's circulation in formal academic discourses is not the originality of his arguments but "the intensity with which he reactivates a fundamental anxiety of the field of African literary studies: that works of literature about Africa may overly cater to 'Western' audiences and consequently present a reified or unfaithful 'image' of the continent" (160). Hence, Ikheloa's online reviews and writings reactivate among contemporary African writers the enduring anxieties about the stereotypic representations of Africa and its literature.

Certain key questions, however, remain mostly unexamined by these positions, including why conventional forms of critical judgment and literary appreciation should be relaxed when dealing with nonexperts and literary bystanders in the field. More importantly, and despite the shortcomings and invisible labors of the academic peer-review system, Ikheloa's important contributions arguably undermine the validity and integrity that result from the careful scrutiny and evaluation that anchors the production of literary knowledge among peers of scholars and writers. If the invisibility of peer review contributes to the symbolic status of publications that become hyper-visible, as Carli Coetzee argues in an African Literature Association lecture, the social media commentator bypasses such gatekeeping protocols and becomes visible through self-focused routes and reading practices (2018). The democratized nature of the medium of literary-critical proclamations demands of us an awareness of a growing interstitial zone of literary criticism, a critical space of reading cultures and literary engagements that may enrich the professional task of literary criticism if well connected to the predigital tradition before it. Also, there is a need to come to terms with the prospect of literary influencers who decenter the authority of trained experts and question established knowledge systems. Ikheloa's praxis demonstrates how the current algorithmic culture accentuates the power of individuals to challenge the elitism of literary networks through influential pronouncements that simultaneous activate what Thomas Nichols describes as the "death of expertise."[11] Unlike the established tradition of Bọ́lẹ̀kájà critics, who spoke from within the ranks of the academy, the current moment confronts us with the outrage of Bọ́lẹ̀kájà readers that profess expertise and spurn the authority of those before them as false or compromised.

There are several other scholars who take Ikheloa seriously as a valuable literary voice whose crucial interventions expand traditional literary criticism and make the field of African literature more inclusive. While scholarly citations may point to the merits of Ikheloa's reviews in formal literary criticism, citational politics is not the only practice that assures his place in contemporary discussions of African literature, nor the sole reason for any academic scrutiny that I am presently undertaking. Along with his intense and forceful dispositions, the relational elements of social media databases, as well as the rankings of recommendation algorithms that suggest personalities to follow and stories to read, also contribute to Ikheloa's social media influence and prominence. The point is that the affordances of social media shape his online personality, visibility, and social prestige.

Moreover, Ikheloa is often perceived, in the words of a reader of his blog, as "writing disparaging articles [that] will bring the much desired [*sic*] fame you covet without going through the rigor of publishing your work."[12] This was the view of a commenter on Ikheloa's 2012 blogpost on the stylistic resemblance between Teju Cole's *Open city* and the writings of the German W. G. Sebald. In a comment to his earlier review of Cole's novel in 2011, Ikheloa himself is similarly patronized by one Adam Slide, who observes that Ikheloa needed to take "a college class in literary criticism in order to learn how to review a book objectively."[13] Of course, the very notion of reading *objectively* is questionable at best, and such critiques invoke an elitism that limits interpretative practices to only a few. While many push back at the confrontational style of a social media critic who has always been coy about describing himself as a literary critic in the professional sense, several other people appreciate his interventions by rewarding his online literary practices through social media gestures of sociality and other mechanisms of recognition. At an institutional level, the James Currey Society awarded Ikheloa the James Currey Lifetime Achievement Award for Literary Criticism for being "a consistent voice in appreciation of literary and artistic work."[14] Under the leadership of Nigerian writer Onyeka Nwelue, the prize was named to honor British publisher James Currey, who collaborated with Chinua Achebe at Heinemann to produce the famous Heinemann's African Writers Series. Like the scholarly affirmations of Ikheloa's online labors in academic publications, the prize, which has had its share of controversies, acknowledges the self-made critic's contributions to the growth of African literary networks on social media. That said, and even if mostly muted, the award for some observers also raises questions about the artifice of personality that affixes itself to the writerly community online and the self-exhibitionist culture of social media that rewards performative circulations online without much attention to established rigors of literary expertise and interpretations.

For someone who has acquired an online reputation among some followers as a crusader for accountability and ethical relations in the African literary space, Ikheloa could be more self-reflexive if not critical of the source of the aforementioned award. The James Currey Society was founded by a writer who, despite being a prolific and fine artist in his own right, opted to credentialize himself as a trained scholar utilizing the instrumentality of a titular PhD, despite only having received an honorary doctorate from a Haitian institution. Despite his unwavering criticisms of public figures and writers such as Chris Abani and the computer scientist Philip Emegwali, Ikheloa ignores the analogous Emeagwali traits in a writer who, in keeping with the politics of vicarious respect and legitimization online, relentlessly cites and launders other writers (such as Flora Nwapa and Soyinka, pinned to his Twitter timeline) as part of the performative politics of a digital identity. Although the writer claims the prizes and literary events he institutes are meant to honor the legacies of these writers—including Flora Nwapa, whose son once accused him of leveraging the legacies of the first African woman novelist to be published in English for his own visibility—the ways in which an avowed literary altruism masks the fact of appropriation remains much entangled to him.

In a 2023 interview, the writer, who never clarifies his use of official terms like "scholar or "academic visitor," consistently gives the impression that he was an actual professor who taught (for free!) at Oxford and Cambridge.[15] Using the images and social prestige of other writers for his own benefit was the norm until he was called out by a student news outlet seeking to hold him accountable for the misrepresentations of his identity, his role at Oxford, and offensive social media posts. While one wonders why affiliations with academia as a principal source of expertise and authority is sought by a popular author, what is precisely dodgy here is the ethics of parading oneself as an academic and the power it authorizes to enter certain institutions and offer literary awards in African literary criticism. This is significant, given the symbolic role that so-called public intellectuals, writers, and book critics and reviewers like Ikheloa and the James Currey Society founder play in our community and the institutions (such as the African Studies Centre at the University of Oxford) that legitimize such roles. Beyond the politics of legitimization, people, of course, do not have to be affiliated to an institution as a formally trained recipient of a doctoral degree to produce knowledge or recognize others as worthy of prizes. But there is something about leveraging the names and insignias of western institutions and the symbolic image of established writers to build a personal brand—in a manner that is consistent with the algorithmic age of personality and its performative politics and excesses on social media.

The source of the literary award, which marks the prestige economies of an influence industry on social media, gestures to Carli Coetzee's argument on the place of academic fakes and fakery in the field of African studies. As Coetzee writes: "we all collude in covering up fakery. Much of what we value most highly is held in place and ring-fenced by the machinery of these fakes. Reputational and professional value is created through our complicit cover-ups of the fakery factories: the intellectual sweat shops, the occult economies through which some toil like invisible zombies while others accrue prestige and resources, and the global 419 schemes that deplete and impoverish many Africa-based scholars" (2021, 272). Silence, whether because of culture or the desire not to be misperceived as envious, thus provides an enabling environment for fakery. Hence, the James Currey Award, with the troubling silence around its activities, invites us to consider how fakery intertwines with the politics of authenticity to accentuate the performance of plastic selves in the attention economy. In this case, fakery is not being covered up since the activities of the award and its organizers are endlessly published on social media; what baffles is the disinclination to ask honest questions about a writer who is using the image and prestige economy of other senior writers as well as faux scholarly and institutional symbols to secure and endow cultural capital. Obviously, much of the award analyses offered here may be dismissed if read as attacks on the deliberately named individuals, but there is something to be said about writers and public intellectuals in a digital age whose established authority is easily erased sometimes in favor of the inchoate ideas of social media influencers. If the writer has any social and ethical commitment, then these narratives matter. Besides, the argument here supports the major thesis of this book, namely, how social media algorithms incentivize an age of personae in African literature that centers on the power of individuals as the locus of cultural analyses. Hence, who gets rewarded and becomes visible is the person who is able to use digital technologies to curate self-exhibitionist performances. Having said this, since there is much value in Ikheloa's literary labors online, it is probably the case that the "critic" deserves the award. Yet, we have to return to questions about the critical parameters and criteria that establish both aesthetic materials and the judgment of expertise. As we ask what constitutes a good Instagram poem, or a flash fiction on a creative Facebook narrative, we are also impelled to ask how the subject of the literary prizes from online literary networks are chosen, compared to professional literary critics who have done equally well for African literature. If anything, Ikheloa's online work serves to show controversies and outrage are intimately connected to the question of literary authority and expertise.

This is not the main question for Nigerian poet Chiedu Ezeanah who, like several people online publicly questioning Ikheloa's literary-critical credentials, has described Ikheloa as "the new Chichidodo of African literature," a reference to the work of the Ghanaian novelist Ayi Kwei Armah.[16] With references to the links between literary feuds and state politics, the context of Ezeanah's post is the inflammatory suggestion that African literature is trashy. As Ikheloa writes, if one man "is killed in America, 100 African writers will write a long heart-felt woke epistle about why it is wrong. In Nigeria, 100 gays could be murdered and African writers would take money from the murderer to organize literary jamborees. Yes, y'all have trashed African literature. Achebe weeps."[17] Here, there is a classic iteration of the generalizations that sometimes manifest in Ikheloa's criticism online. But his queer solidarity is an admirable path that the writers who condemn him hardly take. After he refused to condemn a Nigerian political aspirant who publicly expressed homophobia and was called out by Ikheloa, Ezeanah described him as "the Chichidodo who feeds from African literature to create a name for himself while wasting no opportunity to abuse and excoriate and destroy the work of any African/Nigerian writer in sight."[18] Ezeanah's criticism, which embeds a troubling politics of location and tension between writers in Nigeria and their counterparts in the diaspora, also promotes a common gossip that brands Ikheloa as a failed creative writer. This appears to be a grossly overstated narrative peddled by those who, most disturbed by Ikheloa's style, constantly resort to when attempting to discredit him. The horror of personal attacks that follow and the commentaries generated on the post are worded in the typical derogatory rhetoric of social media outrage culture, which, as the Romantic-era feuds and scandals also demonstrate, often cohere around strong personalities and influencers.

Despite this ambivalence and misgivings that surround his online personality and manner of intervening in the public space, academic engagements with Ikheloa persist. For instance, Krishnan relies on Ikheloa's writings in sections of her 2014 publication, *Contemporary African Literature in English*. In this work, she repeatedly draws on Ikheloa's famous blogpost, "The Trials of Chris Abani and the Power of Empty Words," in which Ikheloa confronts writer Abani about an allegedly fabricated biographical documentation. Krishnan reads Ikheloa's argument as based on a "curious lack of official documentation" of claims made on Abani's printed work that he had been sentenced to a maximum security prison for alleged involvement in a failed military coup in Nigeria (23). Writing on how Ikheloa links these to a broader charge of authorial exploitation of Africa because of international literary prestige, Krishnan explains that:

> Ikheloa's criticisms of Abani, along with the often-vitriolic debate they have sparked within the African literature community, indicate the level of unease and suspicion with which an attempt at a conscious separation of artistic re-presentation and social representation is met. The truth of Ikheloa's allegations and the details of Abani's early biography will likely be known by no one but the author himself. Nonetheless, the attacks against Abani illustrate the ways in which the demand for some level of verifiable proof of the author's status, and therefore legitimacy, as a representative of African conflict emerges as a central concern tied directly to the literary value of his work. (23)

While Krishnan interprets the attacks against Abani as illustrating how the incessant call for proper authorial recognition legitimizes their identity and work, which significantly connects to the literary value of his work, the central issue, as I see it, is to establish the ways Ikheloa's "strong opinions," as he writes on his blog profile, contribute to the algorithmically influenced networks of conflict in African literature online.

"Reading and Writing . . . Loudly," as Ikheloa names his blogging space for the stories of Africa, compels not only our attention, but also the sensibilities of the many writers and public intellectuals with whom he often spars online. The figure of the public intellectual on social media is, like the social media influencer, a vital actor in these analyses. My use in this book of the ideas of publics and publicness relies, in part, on what Moradewun Adejunmobi describes as the different ways of being in the public (2020). As Adejunmobi explains in regard to African letters, the different guises "in which subjects and objects appear in public are often, though not necessarily bound with a medium or conveyance that facilitates an encounter between a text or creative work and a public. Variable forms such as print book publication and small print magazine publication among many other possibilities represent specific forms of publicness" (80). We may add social media and digital literary magazines as new spaces for the conveyance of the social communion between the public and various kinds of textual and discursive formations. While Ikheloa does not self-define as a public intellectual, there is a certain publicness to his ideas that is made possible through the medium of blogging and the social media spaces he inhabits. It goes without saying that the process of his writing is, therefore, public.

Even if perceived as a curmudgeon by some, Ikheloa's work of public debates, from his days in the print networks of the defunct *NeXT* newspaper and on social media, is nonetheless invaluable. As Syed Hussein Alatas notes, a society that lacks "a functioning group of intellectuals is deprived of a certain level of consciousness and insight into vital problems" (1977, 10). Hence, even if his style irritates some, Ikheloa's interventions can be understood in relation to this consciousness-raising value of public commentary discourses. But besides social media, what explains the emergence of actors like Ikheloa? One possible answer lies in the strategic way in which Ikheloa plugs himself into the gap produced by the deterioration of the intellectual class after the structural adjustments program era, a major argument in Ebenezer Obadare's *Pastoral Power, Clerical State*. In his study of the social origins of a religious authority that has ostensibly displaced a formerly vibrant intellectual elite that enjoyed social prestige, Obadare explains that "as Nigerian universities fell on hard times, prompting the attrition of leading academics to European and

North American universities, the reputation of Nigerian intellectuals as respected occupants of rarefied ivory towers took a corresponding nosedive" (2022, 28). With the cultural status diminished, the intelligentsia's ability to offer any liberatory vision for society became almost nonexistent. At the same time, a concurrent rise in the social prestige and influence of a pastoral class (mostly of the Pentecostal groups) became ascendant in politics and social life. In the age of social media, however, pastors also have had to concede a portion of their religious authority to a new class of digital actors that command huge followership online. The social media influencer, whether as popular entertainers or public intellectuals in online spaces, often goes as far as to challenge social norms that once made the contemporary Pentecostal pastor "an existential micromanager" capable of blending an array of social roles and functions (6).

That said, it is perfectly reasonable to wonder if the decline of the intellectual class in Nigeria—also marked by the emigration of writers and literary critics to the West—did not, in fact, also produce a dearth of literary criticism that continues to this day. In other words, while religious leaders become dominant as leading social voices because of the nosedive in the cultural value of the intellectual elite in the country and because of the equalizing power of social media platforms, it is not only in the domain of religion that the consequence of that decline is evident. In the particular frameworks of the ivory tower itself, the condition for the emergence of online literary reviewers like Ikheloa is arguable both a response to a passive intelligentsia in Nigeria and to the social media platforms that facilitate new forms of authorial visibility and social prestige. This is not to suggest that there are currently no intellectuals in Nigeria who visibly shape public discourses or produce robust literary scholarship that garners critical attention. On the other hand, like Obadare, I am merely suggesting that social media actors like Ikheloa, who write literary and cultural reviews, are much more dominant and gain popularity as vectors of viral ideas because of the decline in the role of an educated class that speaks to the public on issues of political or ideological significance. Beyond the brain drain and the capitulation of the intellectual class is also the relative youth of the participants in African digital cultures.

Having said that, we cannot also romanticize the social media influencer, for the digital landscape of these savvy online actors occasionally yields to a hollowness in politics that suggests their digital performances as frequent exposures of the artificiality of the digital world. Even if they don't acknowledge it, social media influencers as literary reviewers and nonprofessional critics of culture aspire to become authority figures whose proclamations need to be taken seriously by others in the writing community. But it is ironic that they seem to want to reconstitute, in that process, the traditional expertise they once despised.

From constantly publicizing Onyango's role in the demise of *Enkare Review* to passionately calling out Nigerian intellectuals and writers and *Brittle Paper* for purported alliance with the Kaduna State government in Nigeria, Ikheloa as a literary influencer is a central actor in African literature's encounters with cancel culture and literary feuds.

Ikheloa, though, carefully makes a distinction between his infamous calls to cancel *Brittle Paper* and holding the literary magazine accountable, writing: "I was for holding them accountable, not cancelling them."[19] What it means to hold others "accountable" and who has the power to perform such a crucial task are, of course, pertinent in the distinction that Ikheloa is making here. Also, his idea of canceling appears to signify a broader call to moral censure that exceeds even the discursive denial of cancelation. In his case, therefore, what constitutes the act of online cancelation also engages a performativity of language that is enacted through a particular set of moral and discursive moves, regardless of the denial of the person performing the canceling. In other words, to cancel another person includes the denial of that very process as a justification of the seemingly righteous investment in moral censure. The blogger had observed elsewhere that the digital world "has democratized the reading and writing culture. Writers are suddenly finding themselves being held more accountable publicly than before. I am excited to be part of that movement to democratize the literary culture" (Iduma 2012). Although the democratization of the digital world is fraught with class politics and challenges to web access that users encounter in many parts of the world, this desire to hold others accountable is ingrained in Ikheloa's vision of social media. Despite its many contradictions and the plastic sanctimonies of some of its proponents, cancel culture, for Ikheloa, names the imperative to hold responsible those who are in positions of power. But he does need to make clearer whether this accountability culture abjures retribution.

Even though cancel culture generally tends to take a political and activist interest in addressing abuses of power, it is not exactly clear in the case of *Brittle Paper* if any abuse of symbolic power was present. In any case, the struggles over morals and social meanings on digital social platforms and the conflicts that accrue from these sometimes enact "commercialized spectacle in the search for accountability" (Lewis and Christin 2022, 1634). Even if there are no broader commercial dimensions to Ikheloa's social media engagements, the symbolic accumulation of followers and subscribers that result from his call to cancel or hold *Brittle Paper* accountable plays into an influence economy that rewards moral policing and censorships on the internet. Being one of the most vociferous actors of the call to cancel the magazine, Ikheloa misreads how the language of boycotting galvanized many of his own followers and fans on Twitter. One of these tweets read: "Let me suggest this to readers of conscience: Boycott @brittlepaper until its 'high' editorial standards stand up for justice and the truth, and do not coddle despots, genocide enablers and rapists. Do not read @brittlepaper until it apologizes for protecting thugs like @elrufai."[20] Responding, one of Ikheloa's followers is "disgusted over the platform's obvious support of violence and rape," an allegation based on mere conjecture and one that proves how social media fails to cultivate close reading and nuance. Ikheloa's tweet serves to remind us of how cancel culture masks itself as a social tool of protest and accountability. While his call for a boycott recognizes and purports to subvert the power of *Brittle Paper*, which, unlike several litmags produced on the continent, is a significant literary space founded and run mainly from the African diaspora, what this tweet fundamentally presents is the foremost logic of cancel culture itself. Equally important, aside from the sentiment of censorship and erasure in Ikheloa's tweet, is the claim that the magazine's attempt to sanitize its publication of the rape story is analogous to "protecting thugs like @elrufai," the erstwhile Governor of Kaduna State in Nigeria. Without providing any documented evidence for these claims, Ikheloa's attacks on *Brittle Paper* demonstrate the lack of the necessary rigor that should normally accompany the literary judgments of professional critics. His views also normalize a new culture of outrage in which participants unwittingly participate in an algorithmically defined shame economy.[21]

Brittle Paper and the KABAFEST Kerfuffle

At this point, it may help to recall that the initial political arguments that prompted the calls to cancel *Brittle Paper* became a literary discussion the moment the litmag decided to unpublish the story that led to Obi-Young's departure. The reason for this connects not only to how the rape joke and its denial implicate the so-called feminist novelist Hadiza El-Rufai, but also to a much broader climate of literary controversy involving KABAFEST, the annual Kaduna Book and Arts Festival. The relevant fact here is the role of the writer and publisher Lola Shoné̩yin, famous for both her own works and the success of another literary and cultural festival, the Aké Arts and Book Festival, as well as being the founding creative director of KABAFEST. Unlike the Aké Festival, which is more pan-African and not limited to Nigeria, KABAFEST was envisioned "to create new and exciting opportunities for social and cultural interaction, the celebration and promotion of creatives in the Northern region of Nigeria and foster tolerance and understanding through dialogue about books, culture, the arts and society" (Utor 2017). With KABAFEST, therefore, Northern Nigeria—a region commonly marginalized in discussions of Nigerian literary and cultural productions—created opportunities for creative avenues for conversations and programs that enabled aesthetic practices.

For critics, however, KABAFEST represented an affective event that politicized art and warranted controversies and contestations because it fostered the conditions under which a certain ethical betrayal of trust by the writing community became possible. Its sponsorship by Nasir Ahmad El-Rufai, a one-time controversial federal government minister and governor of Kaduna State, fed suspicions among the festival's critics that its organizers aimed to co-opt writers into the task of laundering the image of the governor and legitimizing him to Nigerians. In all probability, this idea of an El-Rufai sponsorship of both KABAFEST and other literary festivals organized by Shónẹ́yìn was an elaborate political ploy and was arguably mere literary gossip among detractors. This is an overreading of the actual situation since the Nigerian political class has always found ways to maintain power without the express approval of writers and cultural producers. While KABAFEST might actually have signaled a genuine interest in literature, based on Hadiza El-Rufai's writerly identity, these conspiracy theories remain commonplace in literary discussions.

But they are also pertinent, given that the relationship between Shónẹ́yìn and the El-Rufais makes legible the tensions between the state and the literary community. Ordinarily, the state and the writers should not see eye-to-eye. But the Nigerian literary community gives us evidence to revise that assumption, a point I will return to in the Kenyan context. It is important to understand how the state legitimizes itself and uses literary festivals to mask its corruption and oppressive regime. As an in-law of the Nobel laureate, Shónẹ́yìn's influence extends to the Soyinka literary dynasty, which others might wish to embrace on the grounds of some social prestige that occludes her own formidable merits as a writer and publisher. With the frequent arrests and disappearances of critics of his government, as well as the large-scale ethnopolitical killings under his watch, Nasir Ahmad El-Rufai is seen as using literature and writers, who may be unwittingly in connivance with him, to sanitize his own morally contradictory identity. As Isaac Otidi Amuke argues, collaborations between politicians and artists in Nigeria bring up various contradictions and incongruities, which, in the case of KABAFEST, center on El-Rufai:

> Governor Nasir Ahmad El-Rufai was nicknamed "The Destroyer" while serving as state minister of Federal Capital Territory, Abuja (2003–2007) due to his merciless flattening of properties that didn't comply with the by-laws. El-Rufai was quoted saying Abuja wasn't built for the poor. He was perceived as President Olusegun Obasanjo's blue-eyed boy and enforcer, deployed to deal with opponents in the pretext of enforcing laws. Credited with fixing Abuja and lauded for improving education standards in Kaduna State, where he recently enrolled his son into public school in leading by example, El-Rufai has been criticized for making religiously inflammatory statements and for mishandling ethnic and other volatile conflicts in Kaduna. It is the baggage of El-Rufai's politics that seems to be weighing down the KABAFEST partnership. (2019)

The prevailing notion around the KABAFEST kerfuffle is the belief that the writers who organize and attend the festival might best be encountered as "engineers of the human soul"—the Stalinist term for "official writers" and other cultural producers who "accord primacy to the ideological concerns of the state-sponsored model of literature" (Thomas 2002, 25). In his book *Nation-Building, Propaganda, and Literature in Francophone Africa*, which maps the relationship between literary productions and the postcolonial political elite in French-speaking Africa, Dominic Thomas characterizes official writers as being "at the service of the government" and as legitimizing their atrocities through literary forms (29).

Literary festivals and the arguably unwitting endorsements of some litmags may be seen as one of the mechanisms through which state power is legitimized and manipulated in postcolonial spaces. In fact, several of the KABAFEST writers may have seen themselves as politically committed writers who questioned repressive political ideologies and challenged hegemonic culture. They would probably have described themselves as producing non-official literature, which is more concerned with the construction of a nation and attacks the state for its failure to recognize autonomous political or literary identities. Yet, their alignment with a state-sponsored festival, especially one by a government serially accused of genocidal desires, brings their work into the orbit of officiality that contrasts with their own personal claim to aesthetic forms that push back against the impositions of power. Hence, KABAFEST makes clear how the political class in Nigeria sometimes uses literary figures and festivals for the production and maintenance of consent, besides also being a part of a much longer history of soft power in Nigeria. In sponsoring writers and their convivial celebration of literature, KABAFEST operationalizes the Chomskyan propaganda model that locates cultural and modular forms like literature and the media as operating through basic institutional structures and relationships that enable them to function as a propaganda system on behalf of the powerful societal interests that control and finance them (Herman and Chomsky 2002).

Despite his own puritanical views and the controversies they frequently generate, Ikheloa is right to insist on a proper and ethical relationship between the state and African literature, especially in terms of how financial resources are sourced for literary events.[22] However, while he is against acquiring funds from state officials in the KABAFEST event, he sometimes overlooks other possibly unethical situations that have the potential to generate conflict in the African literary scene. A case in point is the James Currey Society Award, whose founder refused to disinvite Ikheloa despite receiving what he described as "protests in my inbox from writers" who believed Ikheloa was not worthy of the award due to its problematic nature.[23]

The question of how *Brittle Paper* is implicated in the politicization of art and state propaganda that KABAFEST appears to manifest is central. Returning to Ikheloa's brawl with the magazine, this becomes legible in his assumption that unpublishing Obi-Young's article was essentially a reiteration of the political sensibilities that produced the literary festival and made writers complicit in the production and maintenance of state ideology. This viewpoint is partly why Ikheloa claims in a series of tweets that "African literature is a victim of perverse gentrification. Many writers tell tall tales for profit with "Africa" as a mere backdrop. Many are enablers of fascists, thieves and executioners of genocide."[24] Ikheloa is referring to the killing of Muslim minorities in Nigeria (the Shites) as well as repeated killings of non-Muslims in predominantly Christian Southern Kaduna. The online critic's argument is similar to the one Soyinka made about those the laureate terms "Establishment intellectuals" in the heyday of the Nigerian military dictatorship (1996). According to Soyinka, these men of letters became the intellectual backbone of state power and were willing to go as far as discrediting "their own race by the attribution of humanistic principles solely to the Western World" in order to defend the prurience of a decadent and violent military class (114). Although he sometimes includes Soyinka in his diatribes online, Ikheloa recapitulates Soyinka's view that the Nigerian literary establishment should be held accountable for colluding with a corrupt government. His accusations may use the fashionably alarmist language of genocide, but Ikheloa's sentiments are shared by others. In 2020, for example, Nigeria's community of lawyers disinvited El-Rufai as a speaker at an event, "canceling" him in response to the furor over his human rights records as governor and his lack of commitment to the rule of law. Yet, without any formal indictment by the justice system in Nigeria against El-Rufai, Ikheloa's allegations remain conjecture.

Even more significantly, from the perspective of literary feuds and controversies, Ikheloa's public antagonism of the Kaduna governor predates KABAFEST and includes social media encounters with some of the most important literary figures in Nigeria's third generation of writers—as Pius Adesanmi and Chris Dunton refer to them (2005). Some of these writers include Ikheloa as a protagonist, Olu Oguibe, as well as the late writers Harry Garuba and Adesanmi himself. In 2013, when Adesanmi, as director of Carleton University's Institute of African Studies, organized a lecture as part of the launch of El-Rufai's book, *The Accidental Public Servant*, Ikheloa was one of the loudest voices to push back, declaring the book as "the subject of much bullshit pontification by rented PhDs" (2017). He wrote both on Facebook and later on Medium that the lecture was

> pompously titled "Post Colonial Writing and the Challenge of Public Service in Africa" in which eminent intellectuals like Professor Pius Adesanmi and Harry Garuba and Reverend Tunde Bakare tried to canonize his pretend-book. This lecture was held at a university in Canada, no less. Intellectuals were flown in to say nonsense about how that silly book is something important in "African literature" . . . They [African writers] are either stuck in corridors of power begging for crumbs from the oppressors or they are fighting over Western literary prizes. As we speak many are in church praying for divine favor in the hands of the gods that give literary prizes.[25]

The backdrop to Ikheloa's acerbic take is what Moses Ochonu described in an Op-ed as "the El-Rufai nuisance," as well as KABAFEST itself, portrayed in the Medium article as a festival that sequesters Nigerian writers and intellectuals (2011).[26] Adesanmi's response to Ikheloa, whose post he reads as disparaging, similarly employs the language of slurs and slights: "There will be room for you to join by google hangout and abuse all the abuse you want to abuse, including making ignorant and dramatic claims that a panel on a memoir that has generated so much heat is hogwash."[27] As is occasionally evident in heated social media exchanges, other writers like Olu Oguibe joined in the intense discussions, with most critiquing El-Rufai's reliance on African literary scholars and intellectuals for public rebranding. Adesanmi's extension of an invitation to Ikheloa is significant because it models a fundamental characteristic of free, rational deliberations that is being undermined in the age of cancel culture. The possibility that Ikheloa and others who questioned the invitation to El-Rufai could be accommodated in 2013, through a Google platform, has to be seen as antithetical to a cancel culture ethos that forbids the voice of anyone who appears to transgress the "social norm" of difference, of an oppositional perspective. In any case, unlike Ikheloa's charge to his online followers to boycott *Brittle Paper*, Adesanmi was willing to accommodate El-Rufai on a debate stage, demonstrating an intellectual generosity that is sufficiently capacious to indulge dissenting perspectives or even a controversial public servant accused of genocidal impulses. But it has to be said that even this gesture is not new. In his response to Ali Mazrui's critique of the TV series by Skip Gates, Wole Soyinka wrote: "In response to Ali Mazrui's challenge, the pages of TRANSITION will be open either from the next issue, or in one single issue (to be editorially decided) to further debate on the Gates series" (2000). As indicated earlier, the *Transition* feuds, though raucous and indicative of the role of powerful public intellectuals in shaping culture, nevertheless created space for productive exchanges.

In a rather recognizable exhibition of self-praise, Ikheloa writes in a 2020 Facebook memory and repost of his 2013 challenge to Adesanmi: "I am very proud of myself, I have changed the culture, there was a time "writers" would go to Kaduna and read mediocre cheesy poetry and prose on the graves of the slaughtered. Not anymore. I changed that. We have more work to do, I have no time to listen to hagiography about a man just as flawed as myself. Pius did his bit, he is resting. I will not rest until I finish my work. Until then, watch out. Lol."[28] Of course, Ikheloa overstates and exaggerates the transformative potential of his own crusade against state cooptation of literature. KABAFEST has continued in recent years and, it might be argued, has gained more attention despite the attempts by critics to undermine it. In fact, it has inspired newer initiatives such as the Kaduna-based Open Arts and the Hausa International Book and Art Festival.

The online controversies around KABAFEST illuminate the connections between offline and online literary networks. Having discussed the Kaduna Book and Literary Festival in the controversial contexts of its state sponsor, it becomes understandable that the call to cancel *Brittle Paper* because of its purported defense of El-Rufai is, in fact, rooted in offline spaces of literary controversies that disclose intimacies between Nigerian literature and state politics. What is also visible is the deep imbrications between online literary networks and the offline politics that sustain them. In this instance, we see one notable function of literary feuds, namely, the way they serve to uncover deeply embedded links and networks between political actors and literary writers who, despite their political consciousness and unbeknownst to them, are working to secure hegemonic consent for state actors. It is true that these feuds are more complex than the binary logic I offer here, but the politicization of feuds is the dominant picture of things.

A scrutiny of nonliterary discourses, such as the social media narratives on the 2023 elections in Nigeria, presents similar censorious proclivities among online supporters of politicians. For example, the so-called #Obidient movement—a highly personalistic and ideological campaign against an old order of gerontocratic and prebendal politics in Nigeria—offers one instance of how social media discourses often yield to moral censorship and cancel culture ethos. The #Obidient movement was so amenable to controversies that, at different times after Nigeria's 2023 elections, pitted admirers of Soyinka and Chimamanda Adichie (and, by a curious ethnic extension, Achebe) against each other. Supporters of both writers on Facebook and Twitter essentially posted deprecating remarks about them, trolling their views on the elections.[29]

Ikheloa's constant haranguing of Nigerian intellectuals also speaks to the role of organic intellectuals, as captured by Antonio Gramsci in his analysis of the relationship between intellectuals and the state. For Gramsci, a state's expression of hegemonic rule is constituted by the interplay of consensus and coercion, with consensus more prevalent to achieve a balance between the two overlapping realms of "political society" and "civil society." Gramsci makes a distinction between traditional intellectuals, organizers of culture who reason with the masses and try to obtain "spontaneous" consent to a social order, and organic intellectuals. Institutions such as the church, trade unions, schools, and the media, which are crucial to the formation of social and political consciousness, are often headed by traditional intellectuals who essentially work to promote the dominance of a capitalist state. On the other hand, for the fulfillment of the task of economic production, every social group, as Gramsci explains, creates its own organic intellectuals who are fundamental to a class's struggle for hegemony. Therefore, one of the most important characteristics of any group "that is developing towards dominance is its struggle to assimilate and conquer 'ideologically' the traditional intellectuals, but their assimilation and conquest is made quicker and more efficacious the more the group in question succeeds in simultaneously elaborating its own organic intellectuals" (Cammett 1967, 204). There is something to be gained from Gramsci's distinction, as it offers a chance for the refutation of Ikheloa's many essentialist propositions that most Nigerian writers and intellectuals are unquestionably compromised. In the self-righteous call for the country's intellectuals to transcend the constraints of dysfunctional and inchoate institutions that characterize the Nigerian public arena, Ikheloa positions himself and other supposedly progressive voices on social media as organic voices that push back on the complicity of traditional intellectuals and writers who manufacture hegemonic consensus for the agents of governmentality, as in members of the political class that are notorious for their prebendal oppression of the masses. But, again, despite his public pronouncements, Ikheloa neither identifies himself as an organic intellectual nor is he universally imagined in that light. Indeed, as the Nwelue Oxford controversy suggests, a selective moralism appears to color his own online crusades despite the appearance of a commitment to progressive cultural and political commentaries on social media.

Despite the aspersions Ikheloa casts on his late colleague, the tag of the organic intellectual is an apt description of Adesanmi, who specifically used social media as a civic space for the displacement of political propaganda and the re-education of a social group with access to the internet. While Adesanmi himself was often, and rightly so, criticized for the intellectual labors that midwifed the popular acceptance (at least online) of the Buhari government, his social media commentaries signaled an intellectual commitment to critiquing the ruling class for their mediocrity and political corruption. Although the everyday culture of corruption was visible, Adesanmi tasked himself with using quotidian popular texts and everyday narratives to interpret the Nigerian condition. In a column written for *Nigerian Tribune* before his death, Adesanmi's prescient voice as an intellectual who expounded the Nigerian reality was strident in its summation of his public interventions:

> I think our people have been psychologically defeated and have come to accept and love these things about Nigeria. They turn on whoever tries to awaken them. Nigeria's irresponsible rulers have us where they want us. I write basically these days for the purposes of archaeology. A thousand years from now, archaeologists would be interested in how some people called Nigerians lived in the 20th and 21st centuries. If they dig and excavate, I am hoping that fragments of my writing

> survive to point them to the fact that not all of them accepted to live as slaves of the most irresponsible rulers of their era. (2019)

Adesanmi described his work in his final article in archeological terms that simultaneously imagine the work of excavation as a redemptive intervention from an external location. It is as if "some people called Nigerians" would themselves not be bothered about the body of work he had left behind. His marriage of both digital and traditional modes of literary engagement was perhaps his most important achievement, as he expertly redrew the critical and rhetorical boundaries between the two forms. Consequently, he can be read as an intellectual who performed the exegetic work of explaining social texts and a prevailing political order of postcolonial messiness.

Karin Barber provides an equally useful term to understand the agent of such exegetic processes. In *The Anthropology of Texts, Persons and Publics*, she identifies in every community "people who you get sent to, to explain obscure texts that other people are baffled by," "local intellectuals" that make "exegesis into an art comparable to poetic or narrative composition" (2007, 98). Adesanmi's copious use of Yorùbá oral arts, humor, and other rhetorical elements position him as a public intellectual who interpreted various social texts organically. His involvement in playful yet acerbic social media commentary facilitated a form of public engagement in line with his vision of a progressive country unshackled from the forces of everyday corruption. Nevertheless, for all his radical ideas, Adesanmi, like Ikheloa, was hardly critical of the space in which his performance of public knowledge circulated. Whereas Ikheola's proclamations about the participatory web and democratization of access to the means of knowledge production online reveal an ardent romanticization of social media, Adesanmi's indifference to the fact of data coloniality and the capitalist social relations that constrain both critical and creative practices was in some respects equally naïve.

At the risk of belaboring the argument, something else about the KABAFEST controversies, besides the courting of Nigerian writers and the interpretive work of public intellectuals, is how the proposed cancelation of an African literary platform signifies the ways in which the divisive politics of the state intertwine with the polarizing culture of digital networks that sustain writing communities. Indeed, there is nothing unique in the allegiances between writers and politicians, whether in the online world or not. There is a long history of such overlapping tendencies between state power and the writing community. For instance, the postcolonial disillusionment that animated the writings of Nigerian writers like Festus Iyayi, Femi Osofisan, and Niyi Osundare in the decades after political independence became intense in the heyday of the corrupt military years because of the entrenched corruption of the ruling military class. As the military's culture of wanton corruption and its arbitrary despotism propelled "the proliferation of literary texts and networks in Nigeria" (Umezurike 2020, 215), writers became engaged in antimilitary sentiments that attracted even more censorship. The many instances of "brutal suppression of public protests by law enforcement agents, arbitrary arrests and detention of the regime's critics, indefinite closure of media houses and seizure of their publications" meant that writers and the state have always been entangled in a tense relationship" (Adeoti 2003, 31). From Soyinka to Osundare, anecdotal narratives proliferate about the precarious conditions that writers seeking artistic freedom from dictatorial regimes often endured at the hands of military rulers. Yet, cultural producers, including those working in Nollywood and the Nigerian music scene, persistently offered works that sought to undermine military power.[30] For instance, in Adesanmi's poem "University of Ibadan, 1994–1997," from the collection *The Wayfarer and Other Poems*, the persona details the gathering of writers described as "weatherbeaten survivors" on the campus of Ibadan. At Ibadan, Nigeria's cultural and intellectual capital, these writers had the chance to "spread the first mat of knowledge," dreaming dreams yet uncracked by "the radar of the sss" (2001, 20). The panoptic presence of the Nigerian state in the proscription of artistic consciousness across the country is present in many other works by the writers of the so-called third generation. That they survived what the persona sees as "the radar of the sss" underscores the determination of a generation's commitment to literature despite the surveillance of military dictatorships. One gets in the poem the sense of censorship from the military governments that sought to regulate cultural productions and creative expressions in Nigeria during the period Adesanmi writes about. With the eventual turn to civilian rule, politicians began to court writers and artists for the cultural legitimacy they offer, especially during electioneering seasons. The Goodluck Jonathan administration created the Project Act Nollywood fund that, under the guise of promoting the film industry, accelerated the cooptation of Nollywood actors into the project of legitimizing state power. Jonathan's gesture itself was a recognition of the power and prestige of the film industry in Nigeria.

In the frame of this sociological account, what may be read as a digital history of Nigerian literary networks and some of their controversial moments is that the online scrutiny of the action by the *Brittle Paper* owner is somewhat understandable, although the call to cancel the literary platform was absolutely needless. Despite the sinister campaign against *Brittle Paper*, there were many in the larger African literary sphere online who saw past the immediate crisis and sought to defend a prominent African literary platform. In this, there is the crucial instantiation of the value of controversies and cancel culture. As there isn't such a thing as bad press, the furor generated around *Brittle Paper* provided a reason to consume more cultural content on the platform.

Hence, to become "canceled" may often redound to the benefits of the actors being censored, besides the potential economic gains that accrue to those who are canceled and their banned platforms or books. The Kenyan writer Mũkoma wa Ngũgĩ was defiant in his support, writing that the platform is "a singularly important African literary platform with a solid history . . . we will not cancel!"[31] On her part, Ukamaka Olisakwe, novelist and founder of *Isele*, yet another digital litmag in a growing number of little African literary magazines, "strongly reject[ed] the call to cancel *Brittle Paper*" and argued that: "I've expressed my disappointment but I will not pull my articles. The editors have done solid work and it'll be a shame to let them take a beating while the vile human being, whose violent tweets triggered all of this, triumphs."[32] That tweets have the capacity to trigger scandalous encounters in African literary networks are telling, but also important is how they converge on "the vile human being" as individuals wielding tremendous and unhealthy influence online over literary collectives.

The irruption of state politics aside, the *Brittle Paper* wrangles were also based on diasporic ties as well as generational and gendered identities. Many who tended to side with Edoro lived outside of Nigeria, and there was also militant opposition from queer people who often disagreed with older feminist women. Hence, factors such as class, gender, diaspora, and the politics of location in African literature actively configure these controversies as well as response to the call to cancel or not. The fact that Obi-Young was located in Nigeria elicited more sympathies from Nigerian digital subjects, for some of whom being a diasporic actor suggested a self-alienating banishment from the politics and culture of their home community. These categories of social identity obviously intersect to frame things. But for those who sought to have *Brittle Paper* canceled, the fact that the litmag was founded by a Nigerian in the diaspora who appeared to be in support of state actors was sufficient reason for animosity and cancelation. Furthermore, the Edoro saga renders legible the constraints of being and becoming a powerful public figure as a woman in Nigeria's male-dominated society. Although she is located outside of

Nigeria, the episode confirms how a successful woman is automatically assumed to have benefitted from political patronage, something that is never attributed to men.

Kwani? and Another Kenyan Writers' Controversy

Controversies in the African writers' circle are not peculiar to any country, whether Nigeria or Kenya—although in the case of the latter country, as suggested by the title of this section (found on Kenyan Twitter), there always seems to be a surfeit of them. So far, I have focused on *Brittle Paper* and the campaign to cancel the litmag because of assumed alliances with state actors and politicians. But the literary platform is not alone in terms of entanglements with state politics and the controversies and scandals that often emanate from this unholy alliance. The case of another Kenyan literary magazine *Kwani?* points to similar tensions in the East-African context. Among others, my main source for this section is Carey Baraka's 2020 essay, "Intimations of an Ending—Carey Baraka on the Unspoken Demise of *Kwani?*, and the Death of a Dream," which was written for the *Johannesburg Review of Books*.[33] While the fact that his narrative is suffused with language such as "rift," "mess," "financial irresponsibility," "protest," and "fissures" also makes it congenial to this book's interest in discussions of literary scandals on social media, Baraka's essay, which was widely shared on several social networking sites, addresses itself directly to the question of *Kwani?*'s diminishment in the African cultural landscape and the literary controversies it left in its wake. Although *Kwani?* is not a digital litmag analogous to *Enkare*, *Brittle Paper*, or other born-digital literary platforms, its creative reliance on the web was as innovative as its founders' creative outputs. Besides its social media engagements and the fact that its first issue was launched online, *Kwani?* has to be credited with the unique use of livestreaming technologies for several editions of their popular Open Mic long before livestreaming literary events became a thing through Instagram Live and other platforms during the COVID-19 pandemic. The digital foundations of *Kwani?* also manifest in its emergence from an "enthusiastic crowd on email" conversation composed of filmmakers, writers, and artists, coordinated by the filmmaker Wanjiru Kinyanjui.[34] We may consider the email technology in the historical emergence of *Kwani?* as enabling a digital literary network that offered a glimpse of the important intersections that continue to exist between offline and online literary communities in the social media age.

As described on their website, *Kwani?* was established in 2003 as "a Kenyan based literary network dedicated to developing quality creative writing and committed to the growth of the creative industry through the publishing and distribution of contemporary African writing, offering training opportunities, producing literary events and establishing and maintaining global literary networks."[35] With two successive Kenyan writers connected to the group and the founding editors Binyavanga Wainaina and Yvonne Adhiambo Owuor winning the Caine Prize for African Writing in the early 2000s, the literary journal began to gain some attention globally. Owuor won the prize in 2003 for her "Weight of Whispers" after Wainaina's "Discovering Home" had won the prize the year before. As its vision was outlined by its dominant intellectual authority, Wainaina, *Kwani?* was "a magazine of ideas, [that] seeks to entertain, provoke and create and is open to Africans on the continent and the diaspora who wished to say something new" (2003, 6). With its ostensible neo-Modernist sensibility for newness in African literary productions, it thus became the case that Kwani Trust and *Kwani?* would become exciting reference points in scholarly works on the state of the production, distribution, and consumption of Eastern African literary cultures.

Along with the Nigeria-based magazine *Farafina*, *Kwani?* came to be seen, as Kate Wallis argues, as placing "a primary emphasis on building communities of writers and readers located in Kenya and Nigeria, reinforcing their agency in publishing from the "local" or "national" while deliberately positioning themselves within a pan-African and "world literary space" (2018, 166). But it is also the case that *Kwani?*'s identity was aided in part by its initial Caine Prize successes, even if its founding ideology was shaped by an implicit hostility toward an earlier generation of Kenyan writers. In the words of Tom Maliti, Kwani Trust's Board Chairman, the literary network began with the frustrating question of why Ngũgĩ wa Thiong'o and Meja Mwangi remained the only writers that Kenyan publishers were interested in. "Why aren't new writers being published in Kenya?"[36] This generational angst about the fathers of Kenyan literature at the heart of the *Kwani?* project was later to be described by Grace Musila as an "Oedipal anxiety" that assumed *Kwani?* "could only legitimize itself by almost undermining or even being dismissive of the generation of the fathers" (2012, 79).[37] Therefore, as this group of writers concerned themselves with the state of literature in Kenya, there was a sense in which they underplayed the historical importance of the earlier generation and the nationalist and decolonizing labors they performed.

To return to Baraka's essay and the way it constructs what its writer describes as the demise of the *Kwani?* dream, it helps to mention that the essay is not without its contradictions and slippages. For example, it incorrectly lists Mahmood Mamdani as one of "the sheer number of people who were published by *Kwani?*, often before they attained big-name status." While the attempt to story *Kwani?* and historicize its emergence and current realities are laudable, the inattention to some essential details undermines it. The most obvious example of this is a comment by Shalini Gidoomal, who commented on the *Johannesburg Review of Books* (*JRB*) website and calls out Baraka for his lack of fact-checking: "Very interesting read and captures much of the essence, but not all the facts. I should say that my falling out with *Kwani?* was not to do with my payment as the Litfest director, but due to the financial irregularities prevalent at the time . . . I have all this information, and when writing such a piece, Baraka, it would have been useful to make direct contact to fact check rather than relying on secondary (and in this case inaccurate) sources."[38] Despite these issues, the Baraka essay is important for three reasons. It underscores the aspiration toward literary prizes and awards as a driving impulse of *Kwani?*. Two, it suggests a crisis over funding and mismanagement of the finances from cultural institutions and literary-cultural NGOs like the Ford Foundation. This funding was integral to the collective's operations at some point.[39] Most importantly, it highlights the personality conflicts about the early beginnings and editorial processes of *Kwani?*.

From Baraka's account, there seems to be a muted controversy about the identity of the most active players in the early days of the journal. In response to Wainaina's ideological leadership, Tom Maliti says to Baraka: "A lot of writing about *Kwani?* has been about Binya, making it seem like he was the sole driver, and I'm not trying to take the credit away, because he did a lot of the lifting, but there were a lot of people willing it to go forward."[40] Baraka similarly identifies a Billy Kahora-led post-founders *Kwani?* that steadied the course of the project as it increased its visibility through festivals and workshops while inspiring other literary groups such as *Jalada*. Irrespective of the historical focus, controversies over class politics remained since *Kwani?*'s "founders had failed to reckon with their own vagaries of class" despite efforts to reach beyond "the class divide of Uhuru Highway."[41] The middle-class politics that Adenekan argues as constraining the literary productions of online Kenyan and Nigerian writers helps account for how "this generation of writers was in large part middle-class or, if you may, upper-middle class: a comfortable, educated and quite 'Westernised' group of people" (Musila 2012, 72). In his conversation with Musila, Kantai, a founding member of *Kwani?*, goes further to explain the private and self-focused fiction produced by this generation as one that neglected to confront the larger political structures that affected the personal literary world being created. Beyond the lack of introspection on the subject of class, *Kwani?* also seemed to have experienced frictions around the vexing entanglements of state politics and literary productions.[42]

The journal's controversial tangle with the political class demonstrates how the political history of Kenya was a major catalyst for the emergence of *Kwani?*. To return to the issue of state politics from the earlier sections, therefore, an example of such unholy intimacies is a controversial and partisan article Wainaina had written for British newspaper the *Guardian* after the election of Uhuru Kenyatta and his then vice president William Ruto (now president of Kenya) to the presidency in 2013. Seen as propagandist by some members of the *Kwani?* community, the article was a major source of tensions as some in the network expected Wainaina to be apolitical in matters involving politicians indicted for violence at the Hague. Even though he was perceived to be affiliated with civil society, Wainaina's views on Kenyata and Ruto in the article did not acknowledge their complicity and that of the state in the postelection violence of that year. In a comment to Baraka, Kantai described the politicization of the literary network as the ultimate tragedy of *Kwani?*, noting that its real failure was that "we got sucked into the banalities of "Kikuyu Power and its version of Kenya."[43] The main issue here is that the political ideologies of Wainaina, the journal's leading intellectual and literary voice, became coterminous with that of *Kwani?*, and this was perceived as a harbinger of its demise. Here, the tension between charismatic personalities and literary collectives becomes evident again.

Additionally, there appeared to have been some subterranean financial scandals in the operations of *Kwani?*. There is some scholarship on the non-African financialization of literary practices on the continent, especially Doreen Strauhs's important study on African literary NGOs or LINGOS. Strauhs provides a comprehensive history of Western funders that sponsor literary activities on the continent and demonstrates how groups like Females Write, Mbari, and Kwani Trust participate in the production of literary culture and the initiation of important sociopolitical dialogues. Thus, as the activities of *Kwani?* and Kwani Trust indicate, LINGOS constitute "noteworthy sites of literary innovation and public opinion making in the field of African literary production," despite the fact that Global North institutions like the Ford Foundation and media corporations (like Twitter) significantly constrain that production (2013, 42). In addition to writing an essay that appears to be sympathetic, as in the KABAFEST allegations, to a political class accused of genocidal intentions, I am interested in *Kwani?*'s financial culture because of the controversies and heated arguments it produced online. Based on what Tom Odhiambo suggests is the journal's "reliance on donor funding" and "its transnational and global tendencies and its editorial practices," perhaps the most controversial aspect of Baraka's narration is what appears twice in the essay as Wainaina's "financial irresponsibility" (2012, 24). Baraka writes:

> *Kwani?* was heavily funded by Ford, but there is a feeling that more of the money could have gone towards putting out more work. The remuneration of the top brass at *Kwani?* was endemic of what one person described to me as "the Ford Foundation lifestyle," whereby the administrators of Ford grantees were heavily remunerated, and the Binyavanga culture of wanton spending was never done away with completely.[44]

Kwani?'s "Ford Foundation lifestyle under Wainaina's leadership"—which in Ikheloa's Facebook response to Baraka's essay reeks of self-imposed colonialism—may have stymied the growth of the platform. However, it continued to shape the journal's development even long after Wainaina had left to take up a position at Bard College. What Shalini described as the "financial irregularities prevalent at the time" did not only precipitate the demise of the platform. It also resulted in a messy personality-based falling out that caused some members of the writing community to part ways with their network at different times. The personality politics here amounted to an individual becoming a stronger institution than the institution within which they operated. In 2018, after the Ford Foundation withdrew as the main funding body for *Kwani?*, a member of the network, Clifton Gachagua, went as far as tweeting about the financial situation of the journal, writing that he didn't "trust the people doing the Kwani trust workshop. they [*sic*] have been lying to a lot of people."[45] He followed this with a series of tweets that exhorted people to "work instead with the folks at jalada and enkare and writivism." And in yet another set of tweets, he acknowledges that Kahora, the editor then "wrote me a cheque for 26k in February, but only after I cursed a lot and resigned." On both occasions, these tweets became the perfect ground for other users to chime in and express their own outrage about *Kwani?*. One Mehul Gorilla (likely a pseudonym) tweeted in response that "everything in the Kenyan lit scene is fraudulent. It is hard to trust or be friends with other Kenyan writers. Most of them are fake personalities."[46] Someone else, writing from a verified Twitter addressed the debate from a gendered perspective, arguing that *Kwani?* was built on the erasure of women's labor. While these tweets, comments, and retweets all signal the need for a more ethical and liberal publishing environment in the African literary scene, they crucially mark for us a literary culture in Kenya (and elsewhere on the continent) that constantly yields to personality conflicts and controversies.

Finally, what is actually to be gained by dwelling on *Kwani?*'s financial messiness, rather than the excellent body of work it produced as well as the generative offline festivals and digital networks it fostered? One answer is that the activities of *Kwani?*, like those of *Enkare Review* and other digital platforms, ultimately coalesced into a forcefield of personality struggles (to rework Bourdieu) that centered on the interventions of prominent voices like Wainaina and, in the case of Nigeria, Ikheloa. Although tweets calling for *Kwani?* to be canceled were largely absent, Gachagua's digital revelations about *Kwani?*'s financial struggles point to the enduring power of digital media controversies to serve as an archive of past and present cultural oppositions and literary conflicts. In activating a Kenyan artistic and cultural renaissance championed by new voices and writers from the millennial turn, the literary journal also participated in the unruly space of literary controversies enabled by the contentious outrage culture on social media platforms.

What role social media commentaries play in shaping African cultural productions and reading practices can be more focalized by returning to Baraka and another essay of his, this time on Ngũgĩ, which generated a storm of controversies on social media because of the essay's politicized mistranslation by some readers and other netizens online. As one of Ngũgĩ's children wrote on Facebook, the online commentaries meant that the original story "was evolving into a fiction into which people wrote their macabre gossipy fantasies, and ethnic, sexist and ageist prejudices."[47] Although Baraka's sensitive and intimate narration not only outlined Ngũgĩ's revolutionary cultural struggle against the colonial state as well as Kenya's postindependence ruling elite, his stylistic reliance on disclosing extremely private information about the playwright's family became the fodder for fake news and gossipy narrative on social media. Mũkoma wa Ngũgĩ wondered on his Twitter page if other people had found an otherwise compelling and graceful story on his father to be rather unethical and gratuitous, riddled with "unnecessary and gossipy excess."[48] Despite its subtle perpetuation of ageist attitudes, the younger Ngũgĩ's

Twitter claim did not go unchallenged by his writer friends and other Twitter interlocutors, some of whom defended Baraka's essay. Whether on Facebook or Twitter, the controversies that Baraka's essay left in its wake are symptomatic of reading practices in the digital age and mark the tendency of online commentaries and algorithmic cultures to mirror the offline politics of those who create or use them.

CHAPTER 3

Achebe's *There Was a Country* and the Ethnopolitics of Bọ́lẹ̀kájà Readers

The controversies and language of combat and feuding surrounding digital publications, like litmags, sometimes manifest in other contemporary locations of African literature, such as the more established print-based works like the novel. For example, Mohamed Mbougar Sarr's 2021 *The Most Secret Memory of Men* similarly tackles a controversial topic in its literary meditation on the famous plagiarism scandal and authenticity debates surrounding a key text of African literature, Yambo Ouologuem's 1968 novel *Le Devoir de Violence* (published as *Bound to Violence* in 1971). Set in contemporary Paris, Sarr's award-winning novel pays homage to Ouologuem, whose disappearance from the literary scene subtly animates Sarr's attempt to recover the genius of an erased and shamefully silenced African voice. The mystery novel is organized around the search for T. C. Elimane, a Senegalese writer from the 1930s whose novel has been forgotten by the public and then makes a rare appearance in the French capital. For the African authors of the narrator's generation to read the resurfaced novelist was to participate in a venomous debate since Elimane offered "the chance to tear each other limb from limb in pious and bloody literary jousts" (Sarr and Vergnaud 2023, 7). For these Parisian literati, a true writer must spark "fatal disagreements among true readers, who are forever at war; if you're not willing to fight to the death for an author's carcass . . . you're anything but a reader, much less a writer" (7). Even as discussions on the novel grow heated and ever combative, to avoid "the impassioned clashes" provoked by Elimane is to dishonor literature itself. The fact that Sarr himself was subjected to a cancelation campaign for sympathizing with the LGBTQ community and repudiating homophobia in his earlier 2018 novel (*De Purs Hommes*) in Senegal suggests an intimate understanding of the perils of mob mentality on the literary imagination. Nevertheless, his novel reveals that the occasionally vexed relationship between literature and politics that manifests in digital literary networks is reminiscent of a print version of the same dynamic. Thus, the novel makes an argument, similar to the one between Soyinka and Mazrui, that print culture also hosts a similar type of outrage culture and combative reading practices to those found on social media. Following this logic, I want to turn in the current chapter to the social media terrain of a controversy that was activated by a work of print. I read Facebook postings and commentaries as texts for understanding the various ethnopolitical arguments that arose from online discussions of Achebe's wartime memoir, *There Was a Country: A Personal History of Biafra*. While ethnicity and historical accuracy, rather than cancel culture, were at the crux of the major debates in 2012, the various positions taken in these debates demonstrate how social media algorithms exacerbate the ethnopolitical susceptibilities of those who engage in platform controversies.

Similar to the way the intersectional paradigm of politics, class, sexuality, and gender shaped the cancel culture contestations around Adichie, social media commentaries on Achebe's book reveal a world of tensions that concatenated different kinds of ethnopolitical subjectivities. Yet, ethnopolitical acrimony in Nigerian literature is not new, even though they are, like most things, much visible and amplified in the social media era. For example, in 2023, the Nigerian poet Chiedu Ezeanah published a post on Facebook in which he called out the Nigerian leadership of PEN, a worldwide association of writers that promotes friendship and intellectual collaboration among writers who advocates for free speech and the role of literature in the development of world culture. Insistent that a politics of ethnicity underwrote much of PEN's activities in Nigeria, Ezeanah went on Facebook to condemn present and former presidents of PEN Nigeria, including Femi Osofisan, Tade Ipadeola, Remi Raji, and Folu Agoi—all past presidents of the organization who happened be from South West Nigeria. In Ezeanah's reasoning, the organization had become "an ethnic enclave for mainly writers from Yorubaland while excluding others from being members. The literary community does not even know if PEN exists in Nigeria. Why? Because you guys have taken it upon yourselves to ethnicize an international organization for writers."[1] Also telling is the exchange between Ezeanah and Remi Raji who wrote in response to other interlocutors in the discussion thread that followed. For Raji, Ezeanah's denunciation might have constituted some "ethnic dirtiness," but this did not stop the edgy and critical exchanges between him and Ezeanah.[2] The Facebook post is particularly instructive and offers some ideas on the role of social media in conducing the Nigerian literary scene in particular to a rambunctious zone of outrage and controversies.[3] This controversy functions to introduce a necessary and, indeed, rare space for discussions about the activities of PEN in Nigeria and pinpoints the connections between ethnopolitics and social media commentary produced by the Nigerian writing community. Like much of this book, this chapter uses online reader responses to Chinua Achebe's *There Was a Country* to highlight the ways in which digital media transforms Nigerian literary audiences and publics. I reflect on the nature and politics of the publics of African literary works circulated on the internet and argue that there is a growing digital public of African literary and cultural forms that deserves scholarly interrogation.

Several questions emerge, though, in considering how digital technologies reformulate the form, function, and audience of African literature. How are we, for instance, to understand the role of digital publics? What kind of ideological terrains emerge in online literary representations? How do digital technologies mediate the changing forms and publics of contemporary writing in Africa? How do the ontologies and affordances of the digital reconfigure the behavior of literary audiences and reading publics in the interpretation of literary meaning, and how might previous scholarship such as those of Karin Barber's on publics and audiences be read in the context of digitality? I aim to tackle these questions by examining some online commentaries as articulations of reader responses on reviewing platforms and social media to Achebe's *There Was a Country*. I hope to use online discussions of Achebe's memoir to track the trajectories of the digital publics of African literature, showing how the ethnopolitics that greeted the publication of Achebe's wartime narrative explicate both wider issues in the Nigerian literary community and the often volatile, conflictual nature of digital publics.

Despite the ascendancy of digital literatures, marked by the publication of Adenekan's *African Literature in the Digital Age*, a neoliberal logic that undercuts the platformization of African literary productions remains a major issue. As Madhu Krishnan writes, with the increase in internet technologies in many parts of Africa, "the situation for the contemporary purvey of African literature has become exacerbated, its global resonances amplified by the neoliberal impulse to telescope context into slogan" (2014, 134). Despite this reductive tendency, instances of inventive experimentations can be found in Teju Cole's adventures with "Hafiz" as a creative exhibit of Twitterature, as well as in the creative outputs and exciting debates on the politics of African literary prizes on literary blogs and platforms such as *Kwani?* and *Brittle Paper*. These, together with new literary voices who use social media to text and promote their craft, may give the sense of feeling that "sound bites on Facebook, one liners easily retweeted and production-laden, feel-good moments of reflection" have indeed "taken the prevalence in the shaping of a collective vision of Africa and the delimitations of the African writer's position" (134). In reality, rather than the pessimistic tone of Krishnan's otherwise solid intervention, these feel-good cultural works online also offer opportunities for various kinds of literary experimentations that signal digital media's expansion of the literary field and its reterritorialization of indigenous aesthetics and imaginative practices. In her examination of serialized fiction from Southern Africa published on Facebook and blogs, Stephanie Santana remarks, for instance, that the digital is "helping to foster multiple cyberplaces in which new literary forms and indigenous languages are thriving," with digital literary forms often having influences from local, national, and regional zones, beside drawing from broader African, diasporic, and global audiences (2018, 187).

Agency in the Age of the Netizen

The audience of contemporary literary forms in Africa has undergone rapid transformations, with social media serving as an incubator of textual performances of writerly selves among readers and user-generated exhibitions of authorial agency. In a keynote lecture delivered by Pius Adesanmi at the 2012 African Literature Association event sponsored by the Graduate Students' Caucus of the ALA, Adesanmi reflects on the poetics and agency of African writing in the age of the netizen. As he elaborates, his "concern is whether we are paying sufficient attention to the extraordinary dilemmas that these writers [who use digital technologies] face in their attempts to write a continent which now possesses the ability to self-write, self-inscribe, and self-globalize even before the first sentence of your novel, poem, or short story takes shape in your head" (2012).

This recovery of narrative agency by new literacy voices online is articulated through different digital genres, including TikTok videos and Instagram stories, that deconstruct stereotypical representations of the continent in a similar manner to how first-generation African writers used the print medium to contest colonial discourse of Africa. The focus of Adesanmi's lecture gestures toward the various ways social media enables literary netizens to unsettle the politics of victimhood, misrepresentation, and the persistent discursive erasure of African agency in the ecologies of world literature. However, his remarks also project a certain romanticization in his project, a techno-optimism that overly idealizes the digital environments in which netizens self-write and self-represent as if without the technical constraints of platform culture. Without being alert to the structured algorithmic determinations of their online engagements, agency in the age of the netizen is already undermined, as the identity and subjectivities of digital actors derive from prior processes that inform both the economic and algorithmic calculations of the corporate owners of these online spaces. These questions are pertinent in the calculus of ideas that form the core of debates that cohere around issues of agency, representation, and identity on the internet, even as they underpin some of the major questions tackled in this book.

But the need for an anti-essentialist and non-romanticizing approach to social media's value for cultural productions and literary knowledge does not negate the extent to which the authorial spaces of social media platforms have rejuvenated African literature in the last decade. Failure to take cultural and literary interventions on social media seriously merely normalizes a false elitism, restaging the hegemonic polarities between high and low culture. To imagine social media, as members of the Frankfurt School might, as just another way the culture industry repositions itself to depoliticize the masses is to neglect to see "the ways in which the culture industry, while in the service of organized capital, also provides the opportunities for all kinds of individual and collective creativity and decoding" (During 2010, 32). Simon During's position stresses the potential of those who consume the symbolic texts of the culture industry to interpret normative culture while operating within the framework of the capitalist machine to destabilize it. Again, it is possible to live with and alongside an invasive algorithmic culture and resist its protocols of interpellation. It is precisely because digital ecologies are not ideologically neutral that resistance to totalities and hegemonic culture is possible. Nigerian netizens, I argue, are using online network platforms as cultural sites from which they assert political subjectivities, voice, and agency. My idea of agency corresponds to the capacity for individual action that social media facilitates for personal communication, convergence, and content sharing.

As Jillianne Code writes, communication is achieved "through Internet-based applications by enabling identity experimentation, social identification, and ultimately enhances self-development through the expression of human agency" (2013, 39). This agential power, which Adesanmi wanted to celebrate, has been the high point of recent scholarship that recognizes how digital technology is playing a role in the actual changes taking place on the continent, both at the level of facilitating more redemptive narratives and concrete material transformations. Narrative agency in the social media field of culture represents the authorial power of new cultural producers to represent self and express difference by incorporating digital technologies into their production of speech. Since user-based content is definitive of the participatory or social web, much has been made of how social media narratives and readership converge within each netizen's online performance and has enabled the dissolution of the boundaries between producers and consumers of textual forms. Motivated by a space that urges performative self-presentations and authentic textual self-representations of individual agency, the reader also becomes implicated in different expressions of literary authorships, permitting the digital's merger of identities. In the context of understanding this poststructuralist convergence of the identities of the reader and writer, Ato Quayson describes Facebook as belonging genealogically to a mode of reader and viewer identification that dates back to oral tales and later shifted to novels, films, and television. He argues that as users have tools at their disposal, they are able "to insert themselves into the circuits of spectatoriality for others to look at," making Facebook a profound "instantiation of a completely new socio-cultural template" (2013).

Hence, digital audiences demonstrate that what is consumed is not merely the spectacle of others, as consumption becomes an act of self-inscription into the performance of another. On social media, to consume or interact with content is to stage oneself and become visible to both others and the machinic assemblage that enables one's self-presentation. To read and share a text on Facebook involves sharing not only in the production and transmission of its meaning but also to supplement it through the extra discourse it acquires and initiates in its digital flows. What I am describing is a regime of agency that expresses itself in the spectacularized means through which individuals function as both writer and reader, as well as spectator and participant in the performative and epistemic zones of authorships on social media. With ideas of trolling, anonymity, and fake news in recent years, this production of agential power that allows a multiplicity of user identities has problematic implications. But I want to focus on how it has generated new publics for African literature. This transformation of the African literary public, enabled as a more engaged one by Web 2.0 platforms, forms the fulcrum of my intervention. I use Achebe's *There Was a Country* to reflect on social media contestations and controversies that emerge from historical literary works and its discussions online. My argument is that the debates engendered by Achebe's war memoir must be understood as both reflecting the ethnic identities of those who participated in the debates and a culture of social media outrage. I hope to use the online comments on Achebe's account of the Nigeria-Biafra war to study and appreciate the nature of Nigerian literary publics in the digital arena, showing how social media's principles of personal communication, interactivity, convergence, and content sharing shape the reading and reception of African literature, with a focus on ethnic disputations and contestations. Before this, however, I want to step back and explain how social media commentary practices come into being in the first place through the digital's capacity to restructure the reading publics and audiences of African literature.

Digital Literary Publics

One of the major arguments in this book is that we need to engage more with the actual digital platforms that support African literary discourses and examine their affordances in the light of the emergence of Bọ́lẹ̀kájà readers—conflict-prone reading publics and controversial members of digital literary networks. It is crucial to critically interrogate the ways design decisions and affordances of specific platforms shape user experiences and understand how they influence the emergence and interactions of literary publics. We ought to be interested, for instance, in what specific affordances make Facebook more appealing than Twitter or Instagram for digital publics in African digital literary networks. Alexander Cho has written, for example, about a "default publicness" in spaces like Facebook, which is oriented to a general publicness that makes the space less desirable for queer participants who choose alternative, activist platforms like Tumblr, whose affordances promote a safer user experience (2018). Cho's argument interrogates default publicness to make sense of the design decisions that enable the context collapse of platforms and "to make strange the idea of the 'public' itself in the 'networked public' formation, indicting a set of hegemonic cultural suppositions baked into the design of these spaces" (3190). Drawing equivalents between the activities of audiences and those of publics, I argue that digital convergences of netizens, as facilitated by interactive and social network technologies, have reconfigured the participation of African literary audiences in the process of textual reception. Audiences bring a text to wholeness and completion, and social media, both in terms of its dialogic structure and authorizing facility, gives this a new meaning.

Barber has written about the active role of the audience in the construction of meaning, as suggested by the Yorùbá proverb: "We say half a word to the wise; when it gets inside him or her, it will become whole" (2007, 137). This tendency is typical of digital publics, as in their inclination to take a published content in different rhizomatic directions to the extent that such texts accumulate new audiences and meanings of their own as they become circulated online. Sonia Livingstone argues that publics and the fora in which they are expressed, together with our understanding of them, "are increasingly mediated [technologically, materially, discursively], moving ever closer to audiences" (2005, 9). For their part, online audiences are increasingly diffused and diverse but no longer contained within the private sphere. With the interactive, expressive, and connective affordances of digital technologies, there is also a change in mediating the transformation of the public.

In other words, digital media technologies have redefined the modalities of public engagements and political participation, leading to the creation of new public spaces and reading publics that enable new layers of cultural encounters and connections. The Habermasian public sphere as a public realm of democratic interaction in which citizens have impartial and rational debates on politics is commonly applied to social media research, although alternative forms of counter publics and non-normative modes of publicness are also activated by different platforms. In a Nigerian digital context, forms like trolling, ethnic fights, and other manifestations of conflicts trouble the possibility of rational public engagements, but social media as a public sphere in such an environment is not in doubt. New media scholars, with Zizi Papacharissi at the forefront, have examined the Habermasian formulation within the context of digital media, exploring the complex relations between political activism on social media and the creation of affective publics whose activities may transcend the internet. Other significant perspectives from critical social theory exist within Habermas's thesis, including Nancy Fraser's enduring reformulations, which I will address later.

Meanwhile, activist forms such as the Fallist movement in South Africa and the #EndSARS campaign in Nigeria underscore the specific ways citizens of various countries use digital platforms to resist oppressive power and alter official narratives. The dynamics of a digital public, animated by the signifying practices and cultural productions of creative netizens, demonstrate the extent to which an aesthetic-cultural sensibility is crucial to the formation of these publics. In the case of Nigeria, literary and cultural engagements invigorate the public sphere and supplement discourses of social movements and activism through different catalogues of popular culture aesthetics, which I have already described as cultural netizenship. Ebenezer Obadare argues that the saturation of public life with humorous texts and performances in contemporary Nigeria is connected to the digital technologies that support the "simultaneous expansion and profanization of the public sphere" (2016, 75). This public sphere is constituted by creative content producers, mostly a young demographic, lending performative agency on YouTube, Instagram, and TikTok to age-old debates on state power and hegemonic culture. Through commentary practices and satirical comedy sketches, a digital public sphere in many African countries is not merely constituted by political participation but yields to the centrality of popular aesthetics as a mode of digital engagement. Through these cultural forms in social media publics, people who have been traditionally marginal to state power revise the messiness of their postcolonial predicament.

Theories of African popular arts and their audiences focalize this distinction, although there is a remarkable range of publics and audiences, even in a digital environment. Barber views publics as constituted by the jointed efforts of cultural producers and their consumers whose interactions, modes of address, and use of space, are all central to this formation of public consciousness. To "uncover histories of consciousness in African popular genres," Barber writes, we cannot afford to ignore audiences who actively constitute performances (1997, 347). Similarly, Onookome Okome, writing on audiences and the sites of consumption in Nollywood, notes that an understanding of the multiple and nuanced dimensions of the audience of popular arts and literature is "indispensable to the goal of problematizing ways in which knowledge is constructed, used, or circulated, dispensed and re-invented in Africa" (2007, 6). With digital publics, there is a more assertive network of participatory audiences for African cultural productions. The new medium of writing accommodates readers whose responses to literary texts are as swift and immediate as the processes of online authorship that produce the works.

The closest parallel to this decentered space is the oral text, whose context of performance includes performers and spectators whose interchanging roles jointly construct the meaning a text or performance communicates. Writing about earlier texts and contexts, Barber intimates that the best reason "for studying audiences is that they have a hand in the constitution of the 'meaning' of a performance, text, or utterance" (1997, 356). Her view is more relevant than ever, as digital audiences, much more involved in the production of cultural forms online, also come together to constitute a public. Their practices and the socio-cultural controversies of the discourses they produce are what this book elaborates in different ways. As new texts and genres are produced online, they convoke and constitute new audiences (or old audiences in new ways), with online users also bringing their expectations to bear on texts. Text and publics respond to each other, even as online audiences reconstitute texts by interpreting, playing with, and sometimes, reworking them. But the nature of the audiences and publics of various African popular arts "cannot be predicted simply from the nature of the medium" (353). With the convergence culture of digital platforms, and the sharing of content, it is fair to expect audiences of popular arts on the internet to, in many instances, perform their consumption of texts through digital habits like retweeting or remixing content.

As the audiences of culture (readers/viewers) become more engaged and assertive in the use of new media, they become producers of content, "authors" whose works—poems, short stories, and comedy sketches—shape cultural and political conversations in digital publics. For instance, a 2016 debate on a public sphere shaped by the participatory energy and outbursts of young people in Nigerian digital publics involves Africa's first Nobel Laureate, Wole Soyinka. Soyinka had expressed his determination to destroy his American residency card if Donald Trump emerged victorious in the 2016 presidential elections in the United States. After a shocking Trump victory, several young people on social media trolled and called out Soyinka for backtracking. Soyinka read their online commentaries as a raucous invasion of his privacy, calling his interlocutors "illiterates who feel they want to make themselves heard" (Ibekwe 2016). In 2023, after Nigeria's presidential elections, Soyinka, again, was the subject of controversies among some young commentators on social media. Although some of his critics in both instances may have been misguided in the whole, the plurality of haranguing Facebook and Twitter commentaries on the various subjects heralded a new order in the nature and constitution of the Nigerian digital public. Soyinka's language regarding social media users who wish to "make themselves heard" aptly frames the impact of a new order of cultural voice available to young people in Nigeria and other parts of the world. In response to Soyinka, one Nigerian writer on Facebook, in a post that captures the collective disposition of what would later be called "a Soro soke generation" during the 2020 #EndSARS movement, offers a sense of a digital public predicated on the dynamism of youth culture:

> Social media is turning out to be the older generation's nightmare. The older generation of politicians, intellectuals, columnists are used to having opinions and making them public without contradiction. They are used to writing in newspapers and declaring their opinions as final without contradiction because [for] some of these young ones, it will take them a year to ever get their opinions published in those newspapers. What social media has offered the youths is the opportunity to challenge every word spoken, the opportunity to talk back, the opportunity to examine every word written and spoken and sieve out the bullshit from the real message. This is very uncomfortable for certain persons.[4]

Rather than an oedipal anxiety to erase the generation of fathers, James Ogunjimi rails against a gerontocratic culture that excludes young people from the Nigerian public sphere and claims social media as a tool to mitigate such exclusion. But he also appears to miss how social media flattens the generational contours of the Nigerian digital public, and it is hardly true that the print space of the newspaper was exclusively dominated by the old. If anything, the newspaper space is open, with its own modes of public engagements and discursivity that permit a wide range of perspectives, regardless of age. Young people may be generally savvier and more adept at digital technology, but social media provides many kinds of self-representational and publishing opportunities for all groups and establishes a continuum of print and online publics. In other words, Ogunjimi romanticizes the category of youth itself in a similar manner to how many other Nigerian writers who romanticize the platforms fail to see the panoptic violence of visibility that is produced by the surveillance economies of social media itself. Hence, what social media offers the young writer is not just the capacity for public speech but an ambivalence that enhances both participatory politics and extractive regimes of capital.

Ogunjimi's account gestures toward a certain hierarchical understanding that dictates the relationship between some African writers and their readers, although the rigid boundaries of the interactions between both groups are increasingly vulnerable, yielding sometimes to mediatized scrutiny. As evidenced by this Nigerian context, my argument is that digital technologies have enabled a digital public that also structures social and aesthetic relations between African literary writers, their textual productions, and the readers that consume their works, with all sharing a complex virtual world of shifting identities. In her remarks on literary valuation and reading publics, Tsitsi Jaji argues that:

> African poetry's reading publics are multiple and fluid. They shift in historical moments, contingent on publishing venues, political contexts, and relative access along the lines of gender, geography, and genre formation. Careful attention to the media of poetry's circulation, and particularly to varying degrees of ephemerality, reveals how malleable its audiences may be. (2020, 72)

As publishing venues for young African writers who test their work on blogging and social media spaces, digital media shape the practices of African literary publics in more ways than we have explored. And here, I return to my claims about the technical structure of the media and the algorithmic environments that impact African literary and cultural discourses and labors of its publics. More engaged literary publics proceed from the connective affordances of digital media as well as the immediacy that governs social interactions on many digital platforms. What brings digital publics "in an immediate relationship to the contents of the medium," as Jay David Bolter and Richard Grusin put it, is a desire for immediacy—one of the central concepts in their book *Remediation: Understanding New Media* (2000, 318). The immediacy of social media commentaries as a public and visible mode of literary engagement is one of the ways social media enacts different forms of reading praxes among literary publics. In this digital public, the reader transitions from the act of interpreting encoded literary meanings to performing writerly roles.

In Ogunjimi's response, as I have detailed earlier with the ascendancy of social media influencers, is also this ability to question the authority of the literary elite, whether from Soyinka's generation or Adichie's. Although writers' private views must always be differentiated from those they offer in their literary works, there is much to be gleaned from the immediacy of the public commentary that engages these writers and their ideas. Writers who use social media to blend their roles as cultural producers and public intellectuals are, therefore, expected to have opinions on politics and culture, which may not always be well received by those literary friends and followers who believe they should also have a say in the public arena.

Therefore, the digital expansion of African literary publics can mean that readers and audiences have new avenues to respond to the texts they consume. It bears reiteration that with social media, the literary gerontocracy represented by writers such as Soyinka is now under scrutiny as the authoritative voices of canonical writers can now be immediately surveyed by engaged reading publics brimming with creative energy and outrage.

The fact that readers *become* literary friend and followers on social media is an indication that the platform transforms the nature and function of audiences, while writers themselves cultivate and perform certain expectations of sociality that support and consolidate their creative engagements with readers. Friendships and followership may be read as ontological markers of both sociality and epistemic relations. Friends socialize, while followers get information from the newsfeed of the person being followed, depending on timeline settings, without encountering the personal lives of the writers they follow. A fundamental feature of digital publics for literature is that scholars have to respond to an ongoing bifurcation of its reading publics into fans, followers, and friends. I will return to the question of literary friendship, but the social ties between a follower, a fan, and a friend suggest that reading publics are indeed fluidly constituted. To follow a writer or to seek friendship with them is a mode of coming to terms with the writer's ongoing literary engagements. Mike Maphoto's "Diary of a Zulu Girl," an example of what Stephanie Bosch Santana calls "Facebook fiction," illuminates this mode of engagement and relationship between African writers and their digital audiences (2018, 187). Aside from the fact that Maphoto constantly received suggestions on the thematic directions and turns in plots for his stories from appreciative readers, he also deliberately engaged them in conversations after each chapter. These conversations produce more perspectives and commentaries on Maphoto's original storylines, taking them in sometimes new and productive directions. Maphoto, therefore, used digitality to acknowledge the participation of readers in the process of artistic production and recognize the more engaged interpretive labors of the reading publics that converged around his literary blog.

Digital publics are integral to what Musila, following Barber, imagines as constituting "a double addressivity" in African writing (2016a, 1454). Musila clarifies the role of the double publics constituted by "ordinary African publics, most of whom could neither read nor afford books" as well as to "international and local elites" whose tastes and preferences writers today "are increasingly forced to prioritize" in their literary offerings (1454). In this formulation are echoes of Peter Ekeh's argument that colonialism in African created two publics—a primordial and civic public whose linked moral politics operate differently from the European public and private realms transported to postcolonial Africa (1975). I have always wondered how Ekeh's analysis of the two publics and its connections to state politics and the moral foundations of the African bourgeoise class might enrich our understanding of digital media and the various publics it creates. For instance, digital colonialism—as the capitalist domination of African internet subjects through data capture—can be read as creating two categories of digital publics: those who are mainly content with using digital media to participate in cultural productions with little interest in the ethical consequences of extractive data relations, and an elite digital publics mindful of the interpellating function of data relations. In the absence of any just outrage over their data vulnerabilities, the overlapping dynamics of these two publics should go without saying that the nonelite publics, ordinary, everyday people with access to the internet, circulate more in one-to-many platforms like WhatsApp, although this app assumedly has encrypted capabilities that this group may care little for. This is unlike the elitism of the more educated middle-class publics who, though they understand the power of data regimes, lack the infrastructural power of intervention to create African technological alternatives for a public sphere.

To return to Musila, the texts and conversations that shape literary publics on social media are increasingly self-conscious of the agency and participation of local audiences, even if more writers now have enhanced visibility to international readers and publishers. As Ikhide Ikheloa frames this argument in a blog post, there is "a new army of storytellers on the Internet and social media; they have become incredibly influential even as traditional writers jostle for space in the cafes of America and Europe to write traditional pieces for literary prizes."[5] Literary prizes and the conflicts around literary personalities they generate online have become a huge source of debate among African digital publics, and will be discussed as a locus of literary outrage in contemporary African literature. In the meantime, the binary understanding of social media writers and traditional writers effaces nuance and the connections that often define both groups. Digital literary publics serve as a shared literary terrain where assertive and involved audiences participate in a writing community whose media is predicated on the agency of multinational companies in Western countries. The illusion of a placeless social media aside, literary publics on digital media complicate what Akin Adesokan, in response to

Eileen Julien, terms "'reversed extraversion'—the centripetal dispersal of influence of a novel first published outside of its author's primary sphere of interest" to mark Nigerian novelists' practice of producing works at home after success abroad (2012, 16). Along with local publishing networks and awards, writers use digital networks and publics to attain some level of influence and visibility from home, before they and their works travel to other locations.

To summarize the argument on digital literary publics, my interest is to call attention to how African writing in a digital age is highly self-conscious of a much more productive reading public that engages with literary works, whether as writers, readers, or producers of commentary discourses. Also crucial in my argumentation is an attentiveness to the capitalist data politics that produces digital publics as a market demographic whose data is minable and extractable. As the locations and spaces of African literature exhibit intense circulations on digital media platforms, digital literary publics are central to readerly interpretations of African texts but are also simultaneously connected to local, nondigital publics. In fact, a vast majority of literary production and interpretation in African writing community happens in demotic spaces, as scholars such as Bosch Santana, Brouillette, and Sacks have pointed out in several works. Hence, my earlier argument that a "lingering print imaginary" characterizes much of the digital literature produced by African authors (Yékú 2020). In the section that follows, I examine commentary practices as some of the most visible means of performing literary publicness on social media, with Achebe's *There Was a Country* furnishing an analytical space to demonstrate ethnopolitcal controversies of African digital literary publics.

Achebe and the Ethnopolitics of His-story

My starting point for this final section is the contention that an ethnopolitical tension permeates social media commentaries on Achebe's *There Was a Country* on several digital locations, including Facebook. As a work of nonfiction, *There Was a Country* bemoans the early decline of post-Independence Nigeria, which precipitated the events of the Biafran war. Besides an Igbo ancestry that accounts for his sympathies, Achebe's lamentation for Biafra is due to what the memoir frames as hostility toward his people whose historical culture of egalitarianism and enterprise, in Achebe's retelling, provoked animosity from other parts of Nigeria.

Rather than a close reading of the memoir itself, I have limited my analysis to online debates on it, without incorporating external perspectives from prior and offline or personal interactions that may exist between the writers whose discussions I analyze (between Achebe and Biodun Jeyifo, for instance). Achebe's final offering was published at a crucial point in the development of digital publics of Nigerian literature. 2012 was the year of the global occupy movements around the world with the Nigerian version of that transnational repudiation of capitalist modernity occurring in the same year. In the words of onetime presidential adviser, these collective "children of anger and distracted crowd of Facebook addicts" were vociferous in the protest against the official narratives of the Goodluck Jonathan administration and would not tolerate fiscal policies that further entrenched their precariousness (Abati 2012). In the context of this chaotic cesspool of economic imbroglio, Jihadist terrorism, and online public outrage came an important publication that reflects on the events preceding the 1966 Nigeria-Biafra war, as well as the postwar politics that led to the decline of a fractured nation.

The specific politics and contestations over historical representations in the text have already been delineated by several Achebe scholars who are on different sides of the debates informed by the book. What has not really been examined by most of these critical works and reviews is the online reterritorialization of these heated conversations in the new digital publics of Nigerian literature. The social media age and the communities it fosters, however, extend the historical logics of fights and contention in pre-Web 2.0 literary communities. As Adesokan writes on Krazitivity in a reflection piece on Biafra:

> At one point or another, virtually every Nigerian-identified writer or intellectual, including some of the most famous in the world today, belonged to that group. Thinking back to discussions on the listserv, one is struck by how they often degenerated into ugly fights over ethnic identity in Nigeria—routinely, tiresomely between the Igbo and the Yoruba, with scant regard for those of other ethnic groups. Long before its members began to yield to the attractions of other platforms on social media, these fights and the controversies arising from them did much to undermine that group. There were active efforts to destroy what had emerged organically as a community of writers, most of them friends of long standing, and those efforts rode on the back of ethnic preference or prejudice, alias tribalism. . . . A community no longer exists, but the rules supposedly governing its existence do. (2017)

In a private correspondence, the events described by Adesokan were confirmed by Remi Raji, who created an informal email list to connect writers and critics in 1999 in order to help resuscitate a PEN Nigeria Centre. According to Raji, the group was later named Krazitivity by the linguist Kole Ade-Odutola after it had been digitally organized by Sola Osofisan.[6] At the turn of the millennium, Krazitivity became a prominent forum for Nigerian writers' debates, but soon began to generate controversies. This resulted, as Raji notes, in the emergence of another digital community, Ederi, formed by writers who found their ideological positions in conflict with those of Krazitivity. It is safe to say that Nigerian digital networks have their roots deep in the soil of animus and controversy. Krazitivity has since become defunct, after Yahoo! Groups and listservs became discontinued, but the central point remains. Like it obtains in Kenya and several other countries on the continent, Nigerian digital communities and networks have always been haunted by all manners of acrimony, including the specter of ethnic politics. Again, social media, through its social-technical affordances, amplifies this wàhálà proclivity in several ways. While I draw on slight perspectives from my own reading of the work itself, my larger intent is to underscore how *There Was A Country* was taken up on social media by readers who subjected its narratives to ethnic politics, making it the most controversial of all Achebe's work.

These exchanges and arguments on *There Was a Country* are typical of an algorithmic age that centers personae politics and the agitation that is often evident in online publics. Aside from a close reading of commentaries on this text from one or two other online locations (Nnedi Okorafor's Goodreads comment, for example), my analysis specifically motivates interest in the interventions of several Nigerian writers on Facebook. Most of these writers and public commentators appear to agree with Jeyifo that Achebe's book is "a direct challenge to Nigeria's community of writers and intellectuals, especially those who see themselves in the progressive and humanistic traditions of intellectualism" (2013, 683). It is in this sense that I exhume the status updates and posts of some Nigerian writers who are also avid social media personalities serving as public intellectuals in Nigeria. Besides social media comments, online book review platforms, such as Amazon Book Reviews and Goodreads (later bought by Amazon), also offer fascinating perspectives for literary analyses, hence my correlation of social media commentaries with book review comments on Goodreads. Although these platforms are limited in the ability to tell us how people actually read, or if at all they read a book before posting comments, they nevertheless make visible "the social lives of books,"[7] which for my present task are necessary to understand reader agency and practices on African writing online. They also help to understand how reviewing platforms are key to the "greatly broadened base of participation" of digital literary publics, even if readers and authors are often entangled on spaces like Goodreads in the politics of negative reviews and personality attacks that also engender controversies and authorial self-censure (Murray 2018, 118). In any case, the public spats that accrue from the weaponization of reviews on the platform are potentially profitable since, as a social platform, "part of what Goodreads is offering is conversation and user engagement, and controversies and censorious debates can drive more comments and time spent on the platform" (Alter and Harris 2023). In other words, whether on social media or book reviewing platforms, controversies accrue a sticky value that affectively ties readers to a platform that extracts capital from their literary labors.[8] This stickiness is anchored on algorithmic systems.

By reader agency, I refer to the capacity of reading publics to interpret texts and express their perspectives irrespective of the structural constraints of digital platforms. Furthermore, the view that social media comments are offering inchoate and often half-baked thoughts laden with sentimentalism is often used to dismiss their contributions to literary meaning-making. With religion, political affiliations, and ethnic filiations—topics that animate Achebe's autobiography—in the mix, online contestations and trolling are seen as the death knell of civil and meaningful discussions in the Nigerian digital public. Yet, the comment section remains an important source of cultural meaning and often reveals the ideological persuasions of readers, more so on Facebook, on which anonymity is sometimes difficult. As with readers who now possess an immediate connection to literary content, digital technologies make it possible for many in the writing community to publish their works and for readers of these works using online reviewing platforms and social media to respond to them.

Acknowledging the strategic doubleness suggested by Achebe's title, Jeyifo begins his critique of *There Was a Country* by highlighting the book's trenchant treatment of "the crises that led both to the creation and the destruction of the secessionist republic" of Biafra as well as Achebe's reference to Nigeria as a country that once was—or at least was on the verge of becoming—but is now vanished (2013, 683). This doubleness invites us to appreciate Achebe's story as both "Nigeria's story" and "Biafra's story" and, therefore, "our story" (2012, 3). That this collective story of ours (as Achebe puts it) fails to include everyone in its remembrance of the Biafran debates is instantiated by the online controversies around the book. But the narrative of *There Was a Country* harbors four dissociated and diverse parts that blur "frontiers between genres in the promotion of its [Biafran] cause. It informs about human attitudes by a participant observer. In this sense, it stands as an anthropological essay that engages trans-disciplinary views" (Mudimbe 2013, 676). In other words, Achebe may call his Nigerian-Biafran story "our story," yet it is evident that the text offers a narrative that is shaped by the particularities of his own self-interest and privilege as a participant in the tale. In any case, that much of the book comprises shorter pieces previously published elsewhere gives the sense of a curatorial approach that makes "our story" a carefully selected narrative organized to serve some interests. In speaking for us or, as a matter of fact, for the Igbo nation, he inhabits a position of narrative power that members of the reading public would lateractively exercise through the expressive affordances of social media.

There Was a Country is Achebe's version of the story we all share as Nigerians, both on Facebook and even offline, before the memoir was published. There is a problem, though, in the practice of speaking for others since it might lead to discursive erasure and is often "born of a desire for mastery, to privilege oneself as the one who more correctly understands the truth about another's situation" (Alcoff 1992, 22). When the Nigerian poet Jumoke Verissimo, writing on the blog Africa Is a Country, wonders for whom Achebe's reflection on Biafra had been written, she essentially began a war of words among some Nigerian writers on social media, some of whom saw her first as an ethnic other. While it is evident from Achebe's words that he is speaking for all of us, this narration is "a personal history" of a collective story and hence raised ruckus about fidelity to historical accuracy. Because we cannot dissociate the writer from the tale in this case, therefore, many Nigerians, including some Igbo commentators, saw his recollection as ethnocentric and highly subjective. One evidence for this may be found in a Goodreads remark by the Africanfuturist writer Nnedi Okorafor, who wrote that Achebe's work is "definitely not objective" and that "the ghost of Biafra haunts every Nigerian."[9] Her view is one example of dissenting perspectives, even among the Igbo literary community, although it was written not as a review but as commentary that was not intended to start what she described as a firestorm. This idea that Biafra's ghost haunts Nigerians in different ways is germane to its narration and the various controversies around its telling. As may be evident from this Goodreads example, the debates on *There Was a Country* generated controversy even among various writers who appeared to shun literary comradeship in defense of Achebe's work.

For instance, writing on *There Was a Country*, Nigerian poet Verissimo suggested that the memoir "reopened old wounds and resulted in widespread debate, whether in op-ed columns, on blogs or on social media" (2012). But it was her commentary on newspaper reviews of the book that irked other writers:

> Achebe's *Guardian article*, for me, seems to have ended up promoting a self-serving perspective that encourages ethnocentricity. It has furthered ethnic cyber-war on social media and online pages of national newspapers like the *The Nation*, *Punch*, and in the *Vanguard Newspaper*, where a review of the book generated hate comments. (2012)

The late UK-based publisher and wriyer Nnorom Azuonye, in a 2012 Facebook post, reads Verissimo's contribution in terms of ethnic chauvinism and an "Achebe bashing," writing of "Odia Ofeimun and other Awophiles(-ists) and Igbophobic human beings using the opportunity of the publication of Achebe's work to make faulty statements and join issues with Chinua Achebe, Odumegwu-Ojukwu and the entire Igbo people."[10] Here, Azuonye is making a reference to support among most people in the South West for Obafemi Awolowo, a Nigerian nationalist and statesman who played an active role in Nigeria's independence movement. He occupies a controversial position among some in the narratives of the Nigerian Civil War and its associated politics because of a notorious starvation policy he, as Finance Minister of Nigeria, implemented against the Igbos during the war. The idea of an Igbophobia is probably an overstretch, but it is a view supported by other writers who agree that Verissimo's review is "an insult on Achebe and his memory," as Azuonye observes. Other responses to the post, by poets Olu Oguibe and Uche Peter Umez, are also similarly fashioned around deprecating language that take umbrage with Verissimo's review. One commenter wrote that the whole Achebe matter "has shown me that our so-called new generation of Nigerian writers are for the most part, empty vessels who just happen to know how to use words. That Verissimo, a lady I think highly of, and all those so-called writers could make such unfortunate comments has made me fall from heaven literally and destroyed the vestiges of hope I have of a Nigerian renaissance."[11] The recourse to attack personally is consistent with the kinds of politics generated by these online debates.

As the slurs and outrage around Achebe memoir indicate, digital literary publics often become zones of conflicts in which consensus on public matters can be difficult to achieve. As evident in the amplification of the literary feuds and controversies I have been tracking in this book, the role of social media in these conflicts is fascinating since the platforms sometimes become noisy agoras saturated with tensions and textual performances of online rivalry. This conflictual possibility aside, the agency and capacity for speech and self-writing in the possession of the literary collectives that constitute digital publics is something that cannot be denied. Verissimo might have it coming, too, as the original post on Africa Is a Country does not reveal much familiarity with Achebe's work as at the time she wrote. Defending her stance on Azuonye's timeline, the poet claims that "many of the readings [by other writers such as Olu Oguibe and Uche Umez] have been done out of context."[12] Verissimo's suggestion that Achebe's audience mainly belongs to a certain ethnic group basically normalizes the same ethnic politics that constitutes the thematic focus of the memoir. What cannot be missed in Verissimo's post is how it mounts a space to contest Achebe's representation of the Yorùbá leader, Awolowo, a theme on which other writers later elaborated on Facebook.

My second example underpins this contentious terrain of literary commentaries on Facebook. Posted by the Nigerian writer Nduka Otiono, the status update launched a scathing attack on those he referred to as "ethnic bigots" who, having not read the book, jumped to conclusions on its contents. In other words, Otiono rightly takes issues with those who judge Achebe's book by the material they encountered only on Facebook and literary review blogs. "There is no greater stupidity than criticizing a book one has never read," Otiono begins, adding that those "ethnic bigots who have risen up in arms against excerpts from *There Was a Country*, the somber new offering by the venerable Chinua Achebe, should take their time to read the book first."[13] Otiono's charge comes across as a sensible recommendation, except that it is also undergirded with the same language and tone that is consistent with the expression of outrage on social media. While one can appreciate his justifiably fervent defense of "the venerable Chinua Achebe," the rhetoric of the post itself mirrors the larger web of disputations of several writers commenting on *There Was a Country*.

My reference to a post Otiono produced, as he later admitted, in an atmosphere of friendly exchanges among online friends, is perhaps more relevant because of the comments it attracted, including the view by the writer Chidi Anthony Opara that "when they have the book, would they read it well before commenting? Even on Facebook and in other internet fora, Nigerians usually react before reading the materials in question."[14] Opara may exaggerate the Nigerian reading culture on social media, but he is right about how people tend to be hasty when they post content online. As some platforms now urge users to read articles before sharing or tweeting them, this impedes the flow of misinformation but also determines readers' comprehension and responses. The impulse to immediately post a comment, like, share, and retweet a social media status update or tweet may be more than an impulsive surrender to the urgings of the medium. When some social media users encounter commentaries online, they encounter them as texts not only to read, but also as information to be shared or liked first, sometimes in solidarity with friends in their networks. Mark L. Lilleleht's response in the thread of Otiono's post is quite revealing, therefore. That the kinds of "knee-jerk reactions" that annoy Otiono are "not the sole province of Nigerians" can enable an appreciation of the level of conflicts that generally circulate on social media globally. Rather than focus on an Achebe-inspired ethnicity as the sole catalyst of this tension, then, it may be worthwhile to look to the medium, which, while promoting participatory culture and user agency, also facilitates tenuous networks of forced sociality, something that speaks to the profit-driven algorithms that propel literary networks and publics.

The tensions around ethnicity that invigorate most of the discussions on Facebook and elsewhere definitely have something to do with Achebe's privileging of an ethnic disposition in what is supposedly his ethical responsibility to retell the despoliation of Biafra that he witnessed. But as Jeyifo writes, Achebe in *There Was a Country* presents himself as a "propagandist, media apparatchik and ideological zealot" (2013, 684), while "all of his speculations in the book, are relentlessly driven by ethnicity, and a very curious conception of ethnicity for that matter" (685). Clearly, Jeyifo's generalization is not something that completely sits well with my own reading of the text. Achebe's retrospective account is an important treatment of a troubling and traumatic period of Nigerian history, but whether most non-Igbos agree with Achebe and a seemingly contrived genocidal understanding among several Igbo intellectuals is another matter entirely. To return to the Awolowo debate, which came up in the charge against Verissimo mentioned earlier, the underlying assumption of that accusation also restates the debate on Facebook about ethnicity and tribalism that greeted Achebe's work. Ikheloa offers an acerbic review on Facebook in response to Jeyifo's claim that *There Was a Country* ignores and obscures class and marks a radical rupture in Achebe's writings in its promotion of Igbo ethnonationalism:

> Jeyifo is trying awkwardly to hide his huge ethnic bias by accusing Achebe of the same and of a lack of objectivity, it is comical, really. The only reason we are reading all this wahala (or trying to, my eyes glaze over the ancient history of alphabet soup parties, UPGA, NNA, blah blah blah) is because Achebe trained his rage on Awolowo. So all the Awoists are being trotted out to write absolutely dreadful "book reviews."[15]

Aside from the irony of dismissing an expert literary critic, Ikheloa's post offers a curious amalgamation of ethnicity with a support for Awolowo's actions and inactions during the Nigerian civil war. These two ideas are not the same. As another Nigerian writer, Adunni Adelakun, observes in her response to the post, Ikheloa is "probably the only one who does not see ethnic bias in Achebe's book." What is important in all of this is how Achebe's book and the debates it engenders demonstrate the transformed terrain of the Nigerian literary audience, with writers and other regular consumers of literature invested in public performances of readings, antireadings, and rereadings in digital environments. Their interpretive views and reviews of literary works may not be anchored on any theoretical perspective, yet these reader-writers and their perspectives contribute to the vibrancy of digital literary publics and expand the circulations of African letters. The act of reading itself for the literary publics of African literature online manifests as a social and contested practice through which people engage with other members of their online networks. Like the Facebook option, which allows users to announce what book they may be reading at any given time, there is the sense that the various publics of contemporary African writing have a need to be seen performing reading as a mediatized event on social media, whether they have actually read the work or not.

A close reading of the eighty-two comments in the discussion thread of Ikheloa's post uncovers a central fact about literary collectives and publics on digital platforms; despite their elitist pretentions and middle-class background, readers come with ideological assumptions—in the case of Achebe's text, an ethnopolitical awareness—that form and inform the core of their consumption of literary works. Without realizing it, some of these readers seek to naturalize these biases in their supposed readings and interpretations of the text for others in their networks. This point leads me to the uncomfortable conclusion that may be self-evident already. The discussions of Achebe's work enact a needless Igbo-Yorùbá dichotomy, which indicts those who circulate such ethnocentric oppositions that mirror the polarization of social media platforms themselves. For example, one commentator wrote that Jeyifo's rhetoric confirms "his normal Yorùbá bitter and envy-filled anger on Igbos," a view supported by several otherwise informed and progressive writers online. The ethnicization of the conversation—based on both the subject matter of the book and the apparatus of its algorithmic production of outrage—was also evident in other media locations outside of Facebook. For instance, in Ipadeola's 2013 review of *There Was a Country*, which he mentions in the thread of Ikheloa's post, there is the indictment of Chimamanda Adichie for her exclusion of what he considered as canonical texts of the Nigeria–Biafra war: Awolowo's *Awolowo* on the Nigerian Civil War and Ken Saro-Wiwa's *On A Darkling Plain*. In the article published in Nigeria's the *Guardian Newspaper*, Ipadeola writes that Adichie's omission of these writers is "a queer choice to make for anyone who wants to be taken seriously as knowledgeable, empathetic and reasonably *ethnically aware*."[16] This inexplicable and problematic ethnical awareness, which emerges every now and again in the Nigerian digital public, is the fulcrum of the Achebe debates.

One of the most rational voices that prevailed in this contest of ethno-nationalist sentiments is probably offered in the Ikheloa thread by Ken Emetulu: "I love and worship Achebe, but I disagree with his opinion, just as I disagree with all the emotive defenders of Awolowo who approached this from the ethnic dimension."[17] This ethnic dimension is probably the reason those who reject the insinuations of Ikheloa's posts have Yorùbá names, while many of their interlocutors have Igbo names. In Otiono's post, for instance, the major resistance to the charge of ethnic bigots accrue from commenters with Yorùbá names. The focus of this Igbo-Yorùbá split may not appear to be personality at first, since voices such as Ikheloa are not Igbo, while the commenter Ade Osijo offers "Kudos to Achebe." But as in most social media fights and arguments, things soon evolve into personality conflicts.

Social media personalities and their engagements matter. In digital publics, the personality of a commenter, together with the strength of their followership, has much bearing on who likes or does not like a post, even as it does on the kind of discourses that become produced. As I conclude my analysis, it is vital to add that whether one agrees that ethnicity motivates Achebe's work or not, there is sufficient evidence to appreciate how it does motivate the core of the discussions of and commentaries on the book on a social media space that is naturally predisposed to enabling and amplifying polarization. Despite the myriad of negative analyses motivated by such factional impulses, there were some members of the online reading public, such as Emetulu who, for instance, was not keen on joining the debate publicly because of the ethnicization of the matter. The politics of ethnicity in which *There Was a Country* became enmeshed overshadowed the literary merits of Achebe's important contribution to Nigeria's postcolonial literary history. The debates reveal how African literature on the internet is troubled by the relationship between personality politics and literary interpretations on digital media platforms built around an outrage economy. That said, there is value in open and nonacrimonious debates, and I shall revisit this.

CHAPTER 4

The Caine Prize Wàhálà and the Algorithmic Rọ̀fọ̀rọ́fọ̀ of Literary Networks

While the chaos and scandals of social media commentaries intersect with the reception and discussion of literary prizes—my focus in this chapter—they also bring to mind a different kind of chaos, one involving the Zimbabwean novelist Dambudzo Marechera. The year was 1979, the setting was in London, and the majority of the British literary establishment had gathered on the day for the Guardian Fiction Prize, which was awarded that year to Marechera and Neil Jordan. As Jordan recounts in a 2023 interview, Marechera followed a very angry speech with tossing furniture around in the room. The "combative speech," as Jordan recalls it, was about how Marechera felt he was "being patronized and how he rejected the colonial atmosphere of the prize" (Osborn and Jordan 2023). In contemporary discussions of literary prizes in African literature on social media, the chaos is of a different kind and rather than the rejection of coloniality, I want to argue that discourses around prize sometimes center and reinscribe a colonial mindset that gestures back to empire. Digital platforms as ideological and political spaces render outrage profitable through a social media culture that captures attention at any cost, including the exacerbation of divisiveness in society. As I showed earlier, social media platforms are sometimes resistant to ethical content moderation because of the focus on profits, encouraging divisive content and the popular rhetoric of cancelation that undermines civil conversations. As outlined earlier, social media is designed to make people vulnerable to intense regimes of feelings, unfeeling, and affectivity. As platform culture stokes outrage, it fosters conflictual networks and polarizing zones of sociality that promote controversies and amplify extreme behavior. Reading how popular commentary on African cultural productions become shaped by this technocratic culture of mostly rhetorical violence, I wish to explore how the cultural functions of awards, such as the Caine Prize for African Writing and the Nobel, inform the contradictory politics of decolonization in online discussions of African literature. Anyone who is familiar with the Caine Prize, the African Booker as some call it, knows that it is a gift that keeps on giving when it comes to the subject of controversy. My argument is that the algorithms and social media clickbait that glue and stick people to online media and the contentious narratives that circulate on them are relevant to online controversies around literary prizes like the Caine Prize. They function as the technical substructures enabling wàhálà and ròfọ̀rọ́fọ̀, metaphors for local accents of impassioned discussions of Western literary prizes and the controversies they engender on social media. Thus, algorithmic ròfọ̀rọ́fọ̀ refers to the outrage culture of literary networks. Specifically, this chapter explores rhetorical tensions on social media that spring from conversations on literary prizes such as the Caine Prize for African Writing, awarded annually for a short story either written in or translated into English by an African writer.

The Caine Prize Wàhálà

After his Booker Prize for Fiction award, John Berger remarked that "the basic cultural value of a prize depends upon what it is a stimulus to" (2016).[1] Berger suggests that literary prizes stimulate different kinds of subjectivities that ultimately reveal their value as consecratory symbols of aesthetic judgment. The controversies, arguments, and scandals they stimulate enhance their importance. Prizes themselves are defined by a certain scandalous value that renders legible their cultural function as an instrument of legitimacy. Whether it is the Caine Prize, the Booker, or the Nobel, the overarching discourse surrounding cultural prizes is predominantly negative in tone (English 2005, 187). As scandal is generally constitutive of the character and function of prizes, we need to understand it as a "system of exchange" that secures cultural esteem "by maximizing the flow of disesteeming discourse through and around it" (189). This is necessary because despite how scandals and controversial discourses are intrinsically attached to prizes, scandal remains "the instrument par excellence of symbolic action" (Bourdieu 1993, 84). Hence, the view by Meredith Goldsmith that "the construction of cultural prestige" often takes place through both the publishing industry and "literary prizes and their attendant scandals" (2016, 233). There are, of course, some significant differences between controversies and scandals. Controversies may proceed from scandals, but scandals are hardly directly coterminous with controversies. For example, the Caine Prize in Africa is consistently framed negatively as enabling the production of single stories of the continent that encourage western stereotypes. This is a controversial view that is not necessarily a scandal that, for instance, is based on judging practices or any ethical breach in the award process. Despite the distinction I make here, repeated perceptions of such controversies persist as a scandal. Sana Goyal uses the expression "scandals galore" in a 2020 *Wasafiri* interview with Ellah Wakatama, the chair of the Caine Prize board while Nathan Suhr-Sytsma in "The Geography of Prestige" similarly describes a controversial statement on the Caine Prize as "a perceived scandal," essentially reflecting the subjectiveness that follows both terms (2018, 1100).[2] There is enormous critical scholarship on the Caine Prize already, particularly on its cultural politics of literary legitimation and its possible reiteration of a condescending Eurocentric paradigm that constrains the formal, aesthetic, and thematic currents of postcolonial African writing. Hence, I won't rehash much of it.

That said, there has been significant attention to Ikhide Ikheloa, a reviewer of literary texts that began to gain academic visibility when he wrote a review of NoViolet Bulawayo's short story "Hitting Budapest," which won the 2011 Caine Prize. Ikheloa, like many online critics of the prize, wrote that many African writers "are skewing their written perspectives to fit what they imagine will sell to the West and the judges of the Caine Prize."[3] Besides the idea that a new generation of African writers produce fiction that is profitable to the West, the Kenyan writer Wainaina published a series of "angry tweets" in 2014, now cataloged at *Brittle Paper*, in which he calls out the prize organizers for "twitter moans about ingratitude" from writers who took aim at the politics of the prize.[4] This narrative, of course, is a single story of the Caine Prize itself. Yet commentators such as Ikheloa famously refer to this process as "poverty porn," something Helon Habila would later describe as one way the Caine has created "an African aesthetic of suffering" (2013), echoing

Frenkel's 2008 claim that Booker Prize-nominated texts are not only "intimately caught up in the mechanisms of empire" and defined by a politics of loss but are, in fact, expected to "communicate a particular idea of history and culture" that she terms "post-colonial pathos" (2008, 87). In this way, just like algorithms have the power to homogenize culture, the Caine Prize also has the tendency to enact a homogenization of literary culture, reproducing similar logics of sameness between algorithms and literature.

The Caine Prize's poverty porn, which is more about the content of the works that win the prize than the form and language of the narratives themselves, explains the anticathartic sensibilities produced from the essentialist representations of misery and stereotypes in African writing and oriented to western audiences. In this popular rendition of the common critique against the prize, a performance of Africa as a place of lack and crises persists even as the judges of the prize shape the continent's artistic quality and taste. Despite having contributed to the so-called reinvigoration of contemporary African literature, Dobrota Pucherová still argues that the Caine has been involved in the "troubled history of postcolonial literatures in English, of which the primary site of evaluation and legitimation has been the West (2012, 13). Although rather than a legitimization of mainly Anglophonic writing as Pucherová suggests, the prize is a continent-wide award that was won by the Sudanese writer Leila Aboulela in its inaugural year in 2000. Pucherová's Bordieuan reading of the Caine Prize as enabling "the monopoly of literary legitimacy" or the dominant power of an award body "to consecrate producers or products" (Bourdieu 1993, 42) partly informs Doseline Kiguru's argument on the ways in which the Caine Prize constitutes a pivotal structure of African literary production that contributes to the canonization of literature while reproducing "unequal representation in the literary canon" (Kiguru 2016a, 205). Beyond the politics of canon formation, the Caine Prize, for Kiguru, is also a major influencing factor for the creation and organization of the judgment of African literary taste.[5]

Despite the various criticisms leveled against it, equally pertinent is its relevance in conducting a new literary aesthetic that prioritizes innovative storytelling, as many winners of the prize have demonstrated through their writings.[6] Hence, there is a critical ambivalence to the Caine Prize that informs Pucherová's view that it constitutes a "system of postcolonial knowledge industry that both values and marginalizes postcolonial texts" (2012, 13). While the politics of poverty porn and literary legitimacy is important, my focus is different, as I intend to use the Caine Prize to understand how literary prizes generally index the power of western prizes to elicit particular forms of affect, subjectivities, and outrage on blogging and social media platforms. Beyond the critical and scholarly discourses by established theorists, what might be gleaned from the literary-critical interventions of digital literary publics, readers who offer perspectives on African literature and expand the interpretive coverage of African writing? The strategic role of social media and internet blogs is captured by Lizzy Attree in the article "The Caine Prize and Contemporary African Writing," in which she argues:

> The online publication of the five shortlisted stories on the Caine Prize website each year sparks quite heated debate among the Facebook, Twitter, and blogging community. Although online community interest is solicited through Facebook and Twitter, and my recently begun Caine Prize blog, the wider blogging response by readers has been completely spontaneous. (2013, 43)

What the expression "quite heated debate," which is somewhat accelerated by digital media algorithms, does to the production and circulation of new African literary returns us to the point about wàhálà and rọ̀fọ̀rọ́fọ̀ fights, given that social media mud-slinging is intrinsic to the various debates. The bloggers who write about western prizes in Africa, as well as the literary networks of writers and readers who produce discourses around prizes, indicate that literary prizes involve, as English argues, a complex interaction that is composed of many formal and informal actors. This complexity sometimes propels a cultural field that is vulnerable to conflicts.[7] How the internet publicly shapes this field as the major terrain of contestations and heated arguments is crucial.

An Act of Mutiny and Manhood-Shrinking Emails

When it comes to the Caine Prize, there are several examples of these conflicts, wàhálàs, and controversies. A former winner of the prize, Zambia's Namwali Serpell went as far as describing her attempt to change the reward structure of the prize through a promise to share the winning as "an act of mutiny."[8] Serpell's socialist vision, which is also entrenched in her fiction, may be one reason for this act of defiance against the Caine Prize, but her protest fits a historical pattern of negative affect that sometimes overshadows the gains of the prize. Having said that, Serpell's mutiny is far from peculiar to her. There are others that involve some other prominent writers, including Adichie, the Nigerian-American Tope Folarin, and a number of others. For instance, in her piece for *Brittle Paper* on the Caine Prize controversy involving Folarin, Tiwaladeoluwa Adekunle reasons along these lines by presenting a textual and visual archive of views and counterviews on the eligibility of the writer based on fervent online discussions that questioned his Africanness as well as the fictional integrity of his work. After outlining what he considered to be the autobiographical elements of Folarin's Caine Prize story "Genesis," the poet Kola Tubosun announced he had been unfriended on Facebook by Folarin. Tubosun's claim may actually have been controversial, if not sensationalist, as writers routinely source fictional materials from the threads of their lives. Amidst the social media debates involving scholars and writers such as Uganda's Bwesigye Bwa Mwesigire and Nigeria's Chika Unigwe, Folarin's wife later tweeted about the hostility toward the writer, who had been subjected to what was perceived as intense and even unwarranted scrutiny on the two occasions he was shortlisted for the Caine Prize.[9]

Similarly, following Nigeria's Rotimi Babatunde's shortlist for the Caine Prize in 2012, a plagiarism accusation by Ahmed Maiwada, a legal practitioner who once served as the legal adviser to the Association of Nigerian Authors, came up on Facebook. Maiwada outlined the similarities between Babatunde's "Bombay's Republic" story and the late Biyi Bandele's *Burma Boy*. Maiwada had posted on Facebook that the storyline of the two works was "too close." He then asks: "how did it manage to make it through to the final stage of the Caine Prize? It is either the judges are not critical readers, or they are no wide readers at all, or they cannot tell between an original story an[d] the plagiarized. Whatever the shortcoming, this is most unfortunate for African writing!" The Facebook post was reproduced by Nigerian poet and a 2013 Nigeria Liquefied Natural Gas (NLNG) prizewinner Tade Ipadeola, who dismissed the allegations and strangely added that Babatunde "happens to be a substantial and stalwart artist and intellectual, far outstripping his accuser in artistic standing and longevity of practice" (2012). Again, in the manner of the algorithmic age of personality, the language is vituperative, and the focus is on the individual and the personal. Babatunde eventually won the prize, but this claim overshadowed online narratives about the year's winning story, producing on Nigerian social media raucous and ethnic politics and religious disputations that are the center of focus at the expense of the aesthetic merit of the story.

If this particular plagiarism controversy was limited to Nigerian online discussions, the same cannot be said of the removal from the 2019 Caine Prize shortlist of Tochukwu Okafor's "All Our Lives." Determining "that there had been a failure to attribute an original source," the judges eliminated Okafor's story for its resemblance to Laleh Khadivi's "Wanderlust," published in 2014. This plagiarism controversy led to a familiar debate on originality and intertextuality in African fiction, with Kristen Stern wondering why "white writers get praised for creative uses of intertextuality, while black writers are condemned for plagiarism."[10] As these plagiarism accusations and controversies fed into the complex socially symbolic system of prizes, they demonstrated that the politics of the Caine Prize transcended its marginalization or marketization of certain authors at the expense of others. Besides the obvious production of cultural value and literary tastes, it is also important to note that the centrality to the production and circulation of disputations that sometimes arise from their symbolic economies and cultural prestige.

In reading "All Our Lives" as marked by scandals and controversies, Kiguru argues that the responses to the plagiarism allegations invokes "questions on originality and credibility" and point to "the impact of scandal as a threat to the currency of prestige in "formal" literary landscapes, while serving to position "the African writer within the international literary markets" (2022, 140). Kiguru's analysis is a formidable account of the story that uses this particular scandal (or controversy, if looked at from the standpoint of the two other literary platforms that refused to pull the work) to read literary scandals as connected to the cultural politics of literary prizes, as well as quoting strategies and citational practices in African cultural texts. My analysis shifts from this latter reading through its focused attention on the social media terrain of engagements on which this scandal and the other controversies I examine play out. Unlike Kiguru's, it is critical in my approach to understand the social and technical world of scandals online, particularly how social media commentary practices regarding literary scandals and controversies by the artistic community often bear the deprecating marks of a polarizing algorithmic culture.

For example, in Mũkoma wa Ngũgĩ's thread on the "All Our Lives" episode, the language of the conversation reflects this antagonistic posture that I argue is inherent to the character of literary commentaries on social media. Ngũgĩ's tweet has a familiar rage that, though aimed at the organizers of the Caine Prize, mirrors the outrage machine of social media: "Shame on @CainePrize for this heavy handed career threatening corporate-like response to what should be a debate about influences, style and form. I am with @ShortStoryAFR and @brittlepaper nuanced responsible responses. We write well when we read and are influenced by others."[11] As if digitally shaming and calling out the Caine Prize is mistaken, he adds another tweet in which he compares Khadivi's "Wanderlust" to another story that incorporates a similar narrative style and then asks if the Khadivi's story should "be canceled for the echoes" that follow both works. The language of cancel culture deployed in a Twitter thread on a major literary controversy on the Caine Prize illuminates the argument of this chapter, and in-deed, this book. Unbeknownst to them, African writers and literary scholars, through commentary discourses on social media, perform an outrage culture that is delimited by algorithms that foster extreme content.

Responses to Ngũgĩ's tweet were varied, with a Caine Prize board member and one of the year's prize judge, Nii Ayikwei Parkes writing "to disagree" and pointing to Ngũgĩ's "fixative" on a pronominal choice in Okafor's story, and Ikheloa, surprisingly, declaring: "The @CainePrize did the right thing by raising the bar and holding the writer accountable."[12] In these responses, censorship and accountability—two correlating poles in cancel culture discourses—play out in a Twitter conversation to mark the intimacies arising from literary controversies, social media outrage, and cultural prizes. The argument may then be made that Western media and cultural institutions are helping to create regimes of rage in the reception of African literature on the internet. While this may not be peculiar to African literature, the fact that the algorithms that sustain these conversations were created in non-African contexts is reminiscent of the enduring complaints about the role of foreign literary institutions and prizes in Africa.

Again, some of these claims have historical antecedents that manifest in other contexts, revealing how the canonization of African writers is modulated by external agents. For example, Caroline Davis's *African Literature and the CIA: Networks of Authorship and Publishing* presents some arguments on how early "African literature" was entangled with Western institutions pulling strings in the background through the sponsorship of arts festivals and the shadow funding of journals and conferences that featured prominent writers like Soyinka. Davis conjectured that "an exceptional degree of support" was given to Soyinka by the CIA and its affiliated institutions, which he allegedly took for granted, "without questioning its source" as he became "the CIA's leading African literary protégé," propelled to global prominence" (2021, 45). Soyinka's riposte to the CIA controversy acknowledges the freedom to make inferences but also outlines a curious desire to "pursue these women, Caroline Davis and Juliana Saphr, to the ends of the earth and into the pit of hell until they reveal to the world, when and where I was meeting CIA agents" (2020). From the CIA to the Caine Prize and even social media itself, Western cultural and media institutions are entangled with the historical evolution of African literature and are often incentivizing sites of controversies.

Perhaps the biggest literary feuds and controversies generated by the Caine Prize in the last decade involve Adichie and the Nigerian satirist Elnathan John, who was described by Adichie as "one of my boys in my workshop" in a takedown of the 2013 Caine Prize shortlist. In an interview with Aaron Bady published online, Adichie seemed miffed by what she thought was "all this over-privileging of the Caine Prize" and proceeded to suggest her email had better stories from her workshop participants than the year's shortlist. Her view that the Caine Prize is "not the arbiter of the best fiction in Africa" prompted a storm of controversies and literary disputations on social media (2013).[13] As with most Adichie controversies, and there are several of them,[14] perceptions of this comment varied online, with her language considered as infantilizing and contemptuous of the prize by many people, including other writers on Twitter. The Nigerian literati on Twitter basically dismissed Adichie and saw her statement as diminishing the prize, but the biggest response came from another writer and former Caine Prize shortlistee, Nigeria's Abubakar Adam Ibrahim, who broke ranks with a colleague and resorted to expletives in his tweet criticizing Adichie: "So the best African fiction is in Chimamanda Adichie's inbox? I hail thee, queen-god mother. Go fuck yourself, Chimamanda. Nonsense!" Ibrahim may have later deleted his strongly worded tweet, but screenshots and online media reports, including one from the *New Yorker*, confirm the proverbial digital cliché that the internet never forgets.

For John, Adichie's comment signposted a paternalistic attitude that he went on to describe in sexist and misogynistic tweets that became fodder for an equally misogynistic blog post—"The Consequence of Loving Ngozi"—which were all later deleted. Although reposted by other blogs, the story is recoverable through the web archive, Wayback Machine, and I believe it is worth quoting a section of the blog post. In his view, to love Adichie meant:

> You imagined her skin in terms of taste . . . that even when she sent you a nasty manhood-shrinking email about you tweeting negative things about natural hair—an email that shocked you because you did not read or realize she had just announced to the world that hair was political—you sent her three even more manhood-shrinking replies, first denials, then explanations, then begging and groveling in ways you would never admit to anyone whose respect you still desired. She ignored it all. The cocoyam's skin would not come off. Not with the hot boiling water of manhood-shrinking pleas. Not with requests for intercession to a mutual friend who simply laughed at you on twitter . . . She sends you a two line mail

> many weeks after you are nominated for a literary prize. It makes you sad instead of happy: it dries out the cocoyam in your mouth instead of adding palm oil to it.[15]

There are at least four apparent references to "manhood-shrinking" in John's short clapback to Adichie's Caine Prize comment, and it is indicative of the highly personalized nature of this social media genre of prize discussions, which, in the case of this response, sexually objectifies a major feminist writer. While the power asymmetries of the writers' relations are obvious, John's need to conjure up eroticism, analogized by some vague and gastropolitical reference to a cocoyam that is desired for food and pleasure, is a pointless attempt at sarcasm and needlessly personalizes the subject matter (like Adichie's reference to "boy" in the first place). It also intensifies the controversy, with Adichie later calling John immoral for writing "a public attack piece" that dehumanizes the novelist.[16]

John and Adam Ibrahim may not have spared the blushes of a fellow Nigerian, but some other African writers were more generous. In an article for *Saraba Magazine*, the Zimbabwean novelist Novuyo Rosa Tshuma, author of the novel *House of Stone* and winner of the 2019 Bulawayo Arts Award for Outstanding Fiction, responded to Adichie's Caine Prize comments, tagging it "the great brouhaha" that requires a distinction between the legitimacy of hurt and the responsibility to hold Adichie "accountable for our interpretation of her comments, for our hurt."[17] Tshuma gets here at a major inclination of the cancel culture era, the conflation of an interpretation with what is actually said.

These controversies and feuds, in terms of their significations, register the notion of a sedimented connection to Western systems of funding and reinforce attachments to colonial metropoles where the judgment of literary tastes still mainly proceeds. This is particularly true of the various arguments and debates about the Caine Prize. Also, the controversies demonstrate how African literature in the digital age is mainly organized by an algorithmic age of personality that demands authors perform sociality on social media and propels literary feuds and debates as strong literary personalities have heated conversations about literature. The sometimes hostile exchanges underscore the persistence of other larger issues, such as class, location, and gender politics in contemporary African literature, even when the operations of these categories are unbeknownst to the participants and bystanders in online arguments.

The particular role of gender and sexuality in prize-based online controversies is underscored by Tsitsi Jaji's observation that "a sharp (often misogynist) tone of much internet commentary can quickly turn social media exchanges to heated language that would be less likely in real-time or print interaction, particularly where rank and age might mitigate implicit gender biases" (2020, 90). Jaji's comment was a reference to online commentaries on another award-derived literary controversy, the 2018 Brunel Prize for African poetry, whose organizers, to the dismay of some commentators, had six women shortlisted for the prize that year.[18] Again, from Adichie's transphobia tensions to the *Enkare Review* debates, which I discussed earlier, the sexual and gendered dimensions to internet commentary confirm this element of misogyny, but it is probably the case that we likewise miss the opportunity to critique the technologies that underpin the production of these divisive commentaries. The essays Jaji discusses may have been short articles for online news and literary platforms, but the digital culture underlying these essays is supported by the workings of the algorithms that shape outrage on social media.

Beyond African literature, Western prizes or award organizations based in the West exert significant influence on other aspects of cultural productions on the continent. The Netflixization of Nollywood, for example, may be read as implicated in the recent controversies over some new Nollywood films. For instance, when the Nigerian Oscars Selection Committee (NOSC) opted not to submit any film for the Best International Feature category of the ninety-fifth annual Academy Awards, there was no small expression of outrage. Eva Irewole wrote that the committee's decision generated heated controversy "with several petitions sent either directly or via social media on why the decision of no-film-is-eligible should not stand" (2022). Additionally, director Kunle Afolayan caused a Twitter furor when he called attention to the fact of his film, *Anikulapo*, was ignored by the NOSC. His tweet caused a ruckus as it became one of the trending topics on Nigerian social media for days.[19] Again, the arguments made clear how foreign awards become entangled with controversies in social media discourses where the rule of algorithms dominantly shapes the expressions of outrage. Cinematography and sophisticated storytelling might be the defining elements of New Nollywood films but in the Netflix era of the Nigerian film industry, it appears we need to consider how foreign awards play significant roles in the production and reception of Nigerian films. The 2018 *Lionheart* controversy over the role of English in Genevieve Nnaji's indigenous-language production is another recent example of how Nollywood seeks to validate itself internationally. In both the *Lionheart* controversy and the one involving *Anikulapo* some years later, social media was the arena of debates, insults, and outrage. These controversies, scandals, and debates point to larger political and social meanings in the critical spheres of postcolonial meaning-making.

As Serpell suggested regarding the Caine Prize, it is as if the organizers of the prize expect a certain tragic representation of African affairs or of messy national politics to the west and, hence, encourage a persistent "philanthropic model" based on a patronizing logic:

> I found it really strange that when I was nominated in 2010 and again in 2015, the exact same set of neocolonial—slash just colonial—aspects to the prize were evident. Five years apart, we were still saying the same things, we were still all being sent to the supposed centre of Empire in London. So when I split the prize in 2015, that was really what I was trying to push back against . . . That sense that we must be grateful because we're being "launched"? I don't know, I find it quite condescending. There's also a kind of NGO-ism about it. I don't know how else to put it. (Goyal 2020, 47)

Serpell's view, offered in an interview with Sana Goyal of *Wasafiri*, provides an illustrative summary of the mostly depressing attitude and perception toward the Caine Prize, particularly on social media, where Serpell also publishes her views on the prize.[20] But there is, of course, the problematic idea inherent in this argument, that of explaining the prize, as many other commentators and scholars tend to do, through a neo-colonial rhetoric that underplays the agency of African writers and suggest African literature is eternally yoked to colonialism.

Decolonization and Ngũgĩ's Nobel Prize Fatigue

In the "Specter of the Nobel Prize," Gabriel Garcia Marquez writes about the Nobel Prize in Literature as an award that resembles a specter that haunts great writers. He describes how the Argentine writer Jorge Luis, "one of the very greatest and also one of the most regular candidates for the prize, once protested in a press interview about the two months of anxiety to which the fates subject him every year" (2016). The perennial inclusion of Ngũgĩ in this annual prediction is reminiscent of the conditions Marquez, also a winner of the prize himself, wrote about in 1980. In addition to the online discussions and arguments about the Caine Prize, the Nobel Prize is another award that, as in many other places around the world, generates controversies on social media. For instance, with the Nobel and other prizes, judging scandals arise from the moment of inaugural award presentation because such scandals emanate from the "very heart of the prize's initial fragile claim to legitimacy. Every new prize is always already scandalous. The question is whether it will attract enough attention for this latent scandalousness to become manifest in the public sphere" (English 2005, 193). In the digital age, the speed at which literary scandals and controversies both around prizes and other aspects of literature circulate means that this implicit scandalousness frequently captures the public imagination. The controversies that erupted online alongside the celebration of an African winner of the Nobel in 2021 is instructive. Online discussions of the Nobel Prize reveal the discursive power of literary disputes, which come out clearly and function to mark a fragmented understanding of any collectivist notion of decolonization and decolonial thinking in contemporary Africa.

At the same time, it is incontrovertible that a project of decolonization in African literature that pushes back against most of the legacies of colonialism and the persistence of its epistemological afterlives is a helpful framework.[21] But online literary disputes and controversies among African subjects undercut that kind of project. In regard to the Nobel Prize, one obvious function of these heated literary debates and controversial exchanges is how they construct an unhealthy Ngũgĩ obsession in some quarters of the African literary community for the Kenyan to win the Nobel Prize. While the consecratory power of the Nobel Prize is incontestable, the anxiety and obsession negate everything Ngũgĩ's history of decolonization symbolizes. This clamor for Ngũgĩ sometimes takes the shape of the puzzling performative process in higher education to diversify things that is sometimes a mere plastic and meaningless prop not structurally backed up by the necessary praxes of inclusive ethics. One writer for the *Washington Post* thought the decision of the Nobel committee not to award Ngũgĩ the 2016 prize "felt infuriatingly myopic" because it was the year the United States became "saddled with a presidential candidate who peddles in misogyny and appeals to white supremacists" (Balasubramanyam 2016). Hence, Ngũgĩ should have won that year because the power of the left was at its weakest and Trump needed to be countered.

With the announcement of Abdulrazak Gurnah as winner of the 2021 Nobel Prize for literature, the argument among many commentators online was how Kenyan writer Ngũgĩ had been sidelined, the idea that the win of an ostensibly obscure writer, Gurnah, was a statement of snobbery directed toward Ngũgĩ. Bhakti Shringarpure, describing this as "the snub to the giant of African letters," observes that Gurnah would even agree with her that Ngũgĩ more than deserves this prize. East Africa, as she writes, has been put on a pedestal and will come to be constituted into the Western prize circuits. But "it has been emptied of its most important, decisively pioneering writer as well as an influential critic and academic: Ngũgĩ. It is a bit surreal but the fact that Gurnah who writes in English was picked over Ngũgĩ, the vocal native-languages advocate also sends a message about the primacy of English language domination in African literature" (Shringarpure 2021). This is despite the recent upsurge in African language literary productions, translation initiatives and a critical return to indigenous aesthetic forms, which all potentially offer "a ready road map outside of the English-only consensus, out of the English metaphysical empire" (wa Ngũgĩ 2018, 57). For Shringarpure and Ngũgĩ, one wonders if the contradiction here isn't as much the case of a decolonization that is undertaken in what used to be the language of the colonizer as the fact of constantly looking to Western literary prizes for symbolic legitimization and affirmation of the social prestige of African writers.

How digital reproductions and translations of new African literary texts re-encode the logics of coloniality is not only manifest in the arena of data sovereignty and the capitalistic capture of intangible cultural productions on social media spaces. We may also find this in the symbolic meanings that proceed from social media debates and arguments about literary prizes like the Nobel. These conversations demonstrate that African literary space is still very much tethered to the West and undermine the decolonization of African letters. There is no doubt that we undermine the discursive and critical power of decolonization itself when we only superficially apply a decolonizing paradigm to everything, without interest in the lived experiences of communities still affected by both the legacies of colonial violence and the prebendal politics of complicit postcolonial rulers. More importantly, courting recognition from western literary awards without much economic investments in our own infrastructures and institutions of reward give the sense that we are not very serious about decolonizing African literature. As Abiola Irele reminds us:

> Because we have not yet been able to establish on anything like a firm footing the institutions and material conditions for the production of knowledge, we are not in a position to command authority even in areas of scholarship pertaining to our

> continent. We do not control the means of production and transmission of our own discourse . . . Because we lack the resources to initiate and sustain research work related to our interests, our priorities are often determined for us by forces outside our control. (1991, 64)

If the Western academe was the major source of validation for African academics over three decades ago when Irele first penned these thoughts in the pages of *Transition*, much has not changed today, as Western technological infrastructure and locations persist as the most abiding points of enunciating the most radical ideas on/by Africans. To be taken seriously as a legitimate site of knowledge production, our epistemic locations and structures of enunciation cannot be mostly dependent on the West. Decolonizing African literature may begin with the language question, but it cannot end there. Without the necessary material investments in publishing technologies and institutions of cultural and aesthetic validation, African writers may yet retain an extraverted gaze that makes Western markets, publishers, and locations a desired haven for literary visibility. Whether in African languages or inherited colonial languages, telling the African story has to be supported by the necessary infrastructures of knowledge production. If the major markets and distribution channels of traditional publishing are in European metropolitan centers, it does not baffle the mind that the celebrated space of digital publishing, including social media and blogging, are owned by media companies in the North. Yet, to decolonize also means recognizing the material and economic price to pay. As bell hooks said in a 2014 conversation at the New School, "there is a price that comes with decentering, decolonizing, and part of what has to happen for us to be free is that we have to create our own standards of how to live" (2014).

To put it rather pithily, if not simplistically, we must be ready to put our own money where our decolonial mouths are. The most effective way to have epistemic freedom is to have economic agency. We cannot decolonize successfully if the financial anchors of our intellectual projects are located elsewhere and their costs, borne by other people. The transmission of our own stories with the discourses we create about ourselves has to take place through the creation of platforms, portals, and infrastructures that permit African agency and our standards of how to live. Facebook controversies about literary prizes demonstrate the absence of a self-reflexive awareness of how we deny ourselves agency when our decolonizing rhetoric obscures the necessity of creating our own technological and cultural platforms, spaces that enable our stories and ways of knowing. In other words, efforts to decolonize African arts and letters can become a powerful legitimization of Western epistemes and values if a potentially radical decolonization merely negates an African agency through a continued reliance on external economic systems and cultural institutions that are often presented as having perpetual control over sovereign African states and their affairs.

To illustrate my point, the death of the British queen, Elizabeth II, in 2022 rightly precipitated calls on social media for true decolonization among African states still symbolically attached to the British commonwealth. A Nigerian scholar went on to cause some mistimed ruckus on Twitter when, in denouncing the evils and legacies of colonial violence, wished the queen excruciating pain just before the monarch passed on. While many commentators viewed her tweet—later deleted by Twitter for violating its rules—as offensive, it was the idea of blaming the British for the Nigeria-Biafra war that got me thinking about the implicit logic of decolonization in the tweet. African states may not be fully autonomous from neocolonial and global economic forces, but being autonomous states since the 1960s means blaming the Biafran war on external actors is a reckless denial of reality. But such a refusal to come to terms with the irresponsibility of our own internal affairs and seeking to lay them at the feet of the British (or the West more broadly) is a major failure of the new decolonization movement on the continent today. To continually blame outsiders for African actions is precisely the conditions for the enactments of our own disenfranchisement. The queen was, of course, symbolic of British policy and a beneficiary of its once vast empire. But for a real decolonization logic to take hold in Africa, we have to retain a strong sense of African agency, one that begins with reversing the present economic misfortunes of the continent and arresting a widespread culture of prebendal politics among the political class in African countries.

Returning to literature, the paradox of the Gurnah debate was not the claim that Ngũgĩ, a pioneering voice on the centrality of language to decolonizing the African mind, was ignored by the Nobel committee; it is that the constant reference to him as worthy of consecration by the Swedish academe reinscribes a Eurocentric logic that negates what decolonization should stand for. At the same time, the argument could also be made that the call for Ngugi to win the Nobel strategically pushes back at the parochialism of the award itself and may be read as an attempt to resignify its alleged universality. Hence, for anyone who endorses the view, the clamor functions to unhinge the notion of universality from its European appropriation and thus mandates a decolonial approach. Yet, the clamor engenders fatigue.

Writing of how Ngũgĩ's hopes of winning the Nobel Prize in 2017 had been sidelined "by the controversial pick of Bob Dylan" in 2016 and Kazuo Ishiguro in 2017, Matt Carotenuto argues that "Ngũgĩ's elusive Nobel Prize puts a spotlight on the unfinished work of decolonization" (2017). This statement is prescient, not for its accuracy but for its irony, given that decolonization, whether Ngũgĩ wins the Nobel or not, remains eternally unfinished as long as Euro-American institutions remain the major measurement and financial anchor of African systems of knowledge valuations of intellectual prestige. A true decolonizing praxis turns Africa's cultural and philosophical gaze inward and builds the requisite local infrastructure and institutions that enable and reward cultural and intellectual productions. If the major ideological idiom and languages of the Nobel Prize are European, to constantly strive for the validation of an African writer who, besides the genius of his literary craft, is best known as a purveyor of decolonization misprioritizes and undermines Ngũgĩ's cultural praxes. In this instance, the Nobel Prize debate curates an annual spectacle of collective anxiety on the Kenyan and signals how literary controversies get to the heart of some of the most important themes of African intellectual history, including the current wave of decolonization and decoloniality.

In what might be considered a subpar article for the online platform *Africa Is a country*, in which he insinuates a reconsideration of Ngũgĩ's body of work, Nairobi-based Rwandan writer Jean Pierre Nikuze improperly suggests a pattern of "numerous repetitions, reviews, and retells in Ngũgĩ's body of work" (2019). In "The Reading Habits of Ngũgĩ wa Thiong'o," Nikuze controversially adduces this as a possible reason why the author has been consistently snubbed by the Nobel Prize Committee. His article, of course, provokes a mini-storm of contentions on social media. To be clear, though, there is little that can be done to contest Ngũgĩ's towering voice in the history of world literature, even more so in African literature. This truth comes across very clearly in the observation of Booker Prize winning author of *The Famished Road*, Ben Okri. In his 2012 introduction to the Penguin edition of *Weep Not Child*, a novel Okri describes as embryonic of the Kenyan's radicalism and campaign for African languages, he perceptively writes that "if Ngũgĩ had published nothing other than *Weep Not, Child*, he would have earned a distinctive place in the African literary canon" (2012, xv). While Ngũgĩ's critical and literary genius speaks for itself, ardent readers in different ideological camps engage in an annual debate about a Nobel win. His son Mũkoma wa Ngũgĩ retorts on Facebook that Nikuze's "essay on Ngũgĩ is so asinine as to border on parody."[22] Pertinent in the light of the theme of this book is both Nikuze's short essay along with wa Ngũgĩ's Facebook call to the editors of the online platform to fact-check a piece that challenges the merits of his father's literary stature. The denial of the Nobel Prize is, again, the pretext for an essayist's unfounded claim and wa Ngũgĩ's seemingly frantic and filial defense on social media.

What is more crucial is that wa Ngũgĩ's Facebook post makes allowance for the interrogation of what he memorably calls the "Nobel Prize for Literature fatigue." Fatigue is an interesting choice of word in this Facebook update and it gestures to the incessant rhetoric for a prize that marks the presence of the colonial exhaustion, which the so-called resurgent decolonization movement locates in most things today. But fatigue is, in fact, a loaded word that has particular meanings, as is evident in Anson Rabinbach's *The Human Motor*. With the beginning of the industrial revolution and under the strain of capitalist modernity, fatigue "became the most apparent and distinctive sign of the external limits of body and mind, the most reliable indicator of the need to conserve and restrict the waste and misuse of the body's unique capital—its labor power" (Rabinbach 1992, 6). Rather than idleness, the ubiquity of fatigue offers evidence of how the body subverts modernity itself. The bodily and mental labor of cultural commentary on social media may not be a direct analogy to physical labor, but it does capture how our digital labor not only produces value for multinational companies but also leads to a fatigue that occasionally appears on our Facebook timelines and Twitter feeds. In the case of the Nobel, it is a fatigue that exhibits the weariness of colonial affirmation and valuation. Together with the constant anxiety over an Ngũgĩ win, an affectivity by which a section of the African literary community on the internet performs an annual ritual of jitters in discussions of the Nobel Prize blends well with the algorithmic power of social media to inculcate and amplify divisive content that mainly leads to exhaustion and all kinds of emotional outbursts.

In 2021, after the announcement of Annie Ernaux as the winner of the Nobel, wa Ngũgĩ published a post on Facebook in which he lamented the small number of African writers that have won the Nobel Prize for Literature since its inception in 1901. That only five writers "for a continent of 55 countries and 1 billion people" have won it was sufficient reason to take a swipe at the prize, although he quickly added that "I am not saying this because my father did not win," and sensibly offered some congratulations to Ernaux.[23] The discussions that followed are mostly respectful, but the pathos of the post is clear in the commentary section and other reactions it generated. As of December 2022, the post had over two hundred likes, thirty-eight comments, and twenty-five shares. Even when most people don't acknowledge it or when a high number of fake social media followers and engagements can be manufactured, numbers matter on social media and are tied to practices of valuation and affirmation online. We may read high numbers of likes, retweets, followers, and commentary practices as examples of the "kinds of currency that participants bring to a cultural transaction," which, according to James English and John Frow, produce symbolic power in their discussion of celebrity scandals (2006, 55). Numbers not only accrue prestige to people and the content they publish on social media,[24] they can be added to the list of the currency that centralizes people as symbolic agents: "the currency of academic credentials, political office, religious rank, a jail record; or of bestseller status, good reviews, honors and awards, social connections, street cred, physical attractiveness or photogeneity" (55). So, when a comment accumulates more likes (662) than the post itself, people notice it, as in this response to wa Ngũgĩ by Hopewell Chin'ono:

> We should create our own institutions, we have the money but zero leadership. Why do we need Western validation? It is because we are led by failures. These awards are funded by Europeans who died decades ago, they had a vision of what they wanted their countries to be doing today. We arrest and murder our writers, shame on us. This is about vision not inclusion. Let Europeans award each other, let us award our own people with great awards. We have failed to have just one international news channel due to failed incompetent leadership. Then we blame western news outlets for not covering us. We need do [*sic*] better than this! Ngũgĩ is one of the greatest Africans to ever live, he doesn't need any Western validation.

For scholars who sometimes display some elitism toward popular culture and the media industry, popular commentaries on social media might be frowned upon as lacking the thoughtfulness required for epistemic productions, but even many in that rank would hardly refute the fundamental premise of this response. Even if anyone queries my recourse to the quantitative power of mass culture to press a claim, undeniable is its articulation of the most undermining agent of African decolonization in the current era: an African ruling class and cultural elite that has constantly affirmed its lack of ideological acuity and vision despite decades since political independence. There is no doubt that complex factors, also traceable to European colonialism and its famed underdevelopment of Africa, as Walter Rodney argues, may account for the kind of leadership indicated in the response. Colonialism cannot easily be forgotten, not with its legacies still very much active in settler contexts. Yet, as Táíwò and other African thinkers have suggested, the leadership question, with its prebendal culture of everyday corruption, remains the most debilitating factor for African agency, whether in politics, literature, or in any other sphere of life.

The controversies, scandals, and ròfọ̀rọ́fọ̀ fights that arise from literary prizes register the notion of a sedimented entanglement of African literatures with Western systems of funding that reinforce attachments to colonial metropoles. At the same time, the arguments and controversies on the Nobel Prize provide all kinds of opportunities, including the possibility of rearticulating the Nobel Prize as a truly universal award. On social media platforms, a rhetoric of fascination with these prizes circulates in a manner that undercuts a simultaneous demand to decolonize African literature. To close by returning to his controversial London pushback against the supposed coloniality of a fiction award, the language of these online debates would have left a figure like Marechera truly miffed. Whether they are based on literary prizes or on hostile exchanges that underscore the persistence of class and gender in contemporary African literature, these controversies are generative for thinking about the relationship between digital culture and African literary expressions and their social worlds.

CHAPTER 5

Thighs Fell Apart, Online Fan Fiction and Literary Friendships

In April 2020, Nigerian writer Lọlá Shónẹ́yìn wrote on Twitter that she and another writer, Molara Wood, "had a huge argument on Krazitivity (listserv for Nigerian creatives) and we didn't speak to each other for 4 years."[1] Shónẹ́yìn then rhetorically shifts a paragraph later from "a huge argument" to a "fight" that started over a short story written by Chude Jideonwo, the youngest of the now-defunct literary community, which at that point was composed of writers as prominent as Remi Raji, Chris Abani, and Adichie. In his response to this tweet, Jideonwo, a lawyer and writer, wrote about being "forged in fire on Krazitivity" with Wood herself also adding that the argument was epic, a "roforofo of gladiatorial proportions, all prosecuted in words, on Krazitivity."[2] Nigerian visual artist and writer Victor Ehikhamenor, who was also a member of the listserv, tweeted in response that "Krazitivity 'fights' were actually epic . . . Lifelong friends were made" as well as "a few fierce eternal enemies."[3] In these accounts and recollections of the "rọ̀fọ̀rọ́fọ̀," "fights," and gladiatoriality of Krazitivity, there is the idea of a literary network whose efflorescence and centrality to the production of Nigerian literary subjectivities on the internet were partly predicated on both literary conviviality and controversies.[4] Social media amplifies these controversies, making them much more visible beyond the backend of a private listserv. In this chapter, I go against the grain of my own analyses by considering possibilities of literary kinship and friendship, the type that inspired the formations of *Kwani?* and Krazitivity. I examine online friendship and fandom as capable of demonstrating intimate connections and the human power to subvert algorithmic productions of outrage through the enactment of reader agency.

Unlike the preceding sections, this chapter focuses on how social media has also been the terrain of new forms of literary sociality and practices that use the authorial affordances of social media platforms to demonstrate the power of productive reading publics and register a desire for literary affinity and kinship with established writers. If, as Madhu Krishnan argues (restating a Bourdieuan logic), that the history of publishing in African literature is "predicated on the fight over positions, positioning, and position-taking" (2019, 3), then it is possible to read the fights and controversies in the preceding chapters as marking a digital culture of outrage that is likewise based on conflictual position-taking online, one that is influenced, as I have repeatedly sought to demonstrate, to a large degree by a subterranean operation of powerful algorithms. This culture of algorithmic outrage informs Tsitsi Jaji's argument that African literary expressions on the internet are characterized by "a decidedly sharper-toned culture of online discussion in the digital sphere" that values "contention and debate" more than celebration and support" (2020, 84). While this conflictual paradigm is largely the case, I want to argue here that in the social worlds of African books online, fans, and followers often become creatively entangled in a mutually created space of socially produced literary conviviality, with a culture that fosters literary friendship, rather than fomenting only controversies and contentions. Online fan fiction as one experimental mode of digital storytelling reveals possibilities of fandom and friendship that deconstruct a culture of outrage. In short, literary fandom is arguably a site of friendship.

For my major example, I focus on a social media enablement of agency for the contemporary fan-reader of Chinua Achebe's *Things Fall Apart* through a critical exploration of Kiru Taye's "Thighs Fell Apart," an online short story that details a fan-writer's imagined account of Okonkwo's erotic life. Taye's portrayal of Achebe's tragic hero demonstrates how the structure and design of digital media democratizes authorial space and enables user-generated reproduction of traditional modes of literary and cultural representations. Taye's fan fiction experiment with canonical African novels, such as those of Achebe (and, later, Adichie), presents ideas on the social meanings of fandom and the possibility of digital friendships in African literature in a digital age. The topic of literary friendship in the African literary space itself is not new, although social media amplifies the intimate kinships and collaborations among African writers in a different way from what is a common practice in the writing community. In Terri Ochiagha's *Achebe and Friends at Umuahia*, she traces the emergence of a Nigerian literary renaissance that began with the friendship of famous writers such as Elechi Amadi, Chike Momah, Christopher Okigbo, Chukwuemeka Ike, and Achebe in 1940s Umuahia. Ochiagha notes that while at Umuahia, the five authors all subverted "the school's British literary and cultural models as they developed hybrid subjectivities and the sense of cultural nationalism that was the fulcrum of their posterior literary careers" (2015, 8). Similarly, in a piece entitled "The Tough Alchemy of Ben Okri," Percy Zvomuya credits the Nigerian writer with the following words, in which Okri recollects his friendship with Dambudzo Marechera and John Matshikiza, a South African theatre practitioner, as young African writers in 1970s London:

> There was a sense that we had to take on the [Chinua] Achebe, [Wole] Soyinka and Ngũgĩ [wa Thiong'o] generation, not in a bad way, not in the way of killing your father . . . We wanted to take the story and run away with it. And, finding ourselves in London, we had to take on the challenge of Western literature. That was a steep challenge. We had to write in full cognisance of everything that had been written. We couldn't write as if [James] Joyce hadn't written *Finnegans Wake* or [Fyodor] Dostoevsky hadn't written *Crime and Punishment*. There was for us a double challenge: the challenge of the older generation of African writers and the challenge of world literature. Maybe the toughest [of the two tasks] was the challenge of world literature at the point we found ourselves. We had to face the challenge and still be ourselves. (2012)

In this chapter, I compare what it means to perform reader agency through online fan fiction to the ways friendship emerges in Ochiagha's analyses of Achebe and his friends as an "adequate epistemic tool to classify the interactions of the Umuahian writers" (2015, 9). I start with the notion of friendship because it occasionally marks the aspirational labors of some fan fiction writers, even if social media blurs the lines between friends and fans. Friendship on social media might be mostly fraught and fake, but the possibility of achieving it sometimes guide the social worlds of literature and its aesthetic outputs.

This role of literary friendship and its epistemic potentials in online writing networks is underscored by Petina Gappah in a 2023 *Financial Times* article: "I read that Chimamanda and Binyavanga had met each other on Zoetrope, an online writing community. I joined Zoetrope too. It is there that I met Molara Wood and Muthoni Garland, a writer from Kenya. We read and workshopped each other's writing. These friendships continued into real life, and with them came a chain reaction of more friendships—Molara knew Chimamanda, and through Molara I became acquainted with Teju Cole."[5] Aside from the intimacies of digital networks and offline contexts, Gappah establishes how contemporary African literature has been digitally shaped by a generation of friendship among several writers. Hence, although digital media amplifies literary feuds, they also foster literary friendships—which sometimes start along the axes of fandom and stan culture. For those who read some of these established writers, however, what is sometimes possible is an aspirational model of writerly friendship that is enacted through fan writing and recognizes the celebrity and social power of canonical writers. "Thighs Fell Apart" illuminates how fan writing as a rich and original literary landscape has the potential to extend critical debates around the contents of the canonical texts of African literature that they rework. The poaching of a source material underscores the value of the original text, reasserts its aesthetic value, and extends its critical universe.

Thighs Fell Apart

Written by Taye, a Nigerian writer who specializes in sensual narratives and romance, "Thighs Fell Apart" is among several works commissioned for *Brittle Paper* several years ago. For the right context, it helps to begin with Edoro's preamble to Taye's 2014 short story in which she cites Achebe and adds that if "you are a true Things Fall Apart fan, you'd know that Okonkwo's second wife, Ekwefi, was previously married to another man."[6] Taye simply expands this thread of the story to include the bits that Achebe left out (Edoro 2014a).

Edoro signals here some of the ways the imaginative contours of online fan writing call upon a diverse "contributory public" on digital media platforms, to reimagine and "(re)write" both the events that surround Okonkwo's maneuverings "around [Ekwefi's] waist" and the sexual performance that accompanies his reach "for the loose end of her cloth." This possible "writerly" intervention of the reader, facilitated by Web 2.0, urges a crucial need in the criticism of contemporary African literature, particularly with regard to the manifestations of its form, function, and audience in digital environments. It is about time the theoretical mapping of African literary experimentations responded to the ways through which digital culture enables a transgressive recrafting of the canonical texts and ideas of African literature.[7]

There is the apparent fact that the collapse of authorial boundaries in digital media facilitates new kinds of praxis for the poststructuralist idea of the birth of the reader who "rewrites" Achebe's pioneering novel. At the same time, there is the salient articulation of the productive reader of cultural texts who contributes to the meaning of text. Literary fandom in the Nigerian cultural imagination is currently being reshaped through the preponderance of digital technologies and the variegated sites of agency and self-representations granted to ordinary and, hitherto, passive consumers of literature. Also crucial for analyses is how the *Brittle Paper*'s Edoro envisions "a true Things Fall Apart fan," as she claims in the preamble and how an understanding of that can enable a critical reflection of literary fandom in regard to African fiction online. Edoro's formulation suggests that literary fandom involves a new form of close reading that is generative of new forms and directions of African writing in a digital age, including an overlapping Afropolitan consciousness, which I shall return to shortly.

As already noted throughout this book, *Brittle Paper* represents an iconic literary blogosphere in which individual readers and writers exchange roles and identities, discussing literary festivals and reviewing some of the finest works from Africa. Its exploration of erotica is one of the many ways the blog is committed to extending the boundaries of genre and form in African writing. The erotic, as Shola Adenekan has rightly argued, thus manifests as a literary mode of "analysing sexual history in Nigerian writing on the internet in particular (Adenekan 2021, 129). By mobilizing explicit rituals around Okonkwo and Ekwefi's sexuality, private details omitted in *Things Fall Apart* (possibly because they do not further the development of Okonkwo's character), Taye articulates a paradigm of erotic fantasy often not explored in canonical African literature. In the process, she "rewrites" *Things Fall Apart* for both digital natives, "native speakers" of the language of the new media and the internet, and also digital immigrants, if we can overlook the binarism of Marc Prensky's argument (2001, 2). The product of this process is a reconfiguration, enabled by digital technologies, of an archetypal African male literary hero in a way that can reanimate debates around masculinity, gender ideologies, and patriarchal hegemony in studies of Achebe from the perspective of the ordinary reader. In creating fan fiction for *Things Fall Apart*, Taye inaugurates an important discursive field. Besides, digital media platforms as spaces and networks for literary and cultural representation function as creative spaces for mini narratives, which urge us as scholars and writers to think of African literature in an age of digital reproduction differently. These online literary spaces (including literary blogs and social media pages of authors) recast the monologic frame and singular authority of print. What results is a decentered medium, structured on the logics of interactivity and participatory culture, ideas that gesture back to the representational strategies of oral literature. They call for an informed acknowledgment of the ways the digital metaphors of new media reimagine significant paradigms of both indigenous aesthetics and the ways they are now being rematerialized in online platforms. In her account of the Yorùbá ewì and its audiences, Rita Nnodim explains that audiences often "elucidated their understanding of ewì in aesthetic terms" as interpretative encounters with oral culture generally provided insights into the ingenious ways in which "audiences engage with, make meaning of, interpret poetic texts, and, in moves of appropriation, make poetry meaningful in their own life contexts" (2002, 307). Social media lives of literary forms like Achebe's fiction reveal a similar dynamic of creative appropriation and repurposing. Taye's "Thighs Fell Apart" may be a rare work of fan fiction, yet to dismiss it as an uncritical work of literature is to restate common condescending tendency in some sections of the African literary establishment toward social media sites of cultural productions. This attitude neglects to foreground the ways online writing can generate knowledge and new identities—as readers become writers online.

For instance, the discourse on Afropolitanism can be understood within the politics of digital flows and their multiple spatialities. As Achille Mbembe and Bregtje van der Haak note in the *Chimurenga Chronic*, besides the transnational cosmopolitanism that is definitive of Afropolitan subjectivities, there is a politics of space in which one of the places on the African continent to which Afropolitans tie their sense of selves and identities is the Internet (2015). Similarly, Miriam Pahl argues that social media's connective, multimedia, and interactive capabilities are key to the creation of shared cultural spaces for Africans at home and in the diaspora, aside from enabling an Afropolitan consciousness (2016). In her exploration of the term, Susanne Gehrmann similarly points out that neither "the success of the Afropolitan generation nor the controversy around the concept would have been possible without the cyberspace as a new venue for mobility in the sense of the circulation of ideas, images, and self-celebration" (2016, 63). Cybermobility is one major condition for what might be called "Afropolitanism's digital other," to the extent that one thinks of the virtual movement of identities, with readers of text now being able to remix and reproduce existing content and therefore signify as "writers." The circulation of self-celebration in cyberspace, affirmed by the metaphor of the selfie on social media, becomes performatively reconstituted by online fan writers in the narrative spaces of others. Cybermobility is essential to becoming a recognized African cosmopolitan subject, whether within Africa or its diaspora in Euro-American locations. In other words, the importance of digital technologies to the movements of people in, from, and within Africa is crucially connected to Afropolitan subjectivities. Internet spaces thus enable digital hubs where Afropolitans connect and exchange cultural knowledge. The digital imagination is also central to how Afropolitans de-essentialize Africa from a discourse of victimhood and agonies, reclaiming critical agency through their user-generated data. However, the limit of this digital sense of the term is the same elitism and classism that define Afropolitanism. An uneven digital access across the continent ensures that the term has little bearing on Africans in the homeland who have no access to the Internet. Besides class and economic elitism, other objections to Afropolitanism highlight its "apolitical narrative of transnational consumer lifestyles" (Pahl 2016, 77) that configures it as "a particular kind of affluent mobility in the global north," especially among diasporic Africans (Musila 2016, 111).[8]

"Thighs Fell Apart" positions us to appreciate a diasporic fan/reader who re/engages with Africa by inserting her own creative space into Achebe's work. As suggested earlier, what sets *Brittle Paper* apart from other online sites of African writing, such as the much earlier *African Online Writing*, is the way the structure and design of Web 2.0 platforms and applications, such as blogs and social media, democratize and decenter authorial space, opening up more user-generated engagements and reformulations of traditional modes of cultural representations. Adenekan's idea of "the internetting of African Literature" speaks eloquently to how these new literary sites of representations, such as *Brittle Paper*, enable a convergence between African literature and new publics in virtual spaces. A critical reflection on Taye's work extends similar perspectives as it demonstrates how a form of online popular imagination activate more African literary experimentations. Adenekan situates sexual politics and class identity in his study of African literary writing on the internet and argues that "the 'internetting' of Kenyan and Nigerian literature arguably started from the mid to late 1990s when writers seeking to draw attention to their printed work started posting poems and short stories on emailing lists such as Krazitivity and Ederi" (2021, 12). Within the context of African cultural forms, these digital platforms can be seen as some of the earliest virtual spaces for the circulation of popular arts and literary forms.

To appreciate these new forms of African writing, we need to be able to look to such digital hubs as social media and literary blogs where the boundaries between readers and writers, between producers and consumers, are toppled by the interactivity and immediacy of Web 2.0. In other words, the literary imagination in modern Africa can no longer be limited to the works produced only through print technologies. There is an engaged, contributory public of contemporary African literature that connects some of the present (and older) voices and faces of African writing on spaces such as Facebook and Twitter. Whereas a digital public appears to be the conventional word to describe this online convergence, I have termed this a contributory public because of the ways digital platforms enable the assembling or bringing together of a diverse demographic of writers and fan/readers discussing and re/engaging with the politics and aesthetics of African writing in digital network communities. A contributory digital public not only adds to the conversation by reading texts, but also does this by disassembling the identity and textual spaces of an admired author, reassembling them as a practice of literary fandom.

Fan Fiction as Textual Poaching

With provenance in Italian 1930s fanzines, modern fan fiction (or media fan writing) is now a ubiquitous element of digital culture, with popular fans converging online for a shared circulation and critique of each other's fiction on more recognized cultural and media productions. Fan fiction thus involves reconstructions of the work of another writer, usually a canonical author, whose text is marginally or completely refashioned by a fan/reader as an act of cultural interpretation. Through fan writing as an important reading practice, writers ultimately distant themselves from the original work to establish their own voice. This is outlined by Diane Lewis in a 2004 essay:

> What fan fiction offers to these young writers is a great, existing storyline; interesting, three-dimensional characters that have already been developed; and a wealth of back-story to both pull from and write about. The inexperienced author

> doesn't have to spend all his or her time developing something original, but instead can focus on the actual skill of writing. It allows young authors to practice their craft without expending huge amounts of time and energy developing something "original." As they build their "writing muscles," their writing improves and they tend to stray farther and farther from the source material. (3)

With regard to the idea of originality, fan writing should not be seen as a new textual material that is lacking in any artistic merit, for the effort of creating a parallel narrative space from existing fictional material demands some level of creativity. In *The Practice of Everyday Life*, Michel de Certeau explains how reading constitutes a silent production, which individuals, poaching in countless ways on the property of others, use as a tactic to contest dominant hegemonies and strategies (1984). He explains that readers are like travelers who move across lands belonging to someone else, like nomads poaching their way across fields they did not write (174). This logic provides a basis for how Henry Jenkins conceives of fan writing, not as an online practice of cultural dupes or mindless consumers but as a creative practice among young and active readers of digital texts (2005). It is one of the many ways in a social media ecology through which the self is written into the text/s of an admired author and involves a process of textual poaching that produces new meanings (251). In a similar war, Taye's reconstitution of *Things Fall Apart* legitimizes a poaching of textual meaning from Achebe's forest of signifiers, an act that could catalyze new interpretations of the novel from the perspective of the ordinary reader not necessarily schooled in literary criticism. Taye's representation of sexual discourse, although reminiscent of Achebe's, could have been a form of writing back to the author and contesting Achebe's portrayal of women and sexuality.

Fan writing, whether in films, videogames, movies, or novels, is then a site of experimentation for the emergent writer who functions in some way as a literary bricoleur, constituting the different voices of an original work in a new textual space. Fan fiction is an original intervention that locates itself within the fictional universe of an existing work. The fan/reader does not displace the author or the author's position but invents in texts something different from what the author "intended." The task of the fan/reader is thus a form of appropriation devoid of theft. Hence, the fan fiction writer combines textual fragments from an author's space to create something new. The reader, in this case, Taye, experiences the author's text as a productive space that generates literary agency. Far from viewing consumption as imposing subjective meanings upon the public, textual consumption for the fan fiction writer, therefore, involves claiming and reappropriating the textual material as one's own "making" and resignifying the linguistic and cultural universe of the parent text by an infusion of the playful imaginations of readerly agency. The effect of this process is not only to poach meaning from the textual space of the original author, but also a nuancing of personal space in the aesthetic universe of an established author.

In his 1992 work on textual poachers, Jenkins explains how the fan operates not from a position of theft but marginality. Like "the poachers of old, fans operate from a position of cultural marginality and social weakness. Like other popular readers, fans lack direct access to the means of commercial cultural production and have only the most limited resources with which to influence entertainment industry's decisions" (1992, 26). With digital media, the fan, in most cases, is interested in a playful engagement with the work they recreate and not any commercial cultural production. Fan writing is then a signifying practice that stages readers' subjectivities and a reinvention of textual space. These processes enable the reader not to obscure but to memorialize the author and the reader's own silenced and silent history. By insinuating "into another person's text the ruses of pleasure and appropriation, the reader poaches on it, is transported into it, pluralizes himself in it like the internal rumblings of one's body" (Certeau 1984, 71). Fan writing is thus a production that is also an "invention" of the memory and aesthetics of an earlier work. "Words become the outlet or product of silent histories. The readable transforms itself into the memorable" (71). On his part, Jenkins's primary concern is with the consequences of fans' production of their own texts from a source/parent text and how such texts are encoded with readers' subjectivities and social experience (2005, 251).

Having said all of that, these criticisms have been updated in more recent years, particularly in an age of social media and the numerous sites of fan art and labor it enables. Bethan Jones remarks, for example, that "fan fic readers and reviewers did some of the work in creating *Master of the Universe*," but E. L James took sole credit for its success by discountenancing the role that "the fannish community played in shaping what would become *Fifty Shades of Grey*" (Jones 2014, 115). Here, the importance of fan creativity both as a site of professional and volunteer labor that is performed by both book influencers and other everyday users of social media is asserted. Jones reiterates an increasingly dominant idea in digital culture studies that demonstrates a reversal of so-called fan poaching and marks fan fiction as a site of exploitation or what Abigail De Kosnik describes as "fan fiction's Sugarhill," the condition in which a popular text makes fan writing popular, draws attention to the genre, yet disregards "the vast communities and long tradition in which that genre emerged and developed" (2015, 117). Creative digital labor might be an important aspect of work under capitalism. But fan writing, through its transformations of canonical cultural forms, also has a subversive power that is not always assimilable to capitalist logics in the sense of the so-called Sugarhill. In Taye's fan writing, for example, what is notable is a more celebratory and transgressive practice than an exploitative performance, since her erotic fiction was produced as part of *Brittle Paper*'s Valentine's Day events. The transgressive feature of the new story manifests in a retelling of Ikemefuna's tragic story in a second installment of Taye's fanfiction erotica, in which queer intimacies and homosexual desires also become imaginable in the friendship between Nwoye and Okonkwo's adopted son.[9] In Taye's first fanfic of Achebe, which is my focus here, she relocates a universe of erotica into the heart of a pioneering African novel, and in the process, using digital media and creative adaptations of Achebe, establishes a connectivity with the writer.

As a literary text that is rather forthright about an overt political commitment, almost devoid of sexual and erotic fantasies as troupes to be developed explicitly as textual elements, the African novel of the first and second generation of African writing would seem to Taye to be sexually restrained. This is despite the fact that Cyprian Ekwensi in *Jagua Nana*, Buchi Emecheta in *Joys of Motherhood*, Teju Cole in *Open City*, and Chimamanda Adichie in *Half of a Yellow Sun*, and several new experimental writers all now provide fascinating examples of overt sexual descriptions in Nigerian fiction. But the culture of sexual restraint remains at a subterranean level with forms such as the erotic not as explored as it could be. Hence, the argument by playwright Femi Osofisan that "the vacancy in our previous literature of the sensual and the erotic, this absence that now seems astonishing to us, had its roots in the conditioning manners of its genesis, and as well in the extant laws of public morality and of creative practice" (2008, 65). The mere presence of a graphical description of steamy sex between Okonkwo and Ekwefi may be a reason to dismiss fan writing for some critics, but that possibly rehashes the Victorian and colonial sensibilities that repress the sensual elements that work like Taye's recuperates. For some, such prudery may be less important than the audacity of recreating Achebe's work. Like a reader of the story commented: "Can u really do this? I love d [*sic*] book by Chinua Achebe and I must say that I have never for once pictured Okonkwo as someone who could kiss his woman."[10] That's precisely the point of the fanfic: to picture Okonkwo differently and present an African literary classic in a different light that is amenable to a more open field of interpretation. What results is a fan writer's rehabilitation of the silences of cultural forms, such as Achebe's.

Taye's erotic re-presentation of Achebe's work is thus a way for the writer to transcend the explicit sociological commitment of *Things Fall Apart*, reinfusing the literary classic with an aesthetic impulse defined by playful imaginings of sex. In this sense, "Thighs Fell Apart," in particular, may be seen as an example of fan writing that inserts itself into a rich literary landscape that introduces Achebe to literary publics beyond Africa. A number of these digital natives and immigrants, both at home and in the diaspora, are able to engage with the African experience in innovative ways facilitated by digital technologies. Teju Cole's Twitter experimentations, for instance, illustrate how some exilic African writers are renegotiating narrative spaces for the homeland. His collaborative Twitter project, in which users retweeted parts of his story, produced the coherent short story "Hafiz." This experimental work is the result of creative storytelling that engages a global network of readers in new and collaborative digital storytelling. Pahl, commenting on Cole's work, suggests that the writer is using Twitter to write African literature for a global audience and "builds an alternative archive of life in Nigeria that contributes to our shared social (online) world, making visible a, from a non-African reader perspective, marginalized component of the international community" (2016, 80). Because these new forms of digital storytelling open up new directions for African writing, Cole's creativity on Twitter is, therefore, as important as Taye's reworking of Achebe's work, with both signposting the ways African writing is being informed by digital media. "Thighs Fell Apart" inspires us to scrutinize the new kinds of responses readers are bringing to African literature in a digital age. The work unsettles a canonical work of African literature on the terms of the reader as a meaning-maker in the symbolic universe of another's text. Taye's "Thighs Fell Apart" imagines Okonwko and Ekwefi's marriage from a sexual point of view and is set before the fight with Amalinze the cat. Although she is married to Maduka, Ekwefi is in "a doomed courtship" with Okonkwo, whom she visits very early in the morning. After they have sex, he informs her with some emotion in his voice that he will be fighting Amalinze the cat and then "take you as my wife" (Taye 2014).

Ekwefi protests that she cannot abandon her husband, but Okonkwo insists that fame and wealth from defeating Amalinze the cat will enable him to marry her. They resume their sexual activities until Ekwefi falls asleep. Taye is inviting readers to think of the events that might have happened before the fight with Amalinze, that are not included in Achebe's original story. It should be noted that the erotica itself is the product of an experimental blog post, "African Fictional Characters in Bed," in which Edoro invites readers of *Brittle Paper* to imagine which male character in African fiction might be sexy. Envisioning Okonkwo "as a man of less talk and more action," Edoro sees Okonkwo's role as embodying cultural resistance and anticolonialism as crucial. She then conceptualizes the character in a way that locates him within more intimate spheres. "Granted, Achebe does not make this point explicitly," Edoro writes excitedly, "but then he makes it quite easy to fantasize about the character. What is Okonkwo like in bed?—a question that lurks in the shadows of the story, hidden behind subtexts inviting us to look at Okonkwo's body and imagine its erotic possibilities" (2014b).

The impulse to excavate Achebe's subtexts may be the logical consequence of Achebe's disproportionate influence on African writing. But here, digital media affordances make it easier for readers to connect with the late writer and his work through their playful and transgressive interventions. Unlike the pressures to participate in social media outrage, fan fiction, in this case, offers the opportunity for literary kinship and friendship. This process is what fan-readers, who are native to digital culture, employ as a way of inserting self and agency into a vortex of past and present narratives of the African experience. While there are a number of issues that might emerge from a close reading of the short story itself, I am fascinated with Taye's problematic language of sexual dispossession, which reopens debates about the social and cultural roles of gender as a construct:

> In the distance, the sound of drumbeats matched his heart rate as he stared down at the beauty lying beneath him. He reached out and untied her hand-woven wrapper, the intricate brocade pattern identifying her status. He refused to let the implications spoil his admiration of the luscious bundle he'd just unwrapped. Her hair was plaited in twirling rows and converged at the top in a crown-like fashion. To him, she was a queen in repose, offering obeisance to her king. (2014)

Taye extends the patriarchal sentiments that mark *Things Fall Apart* as a text rife with contradictions about the social roles of women as priestesses, wives, or the protective mother to whom Okonkwo returns in *Things Fall Apart*. Her graphic erotic fantasies about Okonkwo's sexual prowess reinforce gender polarities by constructing the woman as the gendered subject whose body is to be relinquished for male satisfaction and pleasure. That the passage is focalized through Okonkwo might be a reason to think more charitably about the admittedly complicated dynamics of this sexual encounter. But even Achebe's Okonkwo is not exactly the type that invites a vision of a gentle romantic who is not cavalier about a woman's pleasure and desire. Taye's reconsolidation of gender stereotypes presents a missed opportunity to contest and subvert a dominant masculinist ideology on Taye's part. The objectification of the female body, reduced to sexual fetish, is presented in lines that portray Ekwefi as closing "her eyes, relishing the sensation that slowly built up within her body. When it came to her body, he was her lord. Every touch, every caress proved his mastery" (Taye 2014). Taye is showing loyalty in her retelling of Achebe's text to Okonkwo's characterization, and her portrayal does not seek to subvert any oppressive male hegemony. Rather, it uses the sexual bed to accentuate the feminine body as an object to be possessed by an African "lord" whose every caress prove his mastery and dominance. While Okonkwo is depicted to own his wife's body, the masculine body is a site of admiration for Ekwefi, who symbolizes here the African woman's lack of agency in the determination of her own sexual identity and pleasure. In these instances, Taye uses "Thighs Fell Apart" to rearticulate the gendered paradigms of dominance in the Achebean imaginary. That her work affirms a subordination of the female body is apparent in the following lines:

> Mindless sensations overtook her body. She writhed, unable to control her body's response as he took her higher and higher toward her peak. As she coasted the wave, he pulled back.
>
> "Please," she whimpered. She didn't mind begging for release. His effect on her was powerful and exhilarating, a potent elixir she needed.
>
> "Please what?" He stood up and flipped her over once more so she lay on her back.
>
> "Please . . . let me have my release." She licked her lips as she watched him, her hunger for him clouding her eyes.
>
> "Not until I'm deep inside you." (2014)

The spectacle of Okonkwo wrestling with Amalinze the cat in Achebe's *Things Fall Apart* is recast in "Thighs Fell Apart" as a sexual contest in which bodies clash in an ideological force field, with phallocentric might triumphing over female desire. In the original text, Achebe describes Okonkwo's response to drumbeats at the *Ilo* as a trembling "with the desire to conquer and subdue" like "the desire for woman" (1959, 42). Taye extends this erotic imagery, but depicts a woman who must be conquered and subdued for the man's sexual satisfaction. Ekwefi cannot have her "release" until Okonkwo is inside of her, an apt metaphor for the sexual dominance used to recall the subordinated role and troubled positions of women in Achebe's work. Because of Taye's failure to contest Achebe's ambivalent representation of women in *Things Fall Apart*, her story evokes the repression of sexual desire, as her representation of Ekwefi as Okonkwo's subservient sexual partner normalizes patriarchal assumptions about female sexuality.

The depiction of the female orgasm in Taye's popular work depicts how a text can teeter at the edge of bliss and precariousness. It is as if the Okonkwo she creates can only take pleasure in Ekwefi's inchoate language of desire, an anxious and whimpering plea for release. Indeed, the erotic language is shown to be incompatible with our encounter with the bliss of the text, the *jouissance*. In *The Pleasure of the Text*, Roland Barthes shows the limits of the textual object in the grip of an erotic paradigm that falters and produces meaning that is precarious and a discourse that is incomplete (1975). When Ekwefi here begs, "Please . . . let me have my release," we are confronted with an elliptical logic for that which is unknown to her and cannot be said even when the text itself inventively sticks itself to the reader's mind. The stickiness here is of a different, sensual kind and is dependent on the power of an elliptical language that breaks down. Ironically, Barthes's argument asserts that erotic desire can never occur in the realm of mass culture, which is the precise location of Taye's fanfic (38). Like Achebe, who subordinates Ekwefi's story to Okonkwo's troubled masculinity, Taye shows fidelity to the gendered contexts of *Things Fall Apart*, extending a persistent regime of female oppression mobilized through the cultural suppression of female bodies. Her version of Ekwefi fails to redeem the fictional character, as eroticism becomes a pretext to construct a needy woman who plays into the stereotype that some hypersexual African women are never truly *released* for orgasmic pleasure by their patriarchal culture.

Yet, an important function of fan fiction is the creation of a community of belonging, one in which members, often women and members of marginalized subcultural groups, seek to transcend the social and cultural alienation that is sometimes informed within dominant representations. In his work on *Star Trek*, Jenkins writes that fans "characterize their entry into fandom in terms of a movement from the social and cultural isolation doubly imposed upon them as women within a patriarchal society and as seekers of alternative pleasures within dominant media representations, toward more and more active participation in a 'community' receptive to their cultural productions, a 'community' within which they may feel a sense of 'belonging'" (Jenkins 2005, 252). For Achebe's *Things Fall Apart*, there are very few active and organized communities of fan fiction writers and readers online, besides a few personal blogs that replot various parts of the novel. This may be due to the predigital history of many of his novels or the lack of playful conversations around African literature—not by theorists, but by ordinary readers who respond to texts through a literary reappropriation and create online communities around them. Taye's work is a single instance of this envisioned community, but it is powerful enough to calibrate a significant moment in the practice and reception of African literature. With a rapidly growing digital consciousness among many African readers of literature and considering the spread of new media's engagement of cultural identities on social media and blogging platforms, fan writing is a practice that might well become a regular online practice.

Taye's fan fiction shows how popular interpretative practices of literary publics can be serious work that, in this case, reclaims Achebe readership from the dominant centers of high theory to a subcultural space of fandom, in which literary elitism becomes snubbed by readers that use the tools and platforms available to them to reengage and remix texts and remake them into something new. What occurs online at the moment are scattered individual efforts of readers who, at various times, are engaged with the content of *Things Fall Apart* to reflect a desire for some kind of connection or friendship—in the case of a living writer like Adichie, who happens to be online. This experimentation with Achebe's work is similar to what Taye does in another fan fiction on Adichie's *Americanah*, in which she recreates Adichie's fictional space to envision and create an erotic text from Ifemelu's love affair with Obinze. Ideas about Achebe's literary mentorship of Adichie, commonly and implicitly expressed by scholarly gossip on the latter's works, take on a new configuration in these associations, as an "ordinary" fan-reader of both writers recreates their work in a manner that gestures at the literary kinship and mentorship between both writers and her own aspiration for connections. Fan writing helps writers to perform a sense of belonging to the social worlds of these writers, while generating friendships with other fans and readers online. The reworkings of novels by both Achebe and Adichie online offer a portal for Taye's performance of her own textual pleasures and politics on *Brittle Paper*.

As Angela Thomas notes, fan fiction functions as a social practice of critically responding to texts. Among other possibilities, an attribute of fan fiction is that "fans of the text can take it and insert characters and plots that are relevant to their own identities and lives, giving them a voice in a text in which they might otherwise be marginalized" (2006, 234). Individual fans who have experimented with the fan writing of Achebe's work, therefore, relocate the individuated and authorial field of *Things Fall Apart* and make it theirs by infusing and repurposing the novel as new texts of their own alternative readings, desires, and judgments. Taye's "Thighs Fell Apart" thus uses Achebe's work as a platform to negotiate her own exploration of sex and sexuality. That said, Taye's exploration of Okonkwo's sex life is a pursuit of the major threads of interests that fascinate many writers of fan fiction. Jenkins explains that the need among the vast majority of female fan fiction writers to "reclaim feminine interests from the margins of 'masculine' texts produces endless speculation, speculation that draws the reader well beyond textual boundaries into the domain of the intertextual" or into an arena of a literary bricolage that envisions contingency as a significant textual attribute for the digital text (2005, 253). Through digital (re)productions, many previously impassive consumers of cultural texts around the world, and in Africa too, are able to regain agency and participate in the public arena. Rather than reclaiming a space of feminine interest, though, Taye's fan writing of *Things Fall Apart* bears the marks of Achebe's influence. Commenting on the subject of Achebe's influence, particularly his most canonized novel, Elleke Boehmer posits "any number of connections and contiguities, at local, regional and international levels. Standing at the head of a tradition or genealogy of writing as Achebe does, he has become a dominant point of origin, a hyper-precursor one might say, in whose aftermath virtually every African author self-consciously writes" (2009, 143). Through digital technologies, we have another way some African writers, mostly a reading public that now writes, relate to Achebe's influence, which, in the case of the fan fiction, is disruptive adaptions of it.

The film critic Didi Cheeka, in a vitriolic response to Taye's work, described "Thighs Fell Apart" as an "infantile expansion" that delegitimizes Achebe's moral position in the way that he is explicitly cast. Cheeka writes that Taye's work "only cheapens the poetry of Okonkwo and Ekwefi's encounter but degrades the latter by turning her into an adulterer."[11] Cheeka is right to the extent that Ekwefi is misrepresented, but to describe Taye's work as infantile is to miss the point. Writers create worlds in their own image, while fans recreate those same worlds as practice of aspirational friendship, a motivation that coverts reading pleasure into a social praxis. This social relationship, though contrived, actually performs a filiation of reading practices as readers operating as fans and "friends" not only write (through avenues such as fan fiction and social media commentary) but also exhibit identities that are descended from sentimental attachments to the fictional worlds of writers and the personae or image politics writers themselves project online. The literary transaction, hence, transcends that of reader and text to include a kinship between reading publics and the social lives of books and their writers. In the fan writing, a synthesis of worlds and ideas emerge, hence the copyright disclaimer on the platform: "Neither Brittle Paper nor Taye owns the two original characters featured on this story. Characters remain the property of Chinua Achebe" (Taye 2014). Taye, a fan who is also a published author herself, engages with and extrapolates meaning from Achebe's work through her fan writing, recalibrating arguments regarding the thematic frames of Achebe's text. The debate "Thighs Fell Apart" initiates in relation to *Things Fall Apart* is an important index of the changing faces of African literature and its reading publics.

Popular works such as this, suggest that, rather than a pernicious culture of deprecations in some section of the artistic community on social media, reader-writers can pay homage to writers (and each other) through social acts that cement bonds of friendship online. Taye's "Thighs Fell Apart" performs the crucial function of signposting how the practice of fandom can animate African literary and reading practices and their social dimensions. Hence, the argument I am making is that fan fiction has the potential to create spaces for literary friendships on social media. In a Twitter correspondence with Taye, she is affirmative about this point, noting that she had "no contact (on social media or otherwise) with Ms Adichie and have no idea of her response to my fanfiction based on her *Americanah*. However, I also wrote a fanfiction based on *Lagoon* by Nnedi Okorafor, with whom I have social media contact. She actually shared the post link on her page at the time."[12] While Okorafor's sharing of her fanfic is not analogous to friendship, Taye is upbeat about how the Africanfuturist writer's response makes possibile intimacies and coalitions that encourage literary friendship. She concludes "that Nnedi was more active on social media than Ms Adichie (at the time I wrote those pieces). Hence more likely to respond to the fanfiction. . . . I'm always happy to support fellow writers on social media and beyond when possible."[13]

Literary fandom, whether through fan fiction or other digital means, is one way some social media users come to terms with the idea of the author as a literary celebrity. For Adichie, her performance of celebrity through pictures on Instagram invites affectionate expressions and words that may convey a desired friendship with her from her fans. But there is also a need to highlight the obsessive iterations of fandom, what is called *stanning* in internet lingo, which manifests a credulous devotion to established writers and other cultural producers. Stanning probably explains why some fans of celebrities like Adichie would never question her pronouncements on postcolonial theory or seek necessary clarification on her views on trans women. In this sense, stanning becomes unquestionable loyalty to a writer. This creates the expectation of uncritical devotion from readers, even if stan culture, like most things about social media itself, could be a force for good.

Dismantling the Canon as the Reader Writes Back

The application of the Western binary of high and low cultures to cultural forms in Africa misreads popular arts in many African contexts, as Karin Barber reminds us (1987). Critical discussions of cultural forms on social media exhibit the high and low culture dialectic that obscures the cultural activities, procedures, and products of the majority of people in present-day Africa (1). It may be useful, therefore, to be responsive to the vast domain of cultural productions available in the cultural spaces of the internet, since whether as "either traditional or elite, as oral or literate, as indigenous or western in inspiration, popular culture in African straddles both and dissolves these distinctions" between the false dichotomies of high and low culture (2). Any anxiety about the authenticity of cultural forms being produced, whether as visual parodies on Facebook and YouTube, or as satirical literary experimentations by ordinary readers on Twitter, may not be sustainable. For instance, a panicky response by critics who object to fan writing instantiates the lack of an understanding of the critic's role in integrating interpretative power into the circuit of mass-produced literary objects circulating on social media. Rather than swiftly dismissing fan fiction as "infantile" or another signifier of a popular practice that unsettles so-called highbrow literary culture, scholars of African literature might do well to become more familiar with the realities of a medium of writing whose publics persistently create and produce texts, while gesturing toward the elasticity of authorial role in the production of literary aesthetics. The African novel of the digital age derives not only content and ideas from social media culture and digital technologies, but also enacts intertextual alliances with the participatory affordances that digital cultural texts enable.

The addition of the voice and agency of the reader who actively shares authorial space with the writer in digital platforms not only constructs fluid and new spaces of literary subjectivity but also affirms how the form and strategies of orature often become reconstructed in African writing on social media. What can be perceived, in other words, is a reconstruction of the performance space in African cultural forms, which exhibits some fluidity in terms of the identity of audience and performer. The digital era reminds us that the modes of experiencing Africa have to be extended to the everyday online practices of its digital subjects as a way of charting the contours of the popular. This reformulation necessitates new ways of engaging with expressive popular forms in Africa. It is made possible because of the notable digital remediation of quotidian everyday life and its aesthetic practices. Web 2.0 platforms have significantly altered the idea of popular culture, as digital social networking sites increasingly position ordinary citizens and decoders of culture to produce and share cultural aesthetics such as internet memes and humorous videos as popular aesthetics of speech. This tendency, cultural netizenship, signals Barber's view that popular arts "play a crucial role in generating and formulating new ways of looking at things" (1987, 74). In this case, whether as Nollywood-derived memes that extend the globalism of Nigerian film culture or a fan fiction that samples and repurposes an earlier work, cultural netizenship presents a continuity between popular culture and social media, opening up spaces for knowing everyday Africa. In their explanation of "the episteme of the everyday," Stephanie Newell and Onookome Okome describe "everyday Africa" as shifting and unstable (2014). The description also fits the provisional and fleeting nature of online popular culture, which the authors suggest share resonances with the unmediated, interactive, and indeterminate nature of African popular arts that Barber had identified before the era of the Internet.

Blogging and social media sites, therefore, not only give young African writers and readers a fluid and dynamic cultural space. They also enable personal agency and provide more platforms to publish works that previously did not (and may never) exist outside of the virtual environment. This is why Adenekan's *African Literature in the Digital Age* is seminal, as it offers a necessary historicity of African digital literary practices in relation to class and sexual politics (2021). His work highlights the emergence of online literary magazines, such as *Brittle Paper*, that focus primarily on the publication of short stories, essays, and poems that appeal to an online reading public. In relation to African literature, it is important to begin a conversation with the medium of the new body of African writing whose publics, thematic currents, and textual impulses are facilitated mainly by digital technologies, born-digital, electronic texts. The implication of this would be to engage with the first-generation African literary texts that have no existence in print technology. Such a dialogue would require us not only to undertake critical analyses of the works produced in online environments but also to investigate the ontology and materiality of the new (electronic) textual spaces of African writing.

African Digital Literature

During the last decade, scholars such as Adenekan, Bosch Santana, Opoku-Agyemang, Cobham-Sander, and, most recently, Adesokan and Sacks have made significant contributions to the field of African digital literature. Whether born-digital literary forms—textual and cultural practices that exist solely and exclusively in electronic environments and without any prior existence in print—or traditional writings in print reconfigured through digital affordances, the role of digital technologies is asserted in these different wide-ranging and innovative studies, many of which I have cited throughout this book.[14] From my analyses earlier, online fan fiction offers a different understanding of the chaotic and messy culture of outrage that is endemic in the social media age. In her article on the formal aesthetics of social media platforms, Ainehi Edoro-Glines argues that social media is "an unruly archive" that accumulates fragmentary literary forms and sensibilities (2022). This understanding is contingent on how some contemporary African writers, as part of their digital performance of authorship, create fascinating content on social media that then create a complex archive of literary materials that potentially unsettles the traditional boundaries between authors and readers. While this sense of unruliness is intimately entangled with the various archives of social and mediatized performances on the platform, ultimately these accumulations enter a dialogue with one another, and rather create a dialogic ecology that prioritizes textual performances in a relational assemblage of multiple voices. And in this multiplicity, the assemblage of voices sometimes belongs to readers who celebrate the writers they admire through adaptive forms like fan fiction. As evident in their social media performances of authorship and narrative selves, the digital spaces of established African writers, as well as their interactions with the digital reading publics who engage with their works in several ways, are worthy of more scholarly attention. Fan fiction is a digital practice that extends critical debates around what counts as canonical in African literature even as it gestures at hackneyed questions on imitation, influence, and originality, which I have only tangentially touched upon. The poaching of textual meaning from a source material is itself a privileging of both the original text and its representational motifs and articulations.

Fan writing has also been shown to be of consequence in how it enables more critical conversations about the nature of African literature in the age of digital technologies. One may wish to examine the roles of authors' Facebook pages and other social media sites, for instance, in the construction of the identity and function of literary practice today. The social interactions between writers and their friends (mostly readers) on social media can mean that literary friendships emerge much more as an important social practice in the artistic community online, and such friendships may sometimes develop through online fan fiction. Even if social relations mostly yield to performativity on social media, the reality of authentic relationships is sometimes a given. How does one justify the interaction between Ifemelu's "unreal" blogging in *Americanah* and the "real" blogging of the same character in "The Small Redemptions of Lagos," a page on Adichie's Americanah WordPress site? Does the unreal indeed hint at and account for the anxieties of the real? The novel, in Pahl's estimation, "explores how the process of writing is democratized, in the sense that Ifemelu and her readers negotiate topics and values together, but also appropriated by the readers on the internet" (2016, 78). By examining Taye's digital fanfic, we might appreciate Achebe's *Things Fall Apart* more, just as Adichie's incorporation of familiar digital spaces into her narrative allows us to appreciate her fictional worlds. For Adichie, her 2013 experimentation with blogging as a formal element of plot makes visible her understanding of the participatory politics of digital media affordances. Just as some members of the older generation (including Achebe and his friends at Umuahia) used print media to subvert the European cultural archive of colonial legitimization, both Adichie's and Achebe's social media fans use digital media to overtly attack the "single story" of African representations from mostly Anglo-American and European media sources. For example, new voices online often attack portrayals of Africans in the West through their Facebook status updates and in much of the online fiction they post on social media networks.

As African cultural productions on the internet have sometimes been subject to ludic suspicions, it is necessary to point out that this generation of African writers who circulate mostly in online communities, and the digital publics that respond to their works on social media, deserve a body of critical responses so literary criticism won't remain an elitist venture unattuned to the new modes and approaches of reading the textual and reinterpreting indigenous forms. In a coauthored article, Adenekan and Helen Cousins, for example, stress the revitalization of oralist modes of representation that is evident in the publishing of poetry online. Social media sites of literary experimentations promote a rediscovery of "orature's art of collaboration between the performer and his audience," which, in their view, a culture of print had relegated (2014, 11). Adenekan and Cousins note that African writing online provides an opportunity for a social network and community of writers and readers who not only have real-time collaboration but also use digital tools to rewrite and revise the margins of textual authority. The digital remapping of African literature reinvented in this way is not completely new, as components of oral literature such as participatory culture are, as I have gestured at earlier, become routinely reconfigured in online spaces. It allows writers to exchange roles with their readers online, reading their own writing and exchanging views on different issues with them on social media platforms. It is the critic's duty then to respond to the cultural politics and the ideologies these spaces materialize. Online fan fiction writing not only enables users to reinsert their subjectivities and reader agency into a network of established cultural producers but also provides a creative space for destabilizing authorial agency by remediating and rewriting traditional fictional works. In "Thighs Fell Apart," Taye is both a producer and consumer of text, a reader who writes, as Jaji argues elsewhere (2020). Taye represents the active reader of African literature who can play with texts in creative ways, performing a creative process within the context of another writer's performance, shifting attention to the way the politics of decoding in African literature can be a participatory praxis of online recreation, with the fan-reader of African writer positioned as a cultural producer who retains their own identity.

Conclusion

In March 2024, Mũkoma wa Ngũgĩ posted a personal story of gender-based violence on social media. In a Facebook update and a post on X, he revealed that his father Ngũgĩ wa Thiong'o physically abused his (Mũkoma's) late mother Nyambura who, as his announcements noted, had been systemically erased from his famous father's legacy. The online response to this revelation was a controversial mix of outrage and solidarity—with many in the literary commentariat either applauding the bravery of calling out Ngũgĩ the elder or criticizing wa Ngũgĩ for publicly airing family issues on social media. As whispers of cancel culture and hasty justification of Ngũgĩ's alleged patriarchal violence confronted distressingly familiar misapprehensions of a writer's personal identity and his artistic creation in unruly comment sections and gossipy literary platforms, the private struggles of a famous African writer once again became visible in an online drama around personae politics. But what became enacted in the Ngũgĩ revelation is not only the algorithmic politics of personality that textures digital performances of authorship and reading, but also how narratives of cancel culture and online controversies shape positive interests in literature or sidetrack the critic from literary and critical engagements with an author's work.[1] Hence, I have sought to demonstrate how the unsettling power of algorithms fosters a culture of outrage and polarizing speech in the African literary ecology as presently constituted and distracts from actual aesthetic evaluation of the literary object. As an intervention in the readership dynamics and literary aesthetics of digital culture, particularly social media sites of critical and literary conversations, it was motivated by the need to understand the operations of online censorship crusades and literary controversies in popular discussions of African literature in its current articulation with algorithmic systems. A full understanding of how African literature takes shape in the digital era requires a critical scrutiny of the role algorithms play in creating and maintaining a culture of outrage online. For many people, there might be a mystification about the workings of algorithms, but it is never in doubt that they are designed to extract profit from the aggravation of different kinds of outrage.

I opened this study with a story that lingered on the question of canceling Chimamanda Adichie from my classroom space, and I wish to conclude on a similar note. Because cancel culture and, indeed, the online world have connections to nondigital spaces, it is essential to understand how the current climate of calling out people whose actions or speech offend or challenge the prevailing political views and sensibilities also percolate into concrete spaces of everyday life such as the classroom. For example, understanding their positionality as a respectful ally of Africa rather than as an interlocutor in an African literature class, an otherwise vocal and brilliant student once told me it was not in their place to speak for African languages when prompted to participate in a class debate about the renewed conversation on the language question in Africa literature. In their view, to withhold their speech and perspectives was a better strategy than to participate in a conversation that simply sought their critical assessment—even if incorrect—on the debate about the continued use of European languages that has recently resurfaced in African literature in an age of resurgent decolonization.

At first, the student's refusal to speak appeared to be a respectful gesture that avoided prescribing what language Africans should have to employ in official communication, but what was really at play in that pedagogic encounter was a reterritorialization of an internalized culture of censorship that deems certain speech problematic and unsayable under the guise of some ethical respect for difference. It is similar to the unspoken ideas of someone who avoids public speech because they know their opinions can be deliberately rendered extreme by an opposing online tribe to elicit political goodwill and solidarity from their ideological camp. Like the maelstroms of cancel culture debates on Twitter and elsewhere, literary controversies about transgender rights among African writers on social media reveal that both what is actually said and what an opposing side interprets to have been said are often two different things. In more severe cases, students in classroom spaces have expressed outrage about characters that are offensive to their own understanding of their democratic freedoms, truth, and social justice, imposing the dominant political doctrines of the day on the fictional worlds they encounter in the classroom.

My interest in African literary controversies and feuds in the social media era was inspired by Adichie's battle with cancel culture on social media and what she considers the puritanical logic of social censure that purportedly imperils literature among emerging writers. In her essay "It Is Obscene," Adichie comes out against cancel culture, addressing her rage against an emergent literary culture and climate of speech that is supposedly undermined by social media discourses on trans rights. The virality of the essay not only forced Adichie's website to crash momentarily due to the interest generated on the subject, but also marked the social capital of a writer whose proclamations as a literary celebrity reflect the current saturation of African literary discourses by the censorious logics of cancel culture with its unabating rhetoric of public invalidation. The subject of cancel culture in African literature matters significantly because aesthetic ecologies are hardly detachable from the broader social matrices from which they emerge. Pierre Bourdieu captures this logic and, indeed, much of the tensions I have presented in this book when he argues that "the space of literary or artistic position-takings, i.e. the structured set of the manifestations of the social agents involved in the field—literary or artistic works, of course, but also political acts of pronouncements, manifestos or polemics, etc.—is inseparable from the space of literary or artistic positions . . . The literary or artistic field is a field of forces, but it is also a field of struggles tending to transform or conserve this field of forces" (1993, 30). Bourdieu did not, of course, write about cancel culture on social media, but the "political acts of pronouncements, manifestos or polemics" that are essentially *related* to the field of literary or artistic production suggest he could have written about it—more so since these political acts and polemical discourses animate a digital culture produced and occupied by social agents operating with different forms of symbolic and cultural capital (30).

What I have attempted to do in this book, therefore, is to draw on the field of digital culture and employ its relationality with African literature as an instantiation of the forcefield of personality struggle. As social media influencers and literary celebrities engage in a culture of outrage over literary prizes and the politicization of social categories such as ethnicity, gender, and sexuality, they manifest the divisive tendencies of an algorithmic culture that prescribes extremism and vitriol. The digital age that produces cancel culture exhibits a practice of *revenge* evocative of what Wendy Brown, in *States of Injury*, theorizes as a culture of late modernity that is marked by the pathos of *ressentiment*. Drawing on Nietzsche's idea that ressentiment is produced by the logics of reaction and a present state inflicted by past memories of hurt and troubling melancholia, Brown argues that:

> Revenge as a "reaction," a substitute for the capacity to act, produces identity as both bound to the history that produced it and as a reproach to the present which embodies that history. The will that "took to hurting" in its own impotence against its past becomes (in the form of an identity whose very existence is due to heightened consciousness of the immovability of its "it was," its history of subordination) a will that makes not only a psychological but a political practice of revenge, a practice that reiterates the existence of an identity whose present past is one of insistently unredeemable injury. This past cannot be redeemed *unless* the identity ceases to be invested in it, and it cannot cease to be invested in it without giving up its identity as such, thus giving up its economy of avenging and at the same time perpetuating its hurt. (1995, 72)

With cancel culture's propensity to adamantly equate identity and the harmful speech of people's past, the reality of an unredeemable history of social injury is even more inescapable, particularly since a mass practice of litigiousness as a worrisome mode of public culture and political life remains attached to the wounds of society, including among the academic left and, in the social media age, the liberals and conservatives who cancel each other, and for whom individual subjectivities remain problematically tied to identity politics. In this framework, something like hate speech is not merely viewed as harmful; it is also subjected to public litigation despite the discursive power embedded in it. With cancel culture—which is sometimes less attentive to redemptive politics and the accountability ethos to which it aspires—the court of litigiousness is not to be found in the formal juridical apparatus of the state but in social media-driven crowds whose first law and instinct is antithetical to both the restoration of the individual and the rehabilitation of social injury. What is thus transformed into a political end for the "resolution of antidemocratic injury" is the court of public opinion rather than the instrumental function of the law (Brown 1995, 28). While generally unsympathetic to cancel culture's language of erasure and faux moralism, I find its threat to rational debates most vexing. For Adichie, what is endangered by cancel culture is not just the capacity to speak—which is shaped by power relations and institutional control—but also the liberty to appear in public discourses without what she calls the "epidemic of self-censorship" (2022b). From the social media posts of writers like OluTimehin Kukoyi and Akwaeke Emezi, though, the argument that cancel culture is an outcome of a social media attack on free speech is merely a pretext to avoid being held accountable for words and perspectives that potentially transform into actual violence for those in the trans community. And these views are pertinent since words are historical sites of political and discursive power. Yet Adichie insists on her right and those of others to express any perspectives, even if they disturb and offend people who identify as trans. For some writers and readers of literature, Adichie articulates a literary humanism that acknowledges that the complexity of the human condition means that we accommodate an inherent ugliness in the human psyche. As Marlow discovers in *Heart of Darkness*, any notion of civilization, absolute truth, and ontological beauty in human nature is bound up with a latent ugliness. Adichie's acceptance of all kinds of speech aligns with Herbert Marcuse's idea of a tolerance that enlarges the range and content of a freedom that is always partisan and intolerant toward the main actors of a repressive status quo (Wolff et al. 1969). As Marcuse writes on the degree and extent of intolerance in established liberal societies, "freedom of speech and assembly was granted even to the radical enemies of society, provided they did not make the transition from word to deed, from speech to action" (97). In other words, there is something about the liberalism of free societies that cultivates tolerance even for the vilest and blasphemous speech, and none should have to self-censure if the expression of an "offensive" speech does not induce any physical harm to anyone.

Why does all this matter in the context of African literature today? The Adichie debates over trans rights transcend discourses of sexuality and identity politics by pointing to the ways in which the algorithmic environments into which African literature is subsumed reanimate questions of free expression and other democratic principles. Another answer is to look at the significant body of works by queer writers and ask to what degree these works are being engaged by scholars on the continent. This is not to suggest that African literary scholars on the continent, like their counterparts in the diaspora, do not condemn, for example, oppressive legislation and physical violence against queer subjects. They do, and some even go as far as boycotting invited lectures to register their just dissatisfaction with the criminalization of queerness. Nevertheless, as a new generation of African writers becomes hypervisible as literary celebrities on social media, African literature is increasingly entangled in the webs of Euro-American culture wars, and their proclamations on these subjects distort perceptions of the social value of African literature. Perhaps with the exception of a queer South African exceptionalism, I am suggesting that African literature has a transgender problem, by which I mean the growing saturation of African literary discourses by transgender writings and ideologies, which a conservative section of the literary community would rather ignore. With scholarly productions on queerness in African (digital) cultures long established and receiving more critical attention in recent years, online controversies around sexualities and transgender ideologies offer more analytical insights into the growing prominence of queer subjectivities in African cultural productions.[2]

Instead of dismissing them as un-African subjects, we do need to be attentive to the new and revitalized terrains of sexuality and gender weaving the tapestries of culture and its symbolic expressions. Taking sides in that debate may not be my focus, yet my task is rather an exploration of the conceptual space these conversations open up for intellectual engagements and debating. Most political persuasions have similar desires, even if their articulations and actors are troubled by ambiguities. Hence, the need for a nuanced and balanced debate on trans identities and other issues that are potentially polarizing. The challenge on both sides is to hold people accountable and respect their differences without assailing their humanity or affronting their individual right to freedoms of any kind. Rather than conflict and controversies, the differences between Adichie and Emezi can produce a humanizing encounter, one that assimilates itself to an ethical accommodation of both identities. Rather than a puritanical zeal on both sides that forecloses the fact of human flaws and messiness, my argument is that the Adichie and Emezi controversy on social media invites more critical reflections on the liberal-democratic ethos of unhindered and democratic speech and its present iterations in African countries, some of which have a long and disturbing tradition of prohibiting free speech based on one's sexual orientation or gender identity. This is a possibility, given an ambivalent social media culture that encourages both cultures of acrimony and visions of nonacrimonious sociality.

When Emezi posts a vituperative tweet about Adichie that simultaneously attacks "other African writers who either quietly or loudly support Adichie,"[3] we are invited to consider the ways in which regimes of silence and nonspeech in some quarters of the African literary establishment are being read as complicit in what is often described as discursive "violence" against trans people. These difficult conversations that are taking place about African writing on Twitter and elsewhere on social media are pertinent for cultural analyses, if only because they alert us to an intensification of gendered debates that require a more self-reflexive critical program. These online controversies shape the African literature curriculum and may determine, for example, whether Emezi's novels are read and taught in Africa-based literature departments or whether Adichie is expunged from the classroom on college campuses in North America. Despite Emezi's oedipal inclination to erase Adichie, which appears to manifest as a lamentation over her mentorship of trans writers through her literary workshops, the works of these two writers need to be taught on the basis of their artistic solidity instead of the identities or politics of the writers themselves.[4]

In a series of tweets responding to Adichie's comments on trans women, Emezi remarks on how traditional media platforms functioned as institutional gatekeepers that support established writers like Adichie rather than join to challenge her freedom to publicly offer ideas deemed harmful by the trans community. Emezi writes that when "Adichie threw her TERF tantrum in June, all these platforms wanted me to comment and I refused because I knew they weren't going to hold her accountable, denounce her bigotry, or protect the trans people harmed."[5] There is iteration here of the belief that constructs cancel culture as a strategy of holding the powerful accountable, even if that perspective elides the power of those calling for this canceling. For Emezi, it is as if media institutions like the BBC and the universities that legitimize Adichie by continually giving her a platform are enablers of what is sometimes framed by many in the trans community as the violent wounding of rhetorical power. By this logic, a progressive performance of a radical queerness would be to publicly insist that Adichie's feminism and LGBTQ advocacy are undercut by an expression of speech that qualifies her for cancelation. But to have her deplatformed from these public spaces and her works thrown out of the academic canon, as is often suggested by some commentators on the internet, would be disingenuous for democratic speech, aside from its denial of the very cultural liberalism and freedom that permits the unrestrained expression of Emezi's legitimate views and pushback in the first place. If, to use John Stuart Mill's controversial remarks, "all silencing of discussion is an assumption of infallibility," such a stance would be awkward and suggest that, despite the combative and censorious tendencies of some in the trans community, their approach is absolutely just and without any mark of its own moral puritanism and hegemonic power (1972,

85). For this vocal section of the trans movement, activism becomes troublingly contingent on the impossibility of constructive disagreement.

Since Adichie's experience with the trans community inspired the core argument of this book, it makes sense to close by reiterating my own position on her views. While having no qualms whatsoever with the rights and choices of trans writers and other individuals in the trans community, I believe it is equally possible to question the assumption that sex, like gender, is a social construction and not a biological category. Also crucial is the need to defend the rights of women to safe space, especially when they feel threatened or their identity erased by extreme and authoritarian trans activism that is indifferent to how, for example, some trans women who retain dominant male experiences and genitalia can be perceived as actual threats. I wrote the last couple of sentences, wondering if they qualify as gender-critical and almost deleted them, but, rather than this act of self-censure, I have left them to underscore a major tendency in the experience of writing this book, namely, my own constant uncertainty as to whether any misreading of the central arguments I have made potentially exposes my major thesis to potential dismissal, or even cancelation. For her trans interlocutors, Adichie might be called a gender-critical feminist steeped in the reactionary politics of fear, what Judith Butler has recently characterized as a phantasm. In this perceived framing, gender becomes a monolith treated by a so-called anti-gender ideology movement as "a threat to all of life, civilization, society, thought, and the like" and gathers up "a wide range of fears and anxieties." (Butler 2024, 5). Rather than this view that writers like Adichie might be gender-critical feminists who imagine gender as an accumulation of several human fears and panic about sexuality, there are merits to her claim that to express caution over any aspect of transgender activism courts personality attacks and regimes of silence among people who don't want to be perceived as anti-trans.

However, the need to critique any work or speech, rather than boycott and label it pejoratively remains sacrosanct, since criticism, rather than merely opposing views one disagrees with, engages in an essential conversation to identify errors. In his Book, *The Constitution of Knowledge: A Defense of Truth*, Jonathan Rauch makes an important distinction between criticism and cancelation. Canceling, as he writes, seeks to "stigmatize conversations and punish the errant. Criticism cares whether statements are true; canceling cares about their social effects . . . Criticism is a substitute for social punishment (we kill our hypotheses rather than each other); canceling is a form of social punishment (we kill your hypothesis by killing you socially)" (2021, 218). Ironically, the existence of cancel culture is often denied and seen as a fantasy of the far right by many on the left who socially censure and morally intimidate anyone of a different ideological persuasion. We are at a point in which African literature, which historically has not been immune from controversial moments, is called upon to respond critically to these important debates occurring in an epoch of unrestrained censure. African literary and cultural discourses need painful, hard, and nuanced discussions about trans activism and its connections to gender-critical feminism, as evidenced by the digital campaign of those who called for Adichie's cancelation. Conversations of this nature must, however, be respectful and empathetic to each individual while still respecting free speech and thought.

Whether it is based on ethnicity or transgender identities, the sociological markers that are part of people's identities online take different shapes and produce different discourses. For example, while the resistance politics of transgender individuals tend to be consistent with the necessary dissidence of other sexual minorities, ethnic clamors, and disputations online often mirror ethnic divisions in nondigital spaces. While these identities also yield to the algorithmic production of outrage online, the points raised by the trans writers responding to Adichie are never to be dismissed, for they signal the power relations involved in who gets to cancel another person and who becomes canceled, besides the enormous power of the platforms that benefit from the proliferation of cancelation discourses. Whether either of these writers is on the side of "truth" or power is not always clear since the claim can be made that the vocal power of the trans community, which is intensely expressed online, is as forceful as what the dominant power of African feminist writers, like Adichie, looks like.

Brown's analysis of Catharine MacKinnon's theory of gender in *States of Injury*, which deconstructs the latter's anti-pornography feminism (1995), might be helpful here. In her project, she suggests that MacKinnon offers a critical and essentialist program of female sexuality rendered as forced subordination, revealing that "wounded attachments" underpin MacKinnon's attempt to censure practices like prostitution and pornography (52). Brown, like other feminist scholars such as Judith Butler, repudiates this approach because of what she reads as an undemocratic tendency to re-inscribe the category of "woman" as an essentialized identity founded on social injury. In other words, Mackinnon's feminist project on female sexuality is based on a normalizing legal structure that sought to use state power to violate the free speech and pleasures of all women as an undifferentiated mass under the yoke of male eroticized dominance. Although I do think Brown's approach that articulates women's sexual expression in the frame of male objectification of the female body lacks some clarity, my point is that the cancelation of Adichie sometimes manifests similar challenges regarding natal women's freedoms. The censorship of Adichie's speech, due to an assumed symbolic power that ostensibly harms trans women, often becomes an anti-democratic violation of Adichie's right to speak for natal women. As with conservative views on the right that are duly disavowed for limiting democratic values, progressive politics, too, cannot become so illiberal that it becomes a pretext for censorship. A culture of no debates is antithetical to all that academic freedom and knowledge production stand for. Indeed, frowning at or outright dissuading conversations about experiences that exist outside the frameworks of heterosexual normativity entrenches bias. But at the same time, how dissenting views about trans subjectivities also become the basis of punitive action in the cancel culture era creates an Orwellian nightmare that hinders speech and critical thought. Whatever the subject—trans rights, anti-racism, or ethnic differences—asking people to stand with free speech and free-thinking norms is one of the most effective ways of building bridges and coalitions.

The role of social media algorithms in the ascendancy of cancel culture is something I have repeatedly emphasized as current conditions bring about literary polarizations in the African literary space online. For Adichie, "social media companies with their mystical algorithms and their lack of transparency exert enormous control on who can speak and who cannot by suspending and censoring the users, something that has been called moderation without representation" (2022b). Since people submit themselves and their privacy to these media entities when they sign up for accounts, this contradicts the logic of representation as being on social media is almost always extractive. But, the algorithmic production of outrage is common, especially in the social science literature. The existence of decision-making algorithms as a supposedly neutral and objective way to limit human bias by delegating decisions and implementations to machines enhances a pervasive presence of digital tools in everyday life, one that unravels the subjectivities of coders and programmers and the vulnerability of users. What Adichie calls "mystical algorithms" to mark a certain vague and esoteric dimension to the algorithms that facilitate the network systems we inhabit is itself problematic. There is nothing mystical about social media platforms and the algorithms that power them. But her fetishization of algorithmic power is consistent with other religious references in some of her recent public talks on cancel culture and social media. To be clear, though, social media platforms are not neutral, as I have repeatedly stressed. Through algorithms created by programmers, social media companies operate as “platforms” that determine what people see and interact with online; hence, they contribute to a culture of outrage and division. Acknowledging here again the role of the designers of these platforms is my way of moderating what may have come across as an overly techno-deterministic analysis of social media, one that ascribes too much agency to algorithms at the expense of the creativity and control of the human agents that both create and co-produce mediatized subjectivities online.

Shaming the Powerful

The performativity of the social media experience, with the fakery of its curated worlds, is not only visible in the digital spectacles of cancel culture and American culture wars, but also translates into a ritual of shaming in which algorithms attract digital subjects to consume the shaming of others, with the publicly shamed becoming objects of our virtual gaze. Besides the fact that social media algorithms foster an economy of lucrative outrage and disputes that transform strangers into moral police of opinions online, they incentivize a performance of shaming that hinders nuanced and civil deliberations. In Cathy O’Neil’s *The Shame Machine*, platforms like Facebook and Google encourage never-ending battles that generate rich advertising revenue for these companies through the data we produce (2022). O’Neil argues that as people “stake out their positions, sharing the posts they agree with and denouncing their enemies,” the platforms, as I have also mentioned, learn from this outrage culture and use the “knowledge to place each user into more finely calibrated subgroups—which makes the targeted advertising even more effective and profitable” (100). What this then means for literary controversies and outrage is that, as in print domains where editors can similarly manufacture a fake scandal to reenergize a weakening readership, there is a peculiar machinic configuration of our outrage. As moral agents who want to hold others accountable, we need to understand the algorithmic-affective workings of platforms that crystalize profitable outrage as complicit in online performances of virtue signaling and shaming. The public shaming of cancel culture fosters what 2017 Nobel Prize winner Sir Kazuo Ishiguro has called a “climate of fear” that forces young writers to self-censor. As he puts it, young writers were avoiding writing from viewpoints outside their own immediate experiences for fear of being canceled by an “anonymous lynch mob [that] will turn up online and make their lives a misery” (Jones 2011). Herein lies the great irony of cancel culture: those who want diversity and inclusion violently exclude rather than engage with uncomfortable ideas, even sometimes making death threats online, in ways reminiscent of totalitarian censorship. While some imagine this as radical activism, it actually indicates a cultural confusion of our age—one that fosters untoward moral aggressiveness as the premise of human relationships.

In the framework of African cultural productions and the public sphere in Nigeria, the first truly viral moment in Nigerian social media—the "Oga at the Top" story—had this element of digital shame, with the government officer at the heart of the episode going viral online for being shamed first in the traditional media and more forcefully by the many satirical discourses and popular humor produced by social media comedians on the story. The same thing can be said of the #BringBackOurGirls hashtag campaign, whose many narratives include a viral theatrical outburst by a former first lady, Patience Jonathan, whose many gaffes animate Nigerian texts of popular humor. Shaming and ridiculing the powerful may be one of the ways the oppressed exact some kind of revenge against the political class, but people who mock oppressive state actors and their excesses, in fact, participate in the performative shaming of an algorithmic culture of outrage. The digital shaming of cancel culture is aimed at the powerful and, in the case of Adichie's cancel culture attack, it is a demonstration of an impressive demonstration of her power and the effect her words have on other African writers today, as the novelist Novuyo Rosa Tshuma argued during Adichie's Caine Prize controversy (Tshuma 2013).

The subject of public shame is one that Achebe addresses in *Things Fall Apart*, and I wish to close by exploring what it might offer in relation to the performative shaming that accompanies cancel culture on social media. Okonkwo is portrayed as a tragic hero who defends the integrity of a society struggling to uphold its traditions in the face of colonial domination, but Okonkwo himself is an imperfect character who, among some of the American students I describe here, might be an agent for cancelation for his abusive treatment of women. To read the protagonist of a literary work produced on the eve of Nigeria's independence in 1960 through the lens of social media cancel culture might be dicey, but it goes back to my point about presentism in the opening of this book. James Chandler prompts us to the importance of locating a work in its actual context of production and interpretation, asking "if there is a politics of literary culture, or a sense of public stakes in literary representation, then what political consequences follow, if any do, from various ways of taking a work's specific time and place into account when we read it?" (1999, xiii). While, as Chandler is suggesting, the saliency of the cultural moment of a work matters, my approach so far has been to center present concerns and read past literary works in the light of the cultural practices of a deterministic algorithmic moment that affects how people interpret cultural and aesthetic forms. Reading Okonkwo and *Things Fall Apart* through a cancel culture framework is in line with arguments in literary presentism that go back to earlier works in the 1990s in Shakespeare studies. As Hugh Grady and Terence Hawkes write in *Presentist Shakespeares*, we "need urgently to recognise the permanence of the present's role in all our dealings with the past. We cannot make contact with a past unshaped by our own concerns" (2007, 3). Hence, what might be tagged as an inattention in this book to the pastness of past cultural forms has informed my reading of Achebe, Conrad, and the other authors whose works I have referenced throughout.

In Achebe's anti-colonial text, Okonkwo is the typical public figure, a kind of celebrity who is well known throughout the nine villages, having acquired fame because of "solid personal achievements" that bring honor to his community, Umuofia (1959, 3). Unlike the gladiatorial discursive fights of literary controversies on social media, Okonkwo is introduced to the reader as actually engaged in combat, during one of which he defeats Amalinze the Cat, a great wrestler whose unbeaten records are shattered by the young Okonkwo. Though prosperous and respected as a lord of his clan, his life is dominated by the fear of failure, a fear that consumes him as a "fear of himself, lest he should be found to resemble his father" (13). Hence, to hate everything his father had loved, particularly Unoka's idleness and laziness, was a lifelong obsession, even though this fear broadly mirrors the huge expectations his society expects of him. Perhaps, what is most relevant to the theme of cancel culture in Achebe's development of Okonkwo's narrative is the fact of the hero's banishment from Umuofia after he accidentally kills a clansman. The shame of being deplatformed and removed from the immediacy of an influential position would definitely be familiar to anyone who has been canceled. Although Okonkwo is forced into exile because of this ethical breach of his society's norms, he ultimately returns after seven years. Here is a major Achebean moral logic that shows the reconciliatory ethos of a redemptive Igbo justice system that could become a model for the contemporary social justice movements. Okonkwo's "cancelation" and readmission back to society, therefore, become the conditions under which the circumstances of his eventual tragic fall become possible.

Of more interest to me, though, is the closing section of *Things Fall Apart*, which enables me to theorize speech as a representative mode of being in an egalitarian Igbo society that values speech and other democratic freedoms. More relevant to my interest in Okonkwo, therefore, is something else that quietly defines his life, namely, "a slight stammer," which, as the novel's diegetic space unfolds, becomes noticeable in moments of anger when he "could not get his words out quickly enough" (Achebe 1959, 4). For a protagonist who is popularly known in Umuofia as a "Roaring Flame," the fact of a speech impairment is one of the fascinating ironies of *Things Fall Apart*. The problematic treatment of women in Okonkwo's patriarchal society is obviously legible in the fists and beatings that are interlaced with this disability, which, as Ato Quayson argues, is "a cultural deficit" that is initially effaced as the narrative establishes Okonkwo's impressive profile (2007).

Just before the climactic moment of the novel, however, Okonkwo's verbal incapacitation returns in the narrative as he kills a messenger from the district office who interrupts a meeting of the tribesmen. Quayson's argument on the tragic seriousness of Okonkwo's verbal facility juxtaposes "the background of his gathered tribesmen coming to *talk* about their most recent humiliation at the hands of the white man" with the descent of a machete that marks Okonkwo's "final severance from a society that has changed imperceptibly due to the colonial encounter" (2003, 217). The tragic hero's personal fate is seen to be at odds with that of a now-transformed society whose acceptance of colonial impositions puzzles Okonkwo to his death. As he stammers, the reality of being "unable to utter a word" before his machete lands on the mes-senger activates his eventual marginality and his tragic ending, with the reader invited to recall ear-lier sections of the narrative (Achebe 1959, 204). The hints at his condition of disability in those opening chapters of the novel become less vague as they come together to clarify his rage and violent treatment of family members. For example, when he hands Ikemefuna over to his most senior wife, "Okonkwo thundered, and stammered," excoriating the woman for asking a question: "When did you become one of the *ndichie* of Umuofia" (14). Okonkwo's attitude to the speech of those who contradict him, whether his wives or other clansmen, is a contemptuous treatment that is evocative of the kind of condescension and censure one sometimes finds on social media, although the natural conditions that produce Okonkwo's speech impairment are different from the ideological forces that threaten speech online. While cancel culture seeks to redress speech others may find offensive—or words that are considered harmful—it is itself a form of speech that, through its ambivalence and occasionally selective moralism, mostly targets people without a monolithic access to power. It has the power to activate an artificial and antidemocratic impairment in speech.

As we read in *Things Fall Apart*, Okonkwo knows how to kill a man's spirit and shame them into silence, particularly men like Osugo who, neither having any title nor influence, offers a viewpoint that contravenes Okonkwo's speech. If we read the *ilo* as a kind of public space for the enactments of play and political deliberations like the type that social media—despite its many contradictions—facilitates, these connections I am making between Okonkwo's speech and free expression on social media are not particularly far-fetched. But rather than algorithms and a polarizing culture, what motivates Okonkwo's public behavior is a disrupted verbal capacity that mixes with anger to structure his social relations and domestic interactions. Since the anger of the online world can be read as of a different kind than Okonkwo's innate disability, what threatens speech in the virtual space is a self-righteous zeal to relate with people based on a bland conformity to one's ideological tribe.

To cancel people by blocking, removing their words, or their capacity for speech from the public arena may not be the explicit goal of Okonkwo in his encounters with contrarian viewpoints, but his troubles with speech in moments of rage and his tendency to constrain the communication of others are reminiscent of what is often found in the tribalist and communal worlds of social media cancel culture. Yet, if among "the Ibo the art of conversation is regarded very highly," as Achebe writes, then Osugo's dismissal by a more powerful interlocutor like Okonkwo registers a breach of an egalitarian Ibo culture that is then rehabilitated through a symbolic act of apology (1959, 7). Hence, the stern intervention by the oldest man present in the meeting and the sympathies of everyone else for Osugo compel Okonkwo's contrition. Here is the point of rupture in my analogy: rituals of contrition, even if sometimes performative and self-seeking, are a rarity on social media. Hence, despite concentrating on a single element from the life of a complex tragic character (the pathology of his slight stammer), a rare moment of penance for a man who lacks "a certain humanity, warmth, and generosity of outlook" that characterizes his father is sufficient to adjust our attention to cancel culture's lack of social grace and its hindrance to free discourse in contemporary times (Palmer 1972, 56). Thus, Okonkwo makes clear to us that people don't have to be perfect humans to be humane and tolerant. As Achebe writes: "An Umuofia man . . . may refuse to do what he is asked; he does not refuse to be asked" (1959, 193). An Umuofia man may not like what is said and may even refuse it, but he always puts himself forward to accommodate what has to be said, even if it is speech that provokes tensions. It is as if Achebe uses Okonkwo to communicate that opposing viewpoints do not have to harm anyone. Hence, the articulation of Okonkwo's character is contingent on an ideology of radical openness in an egalitarian society whose ethos sometimes runs contrary to Okonkwo's sensibilities as a tragic hero.

Epilogue

As public shaming or an outright rejection of a dominant group in the name of social justice, cancel culture becomes self-negation—a conditional affirmation of multiplicity that transforms difference (in thought or belief) into an offense. Collective knowledge production is often based on differences and being able to challenge one another, as well as eschewing a plastic consensus rather than po-licing speech. This is the cornerstone of all democratic cultures, whether among the Ibos or the Greeks. In this sense, canceling people posits that they cannot be reformed and are incapable of recompense in public life, or that they are beyond fallibility or an ethic of compassion that we all need from time to time. Yet, as analyses such as those by Nussbaum indicate, compassion itself in the public culture of liberal democracy is not without its imperfections and limitations and is often the affective locale of philosophical controversies. Nussbaum's work is probably more beneficial to the argument on cancel culture and public life more broadly, but I wish to return to Adorno and his conclusion to *Minima Moralia*, in which he writes: "the only philosophy which can be responsibly practiced in face of despair is the attempt to contemplate all things as they would present themselves from the standpoint of redemption" (2005, 247). Without redemption, all else is an endless reconstruction of grievance. What is meant here by redemption is probably of a transcendental import that is beyond the scope of my analyses, but I am literalizing it as a culture of public tolerance and compassion that may be premised on the Yoruba saying that *orí kì í burú kó má loorùn*. However bad a person's situation is, there is always a redeeming presence around it. This may appear alien to the self-focused habits of thoughts produced by the social media rage machine, but it is precisely its gesture toward restorative justice that makes a politics of redemption appealing.

Like Adichie's, my recourse to metaphors of religion in this closing stage is intended as a commentary on the quasi-religious nature of social media ideological tribes—whether liberals or conservatives. Particularly, it highlights the manner in which the espousal of what manifests as ideological doctrines prescriptively sticks to a culture that prefers a puritanical moralism to progressive political thinking. I am not alone in this understanding of cancel culture and, indeed, a so-called Woke culture as demanding performative contrition in the public. Cancel culture and the spirit of wokeness, as Ian Buruma argues in a *Harper's Magazine* piece that draws extensively from Max Weber's Protestant work ethics, derive from the punitive and confessional logics of early Protestant puritanical cultures (2023). Buruma attributes what he sees to be the coerced public apology that is demanded of popular figures who violate the cultural norms and politics on race and sexuality to early modern Puritanism that was based on the ritual performances of public avowals. At the same time, he misreads the inherent diversity of Protestant cultures of public contrition over sin and lumps an entire religious tradition into an uncritical fundamentalism. Based on his major thesis, individuals who say or do things that violate the public ideal are called upon by a woke collective, the Elect—"highly educated urban sophisticates" who work in elite institutions like museums and literary magazines—to apologize publicly (2023). Like internet cultures, more broadly, there is a social class dimension to cancel culture, but rather than Buruma's suggested notion of cancel culture as a secular inheritance of an irrational culture of Protestant modernism and religious morality, its secularized iterations are not always antithetical to progressive political thoughts. They have historically evolved in constant tension. But the arguments are clear: ideological movements, both in the critical social justice and ultra-right frameworks, tend to exhibit cult and religious tendencies that are driven by powerful interests along the lines of class, neoliberal capital, and the outrage economies of an algorithmic culture.

Returning to Adorno and his theological rubric, therefore, we further understand what he argues to be the tasks of philosophy and knowledge in his reasoning. According to him, "perspectives must be fashioned that displace and estrange the world, reveal it to be, with its rifts and crevices, as indigent and distorted as it will appear one day in the messianic light. To gain such perspectives without velleity or violence, entirely from felt contact with its objects—this alone is the task of thought" (2005, 247). Instead of calling out public actors who breach the norms of the times or whose past beliefs become sanctimoniously excavated as the basis for holding them accountable in the present, a redemptive sensibility is more humanizing. My argument is that a redemptive gesture that fosters a reconciliatory ethos and tolerance works more effectively for public debates, especially when the offender realizes their misdeeds and possesses a will to moral atonement and accountability. This necessary sense of empathy proceeds from a recognition of the ambiguities and messiness that is inherent in all humans and undercuts the tyranny of uncritical censure.

While to imagine cancel culture in the manner I have described it so far may appear utopian to some, Adorno places much demand on the power of philosophical thinking in his disjunctive articulation of the current state of the world and how it could be from the standpoint of an external, messianic epistemology. In that paradigm, thinkers are therefore tasked with distancing themselves from their own culture and historical moment, and, in the case of social media, from its structures of feeling and mechanisms of rewards. This distance allows them to properly discern its algorithmically inspired crises and lay bare its contradictions and despair. Even when the process is streaked with challenges, the goal is to make rational thought diverse and plain without any hierarchical grids from within us. But even a messianic paradigm does not always have to be transcendental in this case, since redemption—while locatable outside the vistas and passions of our own immediate realities—is often, in the words of Ghanaian poet Frank Kobina Parkes, a "search [in] wide heavens for a sign not written there" (1965, 52). The signs that redeem a person or a culture may, similarly, be searched out in the humanistic philosophies and capacious ethics that prioritize the best ideals of our collective fate as humans.

I believe this was what Loretta Ross was getting at when she wrote in her *New York Times* article that society can address complex issues, such as sexual abuse, without resorting to the disciplinary methods and logics of the prison industrial complex. As she notes, we should never have to "use social media to rush to judgment in a courtroom composed of clicks lest we "run into the paradox Audre Lorde warned us about when she said that 'the master's tools will never dismantle the master's house.'"[6] At the heart of this plea is a restorative and redemptive approach to social justice that is sometimes absent in the online haste to cancel or to author new ideas and social meanings. Whether located in the philosophical traditions of the Ifá corpus or in a Nietzschean thought system, to redeem the past and offenders from it, rather than to pursue a campaign of public revenge for social misdemeanors, is a more ethical practice that affirms life in all its beauty, freedoms, constraints, and messiness. At the same time, as the messy and the vulnerable become the conditions under which redemption may emerge, the possibility that not everyone has any qualms with an unredeemed society must be equally accepted rather than judged as prejudiced.

Irrespective of its ideological provenance and platforms of circulation, cancel culture mobilizes social shame in a manner that would be untenable, for instance, in Yorùbá pragmatics of sociality—which promotes an ethic of redemption and radical openness. In any case, even offending actors and ideas can be redeemed, according to the Yorùbá proverb, *bí a kò bá gbàgbé ọ̀rọ̀ àná, a kò ní rẹ́ni bá ṣè mín-in.* In other words, if we don't forget past misdemeanors, creating new alliances and pleasures will be rendered impossible, as an unforgiving culture ultimately undermines critical engagement and silences people. Drawing from an indigenous Yorùbá worldview is partly my acknowledgement of the limits of a Western-style liberal democracy, which is admittedly not without its contradictory logics. It is also intended to urge an online public sphere capacious in its ethical respect for difference and a humanist tolerance for individual liberty and free speech. While it might be idealistic to think such a digital public sphere can totally escape the negativity of social media algorithms and its outrage culture, it can at least yield to reasonable debates that rightly negotiate the dominant codes of algorithmic power. Put differently, algorithms should not necessarily stand in the way of the democratic agon. As the online world offers a persistent model of what Chantal Mouffe describes, in the contexts of democratic politics, as the ineradicability of antagonist forces and of "the conflictual dimension of social life," the role of algorithmic cultures in encouraging conflicts and outrage is even more apparent (2005, 4). However, as I argued in the introduction, humans have power over the algorithms they create, and even everyday users of online platforms can resist the capitalist capture of their digital lives. Hence, users retain the power to extract agonistic relations that foster democratic cultures from algorithmic systems rather than surrender to a mindless regime of digital outrage that is unproductive and intolerant. The challenge is to avoid being assimilated into the outrage culture of algorithmic power, as people can find more ways to disrupt the various systems of artificial intelligence and machinic assemblages that threaten to colonize the human experience for corporate interests. Instead of a digital public sphere that cancels others and censures antagonism, our discursive interactions online can engender a plurality of perspectives and foster a humane space where participants in public debates transcend Habermas's unitary formulation of the public sphere to constitute a plurality of contesting publics, including subaltern counterpublics, accommodating multiple identities and alternative histories. To articulate antagonistic elements in online spaces along with a redemptive rationality of compassion might be a tough goal, but it is not undoable.

Whether on social media or not, compassion may be controversial—as Nussbaum suggests—but it can also be contagious and go viral, since social media algorithms also amplify positive outcomes. While the technical structures of this online public sphere remain ambivalently anchored on the logics of the market, its members are, hopefully, sufficiently self-effacing to accommodate differences and disavow any appearance of the unsayable, especially in a work of art. We could indeed use a widening yet humble capacity for patience and openness in digital public spaces—one that disavows the chronic self-righteousness and moral censorship of those who disagree with others' views, using divergence as a basis of public shaming and erasure. The art of humility, which in the liberal tradition yields respect for individuality and difference, remains key to human connections and empathy, particularly in the gray and ambiguous zones of our shared ontological frailness. Through such a disposition of mind, we may perhaps be able to discern clearly how the pursuit of justice and truth undergirds public interactions. Whatever tyranny exists in online discourses isn't just that of a vast ignorance that proceeds from the throes of thoughtlessness, powerful algorithms, or digital design injustices but also that which cruelly imposes our own versions of truth and mythologies of living on others, declaring them as the primal mode of public engagement. Only those who aspire to such micro-fascist totalities fail to grasp how a constraining rationality activates rage and divisions.

As Hans-Georg Gadamer's philosophical hermeneutics makes clear, even when faced with difficult subjects, it is "through a work of art a truth is experienced" and the fact that we cannot attain this truth "in any other way constitutes the philosophic importance of art, which asserts itself against all attempts to rationalize it away" (Gadamer 2004, iii). The tendency to rationalize away the truths of aesthetic works that appear to breach the dominant view, or to abjure beliefs and points of view that are contrary to our own because of the perceived moral failings of their owners, suggests an attack on the democratic and rational circulation of ideas expected of all free societies. In the name of free speech, we cannot, of course, offer a platform of debate to anyone advocating toxic ideas or any speech that actually harms anyone, nor can free speech or the careful and rational exchange of ideas speech be seen as the solution to all human problems. At the same time, an excavation of past wrongs or the recognition of current misdeeds cannot always be a retributive excuse for excluding people—whether from marginalized or dominant groups—from participating in public life. Those whose rights to public expression are guaranteed cannot demand silence from those with whom they disagree in the name of a vague construction of harm.

In *Things Fall Apart*, Okonkwo's apology to Osugo essentially rescues a public conversation from atrophy, demonstrating the subsumption of the personal by the overarching communal ethos of Umuofia. There is much to learn in that singular enunciation of humility—something that is often absent in some sections of a vibrant African digital public that often surrenders critical discussions of the formal techniques of African texts on the altar of heated debates and controversies over authors whose performance of personality and celebrity on social media becomes a source of personality conflicts and tensions. As I have sought to show throughout the book, whether one gets canceled or canonized in contemporary African writing is increasingly a function of the politicization of identity in the social media age. Yet, the fact remains that literary controversies are merely amplified, like many other things, by social media algorithms and publics. From Achebe's controversial critiques of Conrad to the combative poetics of Bọ́lẹ̀kájà critics and and the rebuff they attracted from writers like Soyinka, and to an unending language question, African literature has had, and continues to have, its fair share of controversies. With digitality in mind, the affordances of African literature become more recruitable to not only the celebration of the digital literary networks, publics, and communities that enrich its scope, publics, and textual aesthetics but also to conceptually map the range of controversial discourses and culture of literary outrage that shapes its social worlds. For every tweet expressing outrage about transphobia, and every Facebook post clarifying a flippant statement on the relevance of postcolonial theory, or every literary prize that courts a scandal, literary controversies also demonstrate how the algorithmic and cultural politics of the digital age configure African literary discourses and reading practices. That is not a controversy.

Notes

Introduction

1. Chimamanda Ngozi Adichie, "The Danger of a Single Story," *TED*, July 2009, https://www.ted.com/talks/chimamanda_adichie_the_danger_of_a_single_story/transcript?language=en.
2. Several Senegalese readers on Twitter used the online campaign #congratulationswithdrawn to attack the writer Mohamed Mbougar Sarr after his antihomophobia novel *De Purs Hommes* (*Of Pure Men*) was cited as the real reason, and not his 2021 novel *The Most Secret Memory of Men*, for his Paris Prix Goncourt award. Also, the social media site formerly known as Twitter is central to the many discussions that are featured in this book. I have left the name of the original platform to reflect the pre-Musk era that was perceived to foster a so-called woke culture that, according to the platform's new owner, stifled freedom of expression. Twitter has since rebranded as X, replacing the popular blue bird logo with a white X on a black background, and *tweets* and *retweets* becoming just *posts* and *reposts*. Since this change in ownership and ideological directions of the platform, many progressive users have since jumped ship, rightly pointing to the escalation of hateful content on X—a name that symbolically mirrors this book's meditation on digital acts of cancelation and the controversial

dramas of censorship and public shaming.

3. In addition to earlier controversies about the language question, Bernth Lindfors recounts how some South African members of the newly formed African Literature Association (ALA) in the mid-1970s were subjected to censorship based on Apartheid politics, causing "lively controversy" and nasty debates (Bernth Lindfors, "Censorship of Public Discourse in the Early Years of the African Literature Association," [*unpublished manuscript*, 2023]). The controversial tensions surrounding the politics of speech and silence provoked a statement from a former president of the association, Emile Snyder: "I see nothing wrong in the linking of politics with literature, during our annual meetings, only insofar as the politics of our opinions do not silence the voices of different and even of dissenting opinion." Emile Snyder, "Strength and Growing Pains in the Life of a Young Association," *ALA Bulletin* 10, no. 4 (1984): 11. The ALA has long gone past this foundational bedrock of controversy and censorious politics. Although, the same cannot be said of African literature itself, which, like other aspects of world literature, manifests several literary feuds, scandals, and controversies that are textured by social media algorithms.
4. Loretta Ross, "I'm a Black Feminist. I Think Call-Out Culture Is Toxic," *New York Times*, August 17, 2019, https://www.nytimes.com.
5. Umut Özkırımlı, *Canceled: The Left Way Back from Woke* (Cambridge: Polity Press, 2023), 14.
6. Frieda Ekotto and Kenneth W. Harrow, *Rethinking African Cultural Production* (Bloomington: Indiana University Press, 2015), 3.
7. Chinua Achebe, "An Image of Africa," *Massachusetts Review* 18, no. 4 (1977): 782–94.
8. I am using *unlike* in the double sense that refers to speech that is disliked and detested for appearing to violate the prevailing orthodoxies, and speech that runs contrary to the normative political culture. Its second use inverses the ritual of liking and gesture toward the performance of displeasure that the thumbs-down button communicates in some online spaces. Dislike buttons were common on YouTube before they were removed in 2021.
9. For Alexander Stern, Adorno's argument helps to clarify cancel culture on Twitter, "particularly the way tweets are taken as immutable expressions of a person's essential being. Thoughts tweeted in the distant past are exhumed to torment people who have risen to prominence. People engage in ritual apologies for innocuous tweets that offend overly delicate sensibilities. Some insufficiently prudent souls even end up losing jobs for tweets that are hardly controversial." Alexander Stern, "Opinion Fetishism: Can We Escape the Reductio Ad Tweetum?," *Hedgehog Review: Critical Reflections on Contemporary Culture*, March 30, 2021, https://hedgehogreview.com/web-features/thr/

posts/opinion-fetishism.

10. The concept of "presentism" arose from Shakespeare studies in the 1990s to refer to a mode of reading past literary texts in a manner that is attentive to the social and political concerns of the present. This perspective in historicist literary studies frames presentism as a less pejorative approach to historical interpretation than its problematic identity among historians who view it as a fallacy to be avoided. For instance, Lynn Hunt, one-time president of the American Historical Society, wrote that "presentism besets us in two different ways: (1) the tendency to interpret the past in presentist terms; and (2) the shift of general historical interest toward the contemporary period and away from the more distant past." Lynn Hunt, "Against Presentism," *Perspectives on History*, May 1, 2002, https://www.historians.org/publications-and-directories/perspectives-on-history/may-2002/against-presentism.
11. I use "ecology" in the sense advanced by Alexander Beecroft in his study of world literature to mark how the complex and heterogenous elements of literary texts are understood through a focus not only on the texts themselves but the roles these texts play in the complex political and cultural arena of their time. Beecroft explains that "texts and literatures thrive in a wide variety of ways," unlike the single adaptive economic model favored by Pascale Casanova in her *The World Republic of Letters*. The social worlds of digital networks and the literary disputations they produce are distinct elements, like the cultural and political domains of African texts, that interact to shape contemporary African literature. Alexander Beecroft, *An Ecology of World Literature: From Antiquity to the Present Day* (London: Verso, 2015).
12. To be fair, in a sense, we cannot really move beyond class, since much of the discourses on cancel culture on social media are highly configured by class politics. The questions of who gets to cancel another person and who is indeed canceled are shaped by class, status, and social prestige. Writers like Adichie and J. K. Rowling are able to survive the attempt to have them canceled by middle-class actors online because they are successful and best-selling authors whose influence transcends the culture industries.
13. Frank Pasquale, *The Black Box Society: The Secret Algorithms That Control Money and Information* (Cambridge: Harvard University Press, 2015), 8.
14. Elnathan John, "The Fourth Republic," Twitter, 2016, https://twitter.com/TheFourthRep/status/765662137159155712.
15. Shola Adenekan, *African Literature in the Digital Age: Class and Sexual Politics in New Writing from Nigeria and Kenya* (Rochester: Boydell & Brewer, 2021); Akin Adesokan, *Everything Is Sampled: Digital and Print Mediations in African Arts and Letters* (; Susanna Sacks, *Networked Poetics: African Poetry's Digital Turn* (Amherst: University of

Massachusetts, 2024).

16. James Yékú, *Cultural Netizenship: Social Media, Popular Culture, and Performance in Nigeria* (Bloomington: Indiana University Press, 2022). Besides *African Literature in the Digital Age, Everything Is Sampled*, and *Networked Poetics*, there have been several journal publications in the last decade exploring African digital literature, including Zahrah Nesbitt-Ahmed, "Reclaiming African Literature in the Digital Age: An Exploration of Online Literary Platforms," *Critical African Studies* 9, no. 3 (2017): 377–90; Stephanie Bosch Santana, "From Nation to Network: Blog and Facebook Fiction from Southern Africa," *Research in African Literatures* 49, no. 1 (2018): 187–208; James Yékú, "Deference to Paper: Textuality, Materiality, and Literary Digital Humanities in Africa," *Digital Studies / Le Champ Numérique* 10, No. 1 (2020): 1–28; Kwabena Opoku-Agyemang, "Digital Cities and Villages: African Writers and a Sense of Place in Short Online Fiction," *Journal of African Media Studies* 15, no. 2 (2023): 217–29; and Sarah Brouillette, "Wattpad, Platform Capitalism, and the Feminization of Publishing Work," *Book History* 26, no. 2 (2023): 419–38. These articles all touch upon different aspects of African digital literatures, including the politics of authorship, textuality, material form, and the question of literariness online and its evaluation. Worthy of mention is the special issue edited by Shola Adenekan, Rhonda Cobham-Sander, Bosch Santana, and Kwabena Opoku-Agyemang that curates some of the most pressing questions in the field: "Introduction to the Guest Issue: Digital Africas," special issue, *Postcolonial Text* 15, no. 3 and 4 (2020).
17. Susanna Sacks and Sara Brouillette, "Introduction: Reading with Algorithms," *Post45*, December 8, 2023, https://post45.org/2023/12/introduction-reading-with-algorithms/.
18. This socio-technological dimension of AI systems emphasizes the ways in which machine learning especially is "structurally dependent on human participation" and is the argument of Rainer Mühlhoff's essay in which he explores the subject of human-aided artificial intelligence, "Human-Aided Artificial Intelligence: Or, How to Run Large Computations in Human Brains? Toward a Media Sociology of Machine Learning," *New Media & Society* 22, no. 10 (2020): 1868–84.
19. Nick Seaver, *Computing Taste: Algorithms and the Makers of Music Recommendation* (Chicago: University of Chicago Press, 2022), 7.
20. In science and technology studies, a coproductionist approach is used to explain the ways in which the social order and technoscientific epistemologies overlap and configure each other. For more on this, see Sheila Jasanoff, ed., *States of Knowledge: The Co-Production of Science and the Social Order* (New York: Routledge, 2004), in which she demonstrates how social identities, institutions, representations shape and are shaped by scientific knowledge.

21. The concept of personality in the African studies literature dates back to E. W. Blyden's theorization. He formulated the African personality around a cultural identity that disavows anthropological views of Black history and culture as inferior and subverts racialized understandings of the African experience. In Blyden's extensive body of works, African concerns, spiritualty and culture are, in fact, fundamental to human existence. See Edward W. Blyden, *Christianity, Islam and the Negro Race* (Baltimore: Black Classic Press, 1994).
22. Samuel Taylor Coleridge, *Biographia Literaria*, ed. Adam Roberts (Edinburgh: Edinburgh University Press, 2014), 28.
23. Mary Ajayi, "Of Kisses, of Sexual Predator, of Chijioke Amu-Nnadi," 9jaFeminista, January 18, 2016, https://9jafeminista.wordpress.com/2016/01/18/of-kisses-of-sexual-predators-of-chijioke-amu-nnadi/.
24. Carl Terver, "Did the NLNG Prize Trend Last Night? I Was Asleep," Twitter, October 15, 2022, https://twitter.com/carlterver/status/1581179627925831682.
25. Although I do not discuss him, the South African anthropologist and activist Archie Mafeje was also involved as a third, principal actor in this historical intellectual jousting. James H. Mittelman writes in 2014 that the "ensuing Soyinka-Mazrui and Mafeje-Mazrui fights turned into slugfests among intellectual warriors" in which Soyinka and Mafeje censured and castigated Mazrui for alleged essentialist views and misrepresentations of Africa. James H. Mittelman, "A Better Intellectual Community Is Possible: Dialogues with Ali A. Mazrui," *African Studies Review* 57, no. 1 (2014): 153–70.
26. Scholarly work on the role of digital media and the social web in generating and circulating literary outrage, disputes, and controversies in African literary discourses has been limited. Building on James F. English's notion of "journalistic capital" and its accumulation of prestige, Nathan Suhr-Sytsma identifies how, as public profile, the "journalistic capital" generated by scandal "serves to convert the economic capital of the prize winnings into symbolic capital" in the artistic community and is "demonstrated through social media trends as much as newspaper coverage." See "The Geography of Prestige: Prizes, Nigerian Writers, and World Literature," *ELH* 85, no. 4 (2018): 1093–122, 1100. My argument in this book builds on the social media side of things by specifically outlining the workings of algorithms in the production of scandals and how controversies issue forth from contestations over reputational capital on social media.
27. Alex Finn (@NFT_GOD), "How Your Tweets Are Ranked," Twitter, March 31, 2023, https://twitter.com/NFT_GOD/status/1641914923826462721.
28. Facebook's legal terms of service page suggests that users "own all of the content and information you post on Facebook, and you can control how it is shared through your

privacy and application settings." In addition, when "you publish content or information using the Public setting, it means that you are allowing everyone, including people off of Facebook, to access and use that information, and to associate it with you (i.e., your name and profile picture)." In other words, while I have provided links to several arguments referenced in this study, there is really no ethical necessity to seek the permission of those whose names and pictures appear here, as they themselves do not intend their data to be private. See "Terms of Service," Statement of Rights and Responsibilities, Facebook, January 30, 2015, http://www.facebook.com.

Chapter 1. Achebe, Adichie, and Conrad's *Heart of Darkness* in a Cancel Culture Age

1. Ezra Klein, "Shame, Safety and Moving Beyond Cancel Culture," *The Ezra Klein Show*, podcast, April 27, 2021, https://www.nytimes.com/2021/04/27/opinion/ezra-klein-podcast-cancel-culture.html.
2. Caryl Phillips, "Out of Africa," *Guardian*, February 22, 2003, https://www.theguardian.com/books/2003/feb/22/classics.chinuaachebe.
3. Loretta Ross, "I'm a Black Feminist. I Think Call-Out Culture Is Toxic," *New York Times*, https://www.nytimes.com/2019/08/17/opinion/sunday/cancel-culture-call-out.html.
4. Chimamanda Adichie, "*Channel 4 News*: Chimamanda Ngozi Adichie Interview," YouTube, March 11, 2017, https://www.youtube.com/watch?v=KP1C7VXUfZQ&feature=youtu.be.
5. Adichie, "*Channel 4 News*," 2017.
6. Chimamanda Adichie, "Clarifying," Facebook, March 12, 2017, https://www.facebook.com/chimamandaadichie/posts/10154893542340944/.
7. See Emezi's initial Twitter thread in which Adichie is accused of inciting a "wave of bigoted violence" from other Nigerians: Akwaeke Emezi, "A Reminder," Twitter, November 12, 2020, https://mobile.twitter.com/azemezi/status/1326911252082397186. These concerns may be far-fetched, but they are not totally unfounded. At the University of Waterloo in 2023, a professor of gender studies was stabbed along with two students, a situation that mirrored Canada's recent history of gender-based violence, especially with regard to missing and murdered Indigenous women. In relation to Adichie and the trans community, one consequence of cancel culture is that it not only silences those with unpopular views but also enables people who can actually act on their harmful rhetoric by encouraging them to convert hate speech into action. Although the definition of "harm" is sometimes unclear in online spats, and cancel culture may silence people, it does not change the fact that problematic views could eventually translate into injurious

social behavior. Rather than deplatform people who disagree with us, we need to listen to them and, without any fundamentalist understanding of free speech, recognize their individual freedom to speak even when they are wrong. The speech that needs the most legal protection is not what can be normally said or what might be considered normal but that which is sometimes deemed unsayable and problematic.

8. Ajayi mentioned this in a personal email conversation. Dami Ajayi, "Yes, It Is Obscene, Ms Adichie, But . . . ," *Yaba Left Review*, July 21, 2021, https://yabaleftreview.com/ yes-it-is-obscene-ms-adichie-but-dami-ajayi.
9. Also see Immanuel Kant and Robert B. Louden, *Anthropology from a Pragmatic Point of View* (Cambridge: Cambridge University Press, 2009).
10. See Martha C. Nussbaum, *Upheavals of Thought: The Intelligence of Emotions* (Cambridge: Cambridge University Press, 2003).
11. Ngũgĩ's critique comes from the essay "The Globalectical Imagination," in which he calls for a globalectical reading of world literature, with globalectics articulated as disavowing the provincial and embracing "wholeness, interconnectedness, equality of potentiality of parts, tension, and motion. It is a way of thinking and relating to the world, particularly in the era of globalism and globalization." This approach involves a theoretical program he calls "poor theory," which is devoid of any ornamentality that confuses a density of words for complexity of thought and is usable for clarifying interactive connections and interconnections of social phenomena and their mutual impact in the local and global ecologies of culture. See Ngũgĩ wa Thiong'o, *Globalectics: Theory and the Politics of Knowing* (New York: Columbia University Press, 2012), 8.
12. See Olúfẹ́mi Táíwò, *How Colonialism Preempted Modernity in Africa* (Bloomington: Indiana University Press, 2010).
13. Adélékè Adéẹ̀kọ́'s article uses the intellectual legacies of Ọlábíyìí Yáì, a Yorùbá/ Beninois linguist and literary theorist, to advocate a truly epistemic freedom or thought rehabilitation that transcends the mere polemic and platitude of a decolonizing rhetoric without attention to indigenous languages and aesthetics. See Adélékè Adéẹ̀kọ́, "Decolonization without a Linguistic Turn Is Like Drinking Sugar without Tea: Ọlábíyìí Babalọlá Joseph Yáì," *Journal of the African Literature Association* 15, no. 2 (2021): 308–20.
14. Rather than inaugurate these critiques, Achebe was lending his voice to those of others who had similarly considered the question of the African image in the European cultural imagination. See Arthur Kemoli and David K. Mulwa, "The European Image of Africa and the African," *Busara* 2, no. 2 (1969): 51–53.
15. This is from later editions of the essay, after Achebe's initial use of "bloody racist," an expression that, as Stephen Ross has noted, was a "remark heard around the world,"

shaping the pedagogical approaches in the African literature classroom as postcolonial theorizing became more prominent. Stephen Ross, *Conrad and Empire* (Columbia: University of Missouri Press, 2004), 4.

Chapter 2. Literary Networks of Conflict and the Politics of the Digital Litmag

1. I am using "genocidal" in this chapter advisedly. Even if seen as a denialist gesture, my stance is that not all mass atrocities qualify as genocide, and this includes the popular reference to Biafra, which Arthur Anyaduba has forcefully argued constitutes a genocidal event—particularly when the definition of the term is socially determined, rather than limited to any legal confines as he argues. In regard to Kaduna's El-Rufai, Anyaduba's work does enable an appreciation of how literary feuds might "participate in the process of producing meanings of genocide and expanding "our understanding of the meanings of genocide produced in literary representations. See Chigbo Arthur Anyaduba, *The Postcolonial African Genocide Novel: Quests for Meaningfulness* (Liverpool: Liverpool University Press, 2021), 4.
2. Abdi Latif Dahir, "The New Magazines and Journals Shaping Africa's Literary Scene," *New York Times*, July 17, 2021, https://www.nytimes.com.
3. Shailja Patel, "Goodbye @EnkareReview," Twitter, January 29, 2019, https://twitter.com/shailjapatel/status/1090478616171941888.
4. "About," *Brittle Paper*, https://www.brittlepaper.com.
5. Ainehi Edoro, "Statement on the Departure of Brittle Paper's Former Deputy Editor," *Brittle Paper*, April 15, 2020, https://brittlepaper.com/.
6. Edoro, "Statement." The relationship between digital shaming and cancel culture that is signaled in the statement is crucial for analyses, and I shall revisit it later.
7. Otosirieze Obi-Young, "Statement on Leaving Brittle Paper," Otosirieze, April 15, 2020, https://otosirieze.com.
8. "Our Story," *Open Magazine*, https://opencountrymag.com. In yet another newly created digital Litmag, founded by Ladi Opaluwa and Oris Aigbokhaevbolo, *Brittle Paper*'s cancel culture experience comes up in an essay by Aigbokhaevbolo who describes the episode as heralding an ending: "Not long ago, there was a Nigerian blog that served as the online drinking hole. We frequently complained about its more or less un-literary methods, but it gave the Nigerian and wider African writing community a centre. A couple years ago, it became involved in an issue concerning a prominent politician's family and quickly fell from grace when its prominent editor departed. . . . I have come to think

of that departure as an ending because the publication is yet to return to its former glory, although the new one started by the departing staff is on the ascendancy." Oris Aigbokhaevbolo, "The Death of Nigerian Literature," *Efiko*, 2023, https://efikomag.com.

9. Ikhide Ikheloa is a popular culture critic on Nigerian social media. His views can be found in several tweets and here: "#EndSARS: On That Open Letter from African Writers," Medium, October 17, 2020, https://medium.com/@ikhide/endsars-on-that-open-letter-from-african-writers-f9dc2f0d3423.
10. In an email interview with Ainehi Edoro, Ikheloa himself admits: "It is correct that I have reviewed several books; however, I do not see myself as a literary critic. Much of what people call reviews are really my commentaries on our condition as Africans, sometimes using a particular book as a launching pad. Many remember me as 'that literary critic' but I do write creative pieces, fiction, nonfiction, prose and poetry. I can't legislate relationships, so I really can't stop people from giving me labels that fit their perceptions of me. How do I see myself? I am a reader who writes." Ainehi Edoro, "The Irreverent Critic: Interview with Ikhide Ikheloa," *Brittle Paper*, February 25, 2013, https://brittlepaper.com/2013/02/irreverent-critic-interview-ikhide-ikheloa/.

    Unlike other social media influencers who outright reject the "critic" label because of the term's so-called elitism and obscurantist language and methods, Ikheloa appears to embrace the term. In his book on *The Rise of the African Novel*, Mũkoma wa Ngũgĩ writes of Ikheloa as "the rare literary critic who is not part of academia." For him, Ikheloa "is an advocate of more African writing on the Internet, he is highly influential, reaching thousands through his blog, Facebook posts (he has close to ten thousand followers), and Twitter account (fifteen thousand). In keeping up with and taking seriously post-Makerere writers across all forms and media, he has built an archive of literary criticism that at some point members of the African literary establishment in academia will have to pay attention to." Ikheloa's social media has, of course, increased significantly since the publication of the book, although designating him as a literary influencer on social media might ruffle some feathers. Mũkoma wa Ngũgĩ, *The Rise of the African Novel: Politics of Language Identity and Ownership* (Ann Arbor: University of Michigan Press), 170–71.
11. Thomas M. Nichols, *The Death of Expertise: The Campaign against Established Knowledge and Why It Matters* (New York: Oxford University Press, 2017). In the context of the religious elite in Nigeria, Ebenezer Obadare similarly tracks the ascendancy of pastors as ubiquitous thought leaders and experts in different domains of life and argues that the authority of the clerical class that challenges established knowledge formations actually antedates the informational nodes of digital technology. See Ebenezer Obadare, *Pastoral*

Power, Clerical State (Notre Dame: University of Notre Dame Press, 2022).

12. Ikhide Ikheloa, "Teju Cole, Palimpsests, and Sebald's Ghost," Pa Ikhide, September 23, 2012, https://xokigbo.com/2012/09/23/teju-cole-palimpsests-and-sebalds-ghost/.
13. Ikhide Ikheloa, "Walks with Julius: Teju Cole's 'Open City,'" Pa Ikhide, November 12, 2012, https://xokigbo.com/2012/03/11/the-2011-caine-prize-how-not-to-write-about-africa/.
14. "Ikhide R. Ikheloa to Receive James Currey Lifetime Achievement Award," James Currey Society, 2022, https://jamescurreysociety.co.uk/blog/ikhide-r-ikheloa-to-receive-james-currey-lifetime-achievement-award-in-literary-criticism. Website no longer available.
15. See Dr. Damages, "Prof. Nwelue on Role of Public Intellectuals in Solving Nigeria's Socio-Political Situation," YouTube video, January 8, 2023, https://youtu.be/0GdHIqM-3_k.
16. Chiedu Ezeanah, "Ikhide Roland Ikheloa, the New Chichidodo of African Literature," Facebook, October 16, 2022, https://www.facebook.com/chiedu.ezeanah/posts/id02omvMQK6k1bcSbXPv5sLH1qAXLNgJENB4MSNYdizEdbB36WqEoHaAbwZBrjuHVG9El.
17. Ezeanah, "Ikhide Roland Ikheloa."
18. Ezeanah, "Ikhide Roland Ikheloa."
19. Ikhide Ikheloa, personal communication to the author, Twitter, September 9, 2020.
20. Ikhide Ikheloa, "Let Me Suggest This to Readers of Conscience," Twitter, April 13, 2020, https://twitter.com/ikhide/status/1249827781246177280.
21. The lack of evidence is one reason the writer Gimba Kikanda reasoned that boycotting KABAFEST was not a good approach, despite the supposedly controversial politics of its organizers and his own strained history with Shónẹ́yìn, which Kakanda recalls in an article posted on Medium: "Ms. Shoneyin and I had a fallout on Facebook—a cause of which is embarrassing to share here—sometime in 2011 and then, being Wole Soyinka's daughter-in-law, she also couldn't stomach—or misunderstood?—my satire on the Nobel laureate . . . That she blocked me from following the Twitter account of her event, even though I've no memory of engaging with the account, is a scary syndrome I elected to take as personal, instead of allowing it to guide my assessment of her art and public engagements. . . . The same Ms. Shoneyin once had me, along with writers B. M. Dzukogi and Ahmed Maiwada, delisted from a cliquey Yahoo listserv of Nigerian writers, Krazitivity, for airing dissenting views." Gimba Kakanda, "The KABAFEST Dilemma," Medium, July 5, 2017, https://medium.com/@gimbakakanda_37996/the-kabafest-dilemma-7303bcef1799.
22. Shónẹ́yìn has consistently denied this controversial claim. In a 2020 Twitter thread, she proceeded to demonstrate the falsity of this common gossip through evidential records, but as if surrendering to the algorithmic machine herself, attacked Ikheloa, presenting screenshots of personal conversations with the late Pius Adesanmi that were damaging

and ungenerous to excoriate Ikheloa. Recognizing the problematic nature of exhuming the voice of the dead to score a point at the living, Shónẹ́yìn later deleted aspects of the thread that referenced Adesanmi but it was almost too late. Red Cap Chief (@007burch), "Dragging Late Pius Adesanmi into This," Twitter, April 18, 2020, https://twitter.com/007burch/status/1251465592294473729.

23. Dr. Damages, "Prof. Nwelue on role of Public Intellectuals." Nwelue read the complaints as not a challenge to his own merits to institute and confer award but as an expression of cancel culture. Hence, he said in the interview, "I am going to use my platform [the James Currey Society] to uncancel the canceled," as if to acknowledge the contradictions that defined the recipient of his prize as a subject that is being "canceled" (mainly ignored) by the literary elite for the kind of controversial pronouncements common to both figures.
24. Ikhide Ikheloa, "African Literature Is a Victim of Perverse Gentrification," Twitter, June 29, 2020, https://twitter.com/ikhide/status/1277562250728034305.
25. Ikhide Ikheloa, "El-Rufai Invites Writers to His Book Festival in July," Medium, June 11, 2017, https://medium.com/@ikhide/el-rufai-invites-writers-to-his-book-festival-in-july-of-oppressors-and-messiahs-the-distinction-c137729a8aa9.
26. Also, a distinction between writers and intellectuals is not something that exists in Ikheloa's world. Both are uncritically lumped together, even though the marriage of both roles then recalls Edward Said's argument that a distinction between both need not be made insofar "as they both act in the new public sphere dominated by globalization . . . their public role as writers and intellectuals can be discussed and analyzed together." "The Public Role of Writers and Intellectuals," in *The Public Intellectual*, ed. Helen Small, 19–39 (Oxford: Blackwell Publishers), 26.
27. Ikhide Ikheloa, "A Premium Times columnist, Pius Adesanmi," Facebook, April 29, 2013, https://www.facebook.com/ikhide/posts/10151907324459616.
28. Ikhide Ikheloa, "I am very proud of myself," Facebook, December 24, 2020, https://www.facebook.com/ikhide/posts/10161750583264616.
29. In one of many derogatory tweets by both camps, controversial Nigerian singer and activist Charles Oputa (Charly Boy) went as far as suggesting that Soyinka could "never be the man Chinua Achebe was," a sentiment shared on other platforms by Ikheloa and others in the writing community who construed Soyinka's view—that the #Obidients were intent on a "fascist" silencing of others—as being in opposition to the movement's promise of progressive politics. In many ways, the online responses to Soyinka ironically and performatively enacted the conditions that produce the censorious and undemocratic tendencies common with cancel culture on social media. Charly Boy Area Fada 1 (@AreaFada1), "The Kin Respect I Had for Dis Man," Twitter, April 8, 2023, https://

twitter.com/AreaFadal/status/1644585830722183169.

30. Other canonical works in this regard include Osundare's *State Visit*, Soyinka's *King Baabu*. In Nollywood, Adewusi's *Babangida Must Go* is another example.
31. Mũkoma wa Ngũgĩ. "@Brittlepaper Is a Singularly Important African Literary Platform," Twitter, April 16, 2020, https://twitter.com/Mũkoma WaNgũgĩ/status/1250762426712113152.
32. Ukamaka Olisakwe, "I Strongly Reject the Call to Cancel Brittle Paper," Twitter, April 16, 2020, https://twitter.com/MsOlisakwe/status/1250820109813387265.
33. Carey Baraka. "Intimations of an Ending—Carey Baraka on the Unspoken Demise of *Kwani?*, and the Death of a Dream," *Johannesburg Review of Books*, August 27, 2020, https://johannesburgreviewofbooks.com/2020/08/27/intimations-of-an-ending-carey-baraka-on-the-unspoken-demise-of-kwani-and-the-death-of-a-dream.
34. "About Us," *Kwani?*, http://kwani.org.
35. "About Us," *Kwani?*.
36. "About Us," *Kwani?*.
37. Musila describes this in another essay as "a desire for novel ways of writing; a robust wrestle with the anxieties of cross-generational influence." See Grace A. Musila, "Archives of the Present in Parselelo Kantai's Writing," in *Popular Culture in Africa: The Episteme of the Everyday*, ed. Stephanie Newell and Onookome Okome (New York: Routledge, 2014), 244.
38. Shalini Gidoomal's comment to Baraka's essay, *JRB*. Shalini Gidoomal's comment to Baraka's essay, *JRB*. Similarly, Baraka again was later called out online for a 2023 essay on Ngũgĩ wa Thiong'o that generated another controversy. Baraka, having spent three days with Ngũgĩ at his California home, wrote what many online commentators, including Ngũgĩ's family members, saw as a gossipy and voyeuristic essay that revealed too many intimate details about the Kenyan writer. See Carey Baraka, "Ngũgĩ wa Thiong'o: Three Days with a Giant of African Literature," *Guardian*, June 13, 2023, https://www.theguardian.com/books/2023/jun/13/ngugi-wa-thiongo-kenyan-novelist-profile-giant-of-africa-literature.
39. Wainaina expressed confidence in the ability of the literary networks he was heading at that point "to create . . . our own aesthetic. Such an aesthetic will not be donated to us from the corridors of a university; or from the ministry of culture, or by the French Cultural Centre. It will come from the individual creations of thousands of creative people." "Editorial," in *Kwani? 01*, ed. Binyavanga Wainaina (Nairobi: Kwani Trust, 2003, 6). Yet, the Ford Foundation and the Caine Prize, it seemed, shaped this aesthetic if Habila and Ihkeloa are taken seriously about the alleged tropes of poverty porn in the fiction being produced by that generation. Although, as Nathan Suhr-Sytsma argues, a

binary understanding of the aesthetic and sociological representations of Caine Prize stories elides the much more complex imbrications between them. "The Geography of Prestige: Prizes, Nigerian Writers, and World Literature," *ELH* 85, no. 4 (2018): 1093–122.

40. Baraka, "Intimations of an Ending."
41. Baraka, "Intimations of an Ending."
42. As the *Brittle Paper* affair with KABAFEST shows, literary magazines and politics in Africa have always exhibited this connection. Mũkoma wa Ngũgĩ comments on how *Transition* in 1967 "almost buckled under the weight of revelations" that it was in part being funded by the CIA through a proxy organization, the Congress for Cultural Freedom, which also funded other literary publications like the *Black Orpheus. The Rise of the African Novel*, 3.
43. Baraka, "Intimations of an Ending."
44. Baraka, "Intimations of an Ending."
45. Clifton Gachagua, "I Don't Trust the People," Twitter, July 6, 2018, https://twitter.com/CliftonGachagua/status/1015286678142013442.
46. Gachagua, "I Don't Trust the People."
47. Tee Ngugi, "How Ngugi wa Thiongo came to be a version of Matigari," Facebook, June 17, 2023, https://www.facebook.com/tee.ngugi.92/posts/myfEWNdzTwM5sKqBpS64sXJMsMTGVWZZvwg6Ck7E5WKLJRtwVMSeassb68RCz1KMl.
48. Mũkoma wa Ngũgĩ, "Am I the Only One," Twitter, June 15, 2023, https://twitter.com/MukomaWaNgugi/status/1669415338402824196.

Chapter 3. Achebe's *There Was a Country* and the Ethnopolitics of Bọ́lọ̀kájà Readers

1. Chiedu Ezeanah, "Pen Nigeria," Facebook, January 31, 2023, https://www.facebook.com/chiedu.ezeanah/posts/id0mQVXo4aMbdyBmXbnhqfcjBTdpLcRbMg27GKYdVRQCTcjmga1ZXvazmNwDfmCuoLpl.
2. Ezeanah, "Pen Nigeria."
3. At the same time, the occurrence of the PEN debate on Facebook also obscures what takes place offline. Ezeanah's challenge to Remi Raji was reprised in another Facebook post calling out Denja Abdullahi, another former president of the Association of Nigerian Authors. But unlike the Raji scenario, Abdullahi was able to elicit a public apology from Ezeanah. This came in the form of a Facebook post, which, as the story goes, was required of him by the police. The point to stress is not only the connections between the offline and online world, but also how much of the controversies that begin or circulate online simultaneously mask their own offline iterations. The

personae politics of the controversy manifests in Ezeanah's later promise to support the Association of Nigerian Authors "without attacking his [Abdullahi's] person or that of any other writer, for that matter." See Chiedu Ezeanah, "Blessed Are the Peacemakers," Facebook, August 28, 2023, https://www.facebook.com/chiedu.ezeanah/posts/pfbid034SmZ1iSaEWbCYLPkcfZVxtWw3RSg4a2iw8PGphujFTmpmCCmAtg9uMGmuhBEms9Fl.

4. James Ogunjimi, "Social Media Nightmare, Nigerian Version of Ageism . . . and the Many Versions of Truth," Facebook, December 9, 2016, https://www.facebook.com/Ogunjimijamestaiwo/posts/10211375897219691.
5. Ikhide Ikheloa, "The Caine Prize: The Burdens of Identity and Fading Memories," Pa Ikhide, June 3, 2016, https://xokigbo.com.
6. Remi Raji, personal communication to the author, November 22, 2023.
7. See Karen Bourrier and Thelwall Mike, "The Social Lives of Books: Reading Victorian Literature on Goodreads," *Journal of Cultural Analytics* 5, no. 1 (2020): 1–34.
8. Another example of how discourses of controversies and cancel culture become profitable for some of the parties involved is seen in the case of British author Trish Lorenz, who appeared to have claimed in an interview that she was the one who named the young Nigerians who protested in 2020 against police brutality the "Soro Soke generation." While many in the #EndSARS movement saw Lorenz's comments and, indeed, her book *Soro Soke: The Young Disruptors of an African Megacity* as another instance of cultural appropriation, the online expressions of outrage and the heated call to Cambridge University Press (the publisher of the book) to pull the book was good publicity for it. Another book edited by the poet Jumoke Verissimo and me, *Sọ̀rọ̀sóke: An #Endsars Anthology*, also benefited from this controversy as it became more visible beyond the Nigerian market because of this particular controversy.
9. Nnedi Okorafor, "Definitely Not Objective," Goodreads, January 14, 2013, https://www.goodreads.com/book/show/13588385-there-was-a-country.
10. Nnorom Azuonye, "Achebe Bashing," Facebook, 2012, https://www.facebook.com/n.o.azuonye/posts/pfbid0ooovaPAXMbfHBbHWpsYuVakEqycLHFhUU7oTCg3jZ2JLUpANbu7FTHRANauCkJqQl.
11. Nnorom Azuonye, Facebook, 2012, https://www.facebook.com/n.o.azuonye/posts/4585161345380?comment_tracking=%7B%22tn%22%3A%22O%22%7D.
12. Azuonye, Facebook, 2012.
13. Nduka Otiono, "There Is No Greater Stupidity," Facebook, 2012, https://www.facebook.com/nduka.otiono/posts/10151129692434107?comment_tracking=%7B%22tn%22%3A%22O%22%7D.

14. Otiono, "There Is No Greater Stupidity."
15. Ikhide Ikheloa, Facebook, 2012, https://www.facebook.com/ikhide/posts/3880601 91284406? comment_tracking=%7B%22tn%22%3A%22O%22%7D.
16. Tade Ipadeola, "The Ogbunigwe Cocktail: Romance, Grundyism and the Old Lie," *Guardian*, February 10, 2013, emphasis mine.
17. Comment on Ikhide Ikheloa's Facebook post, 2012.

Chapter 4. The Caine Prize Wàhálà and the Algorithmic Rọ̀fọ̀rọ́fọ̀ of Literary Networks

1. Also, John Berger captures this negative sentiment in 1972 when, upon winning the Booker Prize for Fiction, he said: "The competitiveness of prizes I find distasteful. And in the case of this prize the publication of the shortlist, the deliberately publicised suspense, the speculation of the writers concerned as though they were horses, the whole emphasis on winners and losers is false and out of place in the context of literature." Berger eventually shared half of the proceeds with the civil rights movements and Black Panthers, declaring his gesture as neither philanthropic nor political. John Berger, "'I Have to Turn This Prize against Itself'—John Berger on Accepting the Booker Prize for Fiction, 23 November 1972," *Verso Books*, November 4, 2016, https://www.versobooks.com/blogs/2317-i-have-to-turn-this-prize-against-itself-john-berger-on-accepting-the-booker-prize-for-fiction-23-november-1972.
2. Sana Goyal, "'Too Much Talking. We've Got Work to Do," *Wasafari*, March 12, 2020, https://www.wasafiri.org/article/too-much-talking-weve-got-work-to-do/.
3. Ikhide Ikheloa, "The 2011 Caine Prize: How Not to Write about Africa," Pa Ikhide, September 11, 2012, https://xokigbo.com/2012/03/11/the-2011-caine-prize-how-not-to-write-about-africa/.
4. The expression "angry tweets" used by Edoro to describe Wainaina's series of tweets captures the affective logic of algorithmic platforms, as anger becomes a feeling that is reproducible online. Ainehi Edoro, "Drama Alert: 'Shine Your Fucking Eyes'; Read Binyavanga's 'Dear Caine Prize' Rant," *Brittle Paper*, October 11, 2014, https://brittlepaper.com/2014/10/binyavanga-dear-caine-prize-rant-1/.
5. See Doseline Kiguru, "Prizing African Literature: Creating a Literary Taste," *Social Dynamics* 42, no. 1 (2016): 161–74.
6. For instance, Irenosen Okojie's "Grace Jones," which won the 2020 Caine Prize, is a brilliant work in experimental language that explores the experience of Blackness in London. Her beautiful style animates her subject matter and shows the diversity of

technique that comes with storytelling on the continent. In this tradition of experimental fiction, Okwiri Oduor's "My Father's Head" also comes to mind. Oduor's 2014 short story exhibits a modernist appeal through an evocative language that blends well with the realism of the story itself. If the language is Joycean, as the prize judges suggested, the narrative world is definitely Achebean in its realist depictions of repressed memory and loss. The point to note is that we can be wary of the politics of the Caine Prize stories while, at the same time, appreciative of their aesthetics. In an age of cancel culture, however, this is sometimes difficult as intense scrutiny is mostly centered on the political and anthropological valences of a particular work. The controversies around the short story "*We Need New Names*," for example, arguably matters more to some commentators than the story itself or even any subsequent necessary engagement with the longer novel derived from it.

7. It may help to recall at this point that the participatory affordances of user-generated media fuse the identities of media producers and consumers, with readers in the comment sections of social media posts also manifesting as writers, editors, or reviewers, depending on the particular media.
8. Namwali Serpell, "Zambian Writer Namwali Serpell to Share Caine Prize Money," *BBC News*, July 7, 2015, https://www.bbc.com/news/world-africa-33424103.
9. Tiwaladeoluwa Adekunle, "#CainePrize2016 | Heated Debate Sparked by Kola Tubosun's Review of Tope Folarin's Story," *Brittle Paper*, June 14, 2016, https://brittlepaper.com/2016/06/caineprize2016-kola-tubusons-controversial-review-tope-folarins-genesis-sparks-debate/. Previous debates about Folarin centered on his diasporic identity, particularly after he was awarded the Caine Prize for his story "Miracle." In this instance, again, there is further evidence of the discursive value of prize-based controversies and debates as they get to the heart of involute questions on the African identity and personality.
10. Kristen Stern, "Plagiarism, Intertextuality, and the Same Old Story: The Caine Prize Controversy Is Not Original," Africa in Words, October 28, 2019, https://africainwords.com/2019/10/28/plagiarism-intertextuality-and-the-same-old-story-the-caine-prize-controversy-is-not-original/. Stern's analysis in the article includes perspectives on Ouologuem's *Bound to Violence*, which was the source of plagiarism accusations after winning a literary prize in France. Her response to the Caine controversy was written for the literary blog Africa in Words, which has been blogging the Caine Prize since 2013.
11. Mũkoma wa Ngũgĩ, "Shame on @Caineprize," Twitter, September 4, 2019, https://twitter.com/Mũkoma WaNgũgĩ/status/1169225189734924288.
12. Ikhide Ikheloa, "The @CainePrize Did the Right Thing," Twitter, September 4, 2019,

https://twitter.com/ikhide/status/1169353528290283521.

13. In fairness, Adichie's controversial view on Western prizes such as the Caine Prize may also be seen in her literary works. In the metafictional short story, "Jumping Monkey Hill," that explores topics such as sexual molestation and trauma, Adichie tackles the perennial question of the white, European expert who gatekeeps culture and who routinely through literary workshops and awards gets to determine the bounds and limits of "authentic" African arts and letters.
14. For instance, Adichie was in Paris in 2018, attending the third The Night of Ideas, a cultural and transnational event organized by the Institut Francais at the Quai d'Orsay and that had taken place in other parts of the world (at about 160 venues). An interview with the French journalist Caroline Broué, scheduled as one of the major highlights of the cross-cultural event, precipitated the coming storm when Adichie was asked by Broué whether there were bookshops in Nigeria. Adichie's response that the question reflected poorly on the French people went viral, so did a later Facebook post in which she sought to defend Broué's attempt at irony. The major controversy of the night, however, was Adichie's response to a question on postcolonial theory that she thought was "something that professors made up because they needed to get jobs." The response to this among many African scholars, both on Twitter and in the traditional media, was loud and intense. Communication scholar Wunpini Mohammed tweeted that we "need to put Chimamanda in rice. How can you shit on postcolonial theory while claiming not to know what it means. The same postcolonial theorists who assign your books & videos in classes." Wunpini F. Mohammed, "We Need to Put Chimamanda in Rice," Twitter, January 26, 2018, https://twitter.com/wunpini_fm/status/956928662481391616.

    In an article for *Aljazeera*, literary scholar Grace Musila wrote that "Adichie's quip about postcolonial theory is revealing about her low regard for academics." What irked many of these scholars the most, and rightly so, was Adichie's negation of the intellectual tradition that, along with her talent, had made it possible for her to become visible as a canonical figure of world literature. Grace A. Musila, "Chimamanda Adichie: The Daughter of Postcolonial Theory," *Aljazeera*, February 4, 2018, https://www.aljazeera.com/opinions/2018/2/4/chimamanda-adichie-the-daughter-of-postcolonial-theory.
15. Elnathan John, "The Consequences of Loving Ngozi," Elnathan John's—The Dark Corner, July 15, 2013, https://web.archive.org/web/20130720222425/https://elnathanjohn.blogspot.com/2013/07/the-consequences-of-loving-ngozi.html?m=0.
16. Edoro Ainehi, "Wow . . . Adichie Gets VERY Candid," *Brittle Paper*, March 12, 2015, https://brittlepaper.com/2015/03/adichie-candid-elnathan-immoral/.
17. Novuyho Tshuma, "Adichie and the Great Brouhaha—a Fine Line Between the

Legitimacy of Hurt and Its Responsibility," *Saraba*, July 20, 2013, http://www.sarabamag.com/adichie-and-the-great-brouhaha-a-fine-line-between-the-legitimacy-of-hurt-and-its-responsibility. Tshuma further elaborates on the personalization that often characterizes literary controversies on social media: "The pressure on Ms. Adichie is not due to her statements, for, if one reads her opinions and views in interviews from the time of *Purple Hibiscus*, they have not really changed; it is due to her status as a prominent writer. . . . I think, perhaps, we have come to confuse Ms. Adichie's writing with her persona. We are assuming a sensitive, dangerous line of public ownership of a person. For though we are entitled as readers to own her work, let us not be arrogant enough to confuse this with ownership of the writer." The focal issue here is the capacity of conflictual narratives on social media to make personalities the crux of literary arguments.

18. While pointing out what appears to him to be the diasporic bias of the prize, Alexander Thandi Ubani excoriates the organizer of the Brunel Prize for the gender imbalance of the shortlist. He writes: "Again, how convenient was it for the organisers to have shortlisted 6 women for this year's prize? Out of all the thousands of applicants, only two men were considered worthy to be shortlisted. The gender bias showed by organisers of this poetry prize is a shameful attempt to favour a gender over another which no reasonable person can take." Alexander Thandi Ubani, "Brunel Shortlist 2018 Controversy: The Politics of Being Too Black," *Information Nigeria*, March 17, 2018, https://www.informationng.com/2018/03/brunel-shortlist-2018-controversy-the-politics-of-being-too-black.html.
19. Kunle Afolayan, "I Am So Pleased and Delighted," Twitter, October 3, 2022, https://twitter.com/kunleafolayan/status/1576832976045756416.
20. Namwali Serpell, "I Explain More," Twitter, September 25, 2020, https://twitter.com/namwalien/status/1309511480602234881.
21. I once had the opportunity to lead some doctoral students from some four African countries on a methods seminar, and the first thing one of them said was something like, "thank God there are no white people here." Frankly, I thought it was an odd thing to say. Not because this statement was offered at all, but because it caused not a small amount of distaste among the other participants. The assumption here is that any African connections to European cultural and intellectual practices (for example, Enlightenment philosophy) has to be naturally and logically perceived as problematic. This is far from what I consider to be my own humane understanding of decolonization. While sympathetic to a movement that queries any harmful remnants of colonialism that marginalize African knowledge forms, I believe, and I think it is the point Táíwò persuasively makes, that Africa is not forever tethered to colonialism. To believe this and

zealously seek to decolonize every phenomenon that gestures at a European connection is to undermine African agency. But I did understand the historical processes that anchored such an outburst in that seminar, for it was expressed by a post-Apartheid subject who still has to confront the tragic legacies of settler colonialism. Of course, decolonizing frameworks are not targeted against white people, many of whom are allies that work to upend structures of systemic racism, but even white colleagues themselves must not be put, or should not put themselves, in a position that bids them to a performative solidarity that lacks any ethical compass. An ethical decolonization is not exclusionary and resists performativity. It is, as the Maori scholar Linda Tuhiwai Smith said, a project of reclamation that centers non-Western theoretical paradigms and favors indigenous ways of knowing and discovering. For Smith, decolonization "does not mean . . . a total rejection of all theory or research or Western knowledge . . . it is about centering our concerns and world views and then coming to know and understand theory and research from our own perspectives and for our own purposes" (*Decolonizing Methodologies: Research and Indigenous Peoples* [Dunedin: University of Otago Press, 1999], 39). Having said this, it is crucial not to confuse decolonization with decoloniality. Explaining the persistent Eurocentric structures that make it possible for colonial powers to dictate social relations along hierarchical lines that converge on the privileges of "Whiteness," Aníbal Quijano frames coloniality "the emergence of a Euro-centered capitalist colonial/modern world power that is still with us" (218). This ideological iteration of an unending colonial legacy in ex-colonial societies calls for a decolonial paradigm that seeks epistemic freedom from the European epistemologies that formed the cultural and ideological base of economic domination of native population. Aside from its tendency to invoke a utopian precolonial order and the fact that it is mostly based on the contradictions of capitalist modernity, a decolonial framework remains important in settler-colonialist contexts, unlike most parts of Africa that did not experience that strain of colonialism. An understanding of colonialism as legally ended in many parts of the world does not refute its ideological continuation, as most decolonial scholars argue. Instead of positing any reductive binary between the two, decoloniality has to be seen as most relevant to settler colonialism. Its cooptation into other contexts that didn't experience this means an uncritical ubiquity that is the basis for its superficiality and diminishing epistemic value. See Aníbal Quijano, "Coloniality of Power and Eurocentrism in Latin America," *International Sociology* 15, no. 2 (2000): 215–32.

22. Mũkoma wa Ngũgĩ, "This Essay on Ngugi Is So Asinine," Facebook, October 16, 2019, https://www.facebook.com/Mũkoma waNgũgĩ/posts/

pfbid0PLNkNcTYj737dwf9qtZVxBy2KJ71wxVZLsfZsvsmtqFg7hJhk2MvBRRGhEtgXQ53l.

23. Before proceeding to offer a list of past winners, he concludes: “The Nobel literature prize should in reality be called the Nobel Prize for European Literature and Occasional Other Friends Prize.” Mũkoma wa Ngũgĩ, “Since 1901 Only 5 African Writers,” October 6, 2022, https://www.facebook.com/photo/?fbid=10158748970821767&set=a.10151308357971767.
24. In the introductory chapter, I cited Nigerian writer Carl Terver’s tweet about Romeo Oriogun, who won the 2022 Nigerian prize for poetry. Terver asked his followers online: “Did the NLNG Prize trend last night? I was asleep. Will the Nigerian literary space ever trend on Twitter when it’s not Chimamanda, or beef?” He then went on to suggest in the exchanges that followed that “our numbers, realistically, is [*sic*] too small to create a trend.” I mention this tweet again to reiterate the point about the power of social media numbers as a marker of literary influence and social prestige in digital literary networks, even if the point in Terver’s original tweet is this fundamental idea that Nigerian literature hardly comes up for conversation on social media if the focus is not on some kind of literary controversies involving famous authors like Adichie. Carl Terver, “Did the NLNG Prize Trend? I Was Asleep,” Twitter, October 15, 2022, https://twitter.com/carlterver/status/1581179627925831682.

Chapter 5. Thighs Fell Apart, Online Fan Fiction and Literary Friendships

1. Lọlá Shónẹ́yìn, “Funny Memory,” Twitter, April 21, 2020, https://mobile.twitter.com/lolaShoneyin/status/1252735158735835137.
2. Molara Wood, “I Posted My Short Story,” Twitter, April 26, 2020, https://mobile.twitter.com/molarawood/status/1254388357490237441.
3. Victor Ehikhamenor, “Krazitivity ‘Fights’ Were Actually Epic,” Twitter, April 26, 2020, https://mobile.twitter.com/victorsozaboy/status/1252925921386004480.
4. While rumors of fights and conflicts in Nigerian literary discourses are sometimes mostly fictional, there is both an underground and open public archive of anecdotes about imaginary conflicts between Achebe and Soyinka, as well as between Flora Nwanpa and Mabel Segun. What social functions these literary rumors and controversial stories have remains undertheorized, and it is one of the gaps I hope this book addresses. On the subject of rumors in African cultural studies, Grace Musila has powerfully reminded us how rumors serve as “a medium that contests the legitimacy of hegemonic ‘truths’ produced through modern institutions in Africa.” Hence, rumors have a functional value that enacts a dialectics with different regimes and versions of truth. See Grace A. Musila,

A Death Retold in Truth and Rumour: Kenya Britain and the Julie Ward Murder (Suffolk: James Currey, 2015), 28.

5. Petina Gappah, "'We Are Daring to Invent the Future'—the Generation That Rewrote Africa's Story," *Financial Times*, March 9, 2023, https://www.ft.com/content/e1fad84a-903e-44ec-b7c5-920e88a91eac.
6. The is the passage to which Edoro refers: "It had been early in the morning. The moon was shining. She was going to the stream to fetch water. Okonkwo's house was on the way to the stream. She went in and knocked at his door and he came out. Even in those days he was not a man of many words. He just carried her into his bed and in the darkness began to feel around her waist for the loose end of her cloth." Chinua Achebe, *Things Fall Apart* (New York: Anchor Books, 1959), 109.
7. In Taye's fan fiction of Nnedi Okorafor's *Lagoon*, the writer similarly reimagines the relationship between Adaora, one of the protagonists of the novel, and Ayodele, an alien emissary. The contrived sexual relationship between both characters, located in the private zones of same-sex desires, is of a speculative kind that essentially transgresses the heteronormative sexualities of Okorafor's novel, but this speculative logic is similar to what Taye does with her reading of Okonkwo and Ekwefi's sexual lives.
8. See also Stephanie Bosch Santana, "Exorcizing Afropolitanism: Binyavanga Wainaina Explains Why 'I Am a Pan-Africanist, Not an Afropolitan' at ASAUK 2012," Africa in Words, February 8, 2013, http://africainwords.com/2013/02/08/exorcizing-afropolitanism-binyavanga-wainaina-explains-why-i-am-a-pan-africanist-not-an-afropolitan-at-asauk-2012/; Emma Dabiri, "Why I Am Not an Afropolitan," Africa Is a Country, October 2, 2014, http://africasacountry.com/2014/01/why-im-not-an-afropolitan.
9. See Kiru Taye, "Thighs Fell Apart: 'Ikemefuna' (Episode 2)," *Brittle Paper*, September 17, 2020, https://brittlepaper.com/2020/09/thighs-fell-apart-ikemefuna-episode-2/.
10. Kiru Taye, "Achebe's *Things Fall Apart* Fan-Fiction Erotica: Thighs Fell Apart by Kiru Taye, *Brittle Paper* Exclusive," *Brittle Paper*, February 14, 2014, https://brittlepaper.com/2014/02/thighs-fell-kiru-taye-fall-fan-fiction-erotica/.
11. Didi Cheeka is a popular film critic from Nigeria. The website containing the response to Taye's work is now no longer available.
12. Kiru Taye, personal communication to the author, Twitter, April 29, 2023.
13. Taye, personal communication.
14. Adesokan's 2023 book draws on distinct but interrelated histories and spaces of textual forms and artistic assemblages to judge our understanding of aesthetics, textuality, and authorship, while Sacks's *Networked Poetics*, the most recent of the scholarship on African digital literatures, centers how digital media reconfigures southern African

poetry scene in Malawi, Zimbabwe, and South Africa. Akinwumi Adesokan, *Everything Is Sampled: Digital and Print Mediations in African Arts and Letters* (Bloomington: Indiana University Press), 33. Susanna Sacks, *Networked Poetics: African Poetry's Digital Turn* (Amherst: University of Massachusetts, 2024).

Conclusion

1. This point was made earlier with respect to Adichie, who, though a survivor of cancel culture, had people questioning the relevance of her work in the classroom because of her speech act. For Ngũgĩ, there appears to be a similar articulation of this sentiment in several tweets. A Jakarta-based book outlet, Transit Bookstore, posted that they would "be taking Ngũgĩ wa Thiong'o's books off of our shelves." Transit Bookstore, Twitter, March 2024, https://twitter.com/transitreads/status/1772389255282593871. Similarly, an Iraqi Theatre scholar Hadeel Abdelhameed wrote stridently: "Thank you Mukoma for sharing this fact about @NgugiWaThiongo_. I just cited him in one of my recent lectures in Iraq. His argument about 'liberating' nations from the 'cage' of colonialism does not resonate with my work anymore. Liberating nations starts from respecting women." Hadeel Abdelhameed, Twitter, March 12, 2024, https://twitter.com/HadeelAbdlhamed/status/1767693599435874625. In the current era of social media, though, individuals who have become the subject of cancel culture often retain their predigital cultural capital and offline platforms and publics. This continuing widespread support effectively renders them immune to complete cancelation in the truest sense of the term. Structured by power dynamics, there is an arbitrariness to the operating rules governing cancel culture that makes certain people cancelable while others continue to be socially accepted despite egregious moral behavior.
2. The online platform *Brittle Paper* has helped to circulate the works and perspectives of different queer writers in Nigerian literature in the last several years. To mark the platform's seventh anniversary in 2017, *Brittle Paper* organized a couple of conversations on Facebook, with one of these having the theme "Un-Silencing Queer Nigeria: The Language of Emotional Truth" and featuring Romeo Oriogun, Arinze Ifeakandu, Kelechi Njoku, and Laura Ahmed, all of whom discussed queerness in Nigerian literature. Scholarly works such as Adenekan's argument in *African Literature in The Digital Age* show that African queer subjectivities have to be seen as fundamental to theorizing African writing on the internet. See also Noah Tsika, *Pink 2.0: Encoding Queer Cinema on the Internet* (Bloomington: Indiana University Press, 2016); Keguro Macharia, *Frottage: Frictions of Intimacy across the Black Diaspora* (New York: New York University Press, 2019).

3. Akwaeke Emezi, "Oh, That Applies to Other African Writers," Twitter, April 7, 2021, https://twitter.com/azemezi/status/1379963419059716096.
4. Freud's Oedipal complex is a useful psychoanalytic framework for making sense of Adichie's brouhaha with both Emezi and Elnathan John. With both writers, the controversial proclamations of the more established Adichie and former mentor both in regard to transgender identity and the Caine Prize arguably produce a sensibility of denial that abandons Adichie's literary mentorship based on an Oedipal rivalry that is effected and exacerbated by a social media age of conviction and cancelation.
5. Akwaeke Emezi, "Adichie Threw Her TERF Tantrum in June," Twitter, 2021, https://twitter.com/azemezi/status/1435440483258535938.
6. Loretta Ross, "I'm a Black Feminist. I Think Call-Out Culture Is Toxic," *New York Times*, August 17, 2019, https://www.nytimes.com/2019/08/17/opinion/sunday/cancel-culture-call-out.html.

Bibliography

Abati, Rueben. 2012. "The Jonathan They Don't Know." *Vanguard*, August 26, 2012. https://www.vanguardngr.com/2012/08/the-jonathan-they-dont-know/.

Abdullahi, Denja. 2023. "Of Literature, Prizes and Their Biases." *The Nation*, October 15, 2023. https://thenationonlineng.net/of-literature-prizes-and-their-biases/.

Achebe, Chinua. 1959. *Things Fall Apart*. New York: Anchor Books.

———. 1965. "English and the African Writer." *Transition* 4, no. 18:27–30.

———. 1976. *Morning Yet on Creation Day: Essays*. New York: Anchor Books.

———. 1977. "An Image of Africa." *Massachusetts Review* 18, no. 4:782–94.

———. 1989. *Hopes and Impediments: Selected Essays*. New York: Doubleday.

———. 2012. *There Was a Country: A Memoir*. New York: Penguin.

Adéẹ̀kọ́, Adélékè. 2021. "Decolonization without a Linguistic Turn Is Like Drinking Sugar without Tea: Ọlábíyìí Babalọlá Joseph Yáì." *Journal of the African Literature Association* 15, no. 2:308–20.

Adejunmobi, Moradewun. 2020. "Abiola Irele and the Publicness of African Letters." *Journal of the African Literature Association* 14, no. 1:72–89.

Adekunle, Tiwaladeoluwa. 2016. "#CainePrize2016 | Heated Debate Sparked by Kola Tubosun's Review of Tope Folarin's Story." *Brittle Paper*, June 14, 2016. https://brittlepaper.

com/2016/06/caineprize2016-kola-tubusons-controversial-review-tope-folarins-genesis-sparks-debate/.

Adenekan, Shola. 2021. *African Literature in the Digital Age: Class and Sexual Politics in New Writing from Nigeria and Kenya.* Rochester: Boydell & Brewer.

Adenekan, Shola, and Helen Cousins. 2014. "Class Online: Representations of African Middle-Class." *Postcolonial Text* 9, no. 3:2–15.

Adenekan, Shola, et al. 2020. "Introduction to the Guest Issue: Digital Africas." *Postcolonial Text* 15, no. 3 and 4:1–19.

Adeoti, Gbemisola. 2003. "The Military in Nigerian Postcolonial Literature: An Overview." *Revista Alicantina de Estudios Ingleses* 16:1–45.

Adesanmi, Pius. 2001. *The Wayfarer and Other Poems.* Lagos: Oracle Books.

———. 2012. "Face Me, I Book You: Writing Africa's Agency in the Age of the Netizen." Pa Ikhide, April 22, 2012. https://xokigbo.com/2012/04/22/guest-blog-professor-pius-adesanmi-face-me-i-book-you-writing-africas-agency-in-the-age-of-the-netizen/.

———. 2019. "An Archaeology of Nigerian." *Nigerian Tribune,* March 10, 2019. https://tribuneonlineng.com/an-archaeology-of-nigeria/.

Adesanmi, Pius, and Chris Dunton. 2005. "Nigeria's Third Generation Writing: Historiography and Preliminary Theoretical Considerations." *English in Africa* 32, no. 1:7–19.

Adesokan, Akinwumi. 2012. "New African Writing and the Question of Audience." *Research in African Literatures* 43, no. 3:1–20.

———. 2017. "Biafra and Other Ghosts." Africa Is A Country, June 5, 2017. https://africasacountry.com/2017/06/biafra-and-other-ghosts.

———. 2023. *Everything Is Sampled: Digital and Print Mediations in African Arts and Letters.* Bloomington: Indiana University Press.

Adichie, Chimamanda Ngozi. 2009. "The Danger of a Single Story." Filmed July 2009, TED video. https://www.ted.com/talks/chimamanda_adichie_the_danger_of_a_single_story/transcript?language=en.

———. 2013. *Americanah.* New York: Alfred A. Knopf.

———. 2017. "*Channel 4 News*: Chimamanda Ngozi Adichie Interview." YouTube video, March 11, 2017. www.youtube.com/watch?v=KP1C7VXUfZQ&feature=youtu.be.

———. 2021. "It Is Obscene: A True Reflection in Three Parts." Chimamanda Adichie, June 15, 2021. https://www.chimamanda.com/news_items/it-is-obscene-a-true-reflection-in-three-parts/.

———. 2022a. "The Fragility of Truth." UCLouvian Honorary Doctorate Ceremony, April 28, 2022. https://uclouvain.be/en/discover/events/2022-honorary-doctorates-the-fragility-of-truth.html.

———. 2022b. “Freedom of Speech.” *BBC Radio 4: The Reith Lectures*. November 30, 2022. https://www.bbc.co.uk/programmes/p0dhrlhm.

Adorno, Theodor W. 2005. *Minima Moralia: Reflections from Damaged Life*. Trans. E.F.N Jephcott. London: Verso.

Ahmed, Sara. 2015. *The Cultural Politics of Emotion*. New York: Routledge.

Ajayi, Dami. 2021. “Yes, It Is Obscene, Ms Adichie, But. . . .” *Yaba Left Review*, July 21, 2021. https://yabaleftreview.com/yes-it-is-obscene-ms-adichie-but-dami-ajayi/.

Ajayi, Mary. 2016. “Of Kisses, of Sexual Predator, of Chijioke Amu-Nnadi.” 9jaFeminista, January 18, 2016. https://9jafeminista.wordpress.com/2016/01/18/of-kisses-of-sexual-predators-of-chijioke-amu-nnadi/.

Alatas, Syed Hussein. 1977. *Intellectuals in Developing Societies*. London: Franc Cass.

Alcoff, Linda. 1992. “The Problem of Speaking for Others.” *Cultural Critique* 20:5–32.

Allardice, Lisa. 2020. “Chimamanda Ngozi Adichie: ‘America under Trump Felt Like a Personal Loss.’” *Guardian*, November 14, 2020. https://www.theguardian.com/books/2020/nov/14/chimamanda-ngozi-adichie-america-under-trump-felt-like-a-personal-loss.

Alter, Alexandra, and Elizabeth A. Harris. 2023. “How Review-Bombing Can Tank a Book Before It’s Published.” *New York Times*, June 27, 2023. https://www.nytimes.com/2023/06/26/books/goodreads-review-bombing.html.

Amuke, Isaac Otidi. 2019. “Politics of Art: The Contradictions of Nigeria’s KABAFEST.” *Elephant*, October 24, 2019. https://www.theelephant.info/culture/2019/10/24/politics-of-art-the-contradictions-of-nigerias-kabafest/.

Anyaduba, Chigbo Arthur. 2021. *The Postcolonial African Genocide Novel: Quests for Meaningfulness*. Liverpool: Liverpool University Press.

Applebaum, Ann. 2021. “The New Puritans.” *Atlantic*, August 31, 2021. https://www.theatlantic.com/magazine/archive/2021/10/new-puritans-mob-justice-canceled/619818/.

Arendt, Hannah. 1951. *The Origins of Totalitarianism*. New York: Harcourt Brace Jovanovich.

Armstrong, Meg. 1996. “‘The Effects of Blackness’: Gender, Race, and the Sublime in Aesthetic Theories of Burke and Kant.” *Journal of Aesthetics and Art Criticism* 54, no. 3:224.

Attree, Lizzy. 2013. “The Caine Prize and Contemporary African Writing.” *Research in African Literatures* 44, no. 2:35–47.

Badim, Noah. 2022. “Meet Post: A Social Platform for Real People, Real News, and Civil Conversations.” *Post*, November 15, 2022. https://post.news/?fbclid=IwAR0t_1KMU_OKK7rAQD8EdW1sg6cu3cCNar77xQzr9774XnsemLrB_OECnTM. Website no longer available.

Bady, Aaron. 2013. “The Varieties of Blackness: An Interview with Chimamanda Ngozi Adichie.” *Boston Review*, July 10, 2013. https://bostonreview.net/fiction/

varieties-blackness.

Balasubramanyam, Rajeev. 2016. "The Nobel Committee Got It Wrong." *Washington Post*, October 22, 2016. https://www.washingtonpost.com/news/global-opinions/wp/2016/10/22/the-nobel-committee-got-it-wrong-ngugi-wa-thiongo-is-the-writer-the-world-needs-right-now/.

Baraka, Carey. 2020. "Intimations of an Ending—Carey Baraka on the Unspoken Demise of *Kwani?*, and the Death of a Dream." *Johannesburg Review of Books*, August 27, 2020. https://johannesburgreviewofbooks.com/2020/08/27/intimations-of-an-ending-carey-baraka-on-the-unspoken-demise-of-kwani-and-the-death-of-a-dream/.

Barber, Karin. 1987. "Popular Arts in Africa." *African Studies Review* 30, no. 3:1–78.

———. 1997. "Preliminary Notes on Audiences in Africa." *Africa* 67, no. 3:347–62.

———. 2007. *The Anthropology of Texts, Persons and Publics: Oral and Written Culture in Africa and Beyond.* Cambridge: Cambridge University Press.

Barthes, Roland. 1975. *The Pleasure of the Text.* New York: Hill and Wang.

Becker, Howard Saul. 1982. *Art Worlds.* Berkeley: University of California Press.

Beecroft, Alexander. 2015. *An Ecology of World Literature: From Antiquity to the Present Day.* London: Verso.

Benjamin, Ruha. 2019. *Race after Technology: Abolitionist Tools for the New Jim Code.* Cambridge: Polity Press.

Benson, Peter. 1986. *Black Orpheus, Transition, and Modern Cultural Awakening in Africa.* Oakland: University of California Press.

Berger, John. 2016. "'I Have to Turn This Prize against Itself'—John Berger on Accepting the Booker Prize for Fiction, 23 November 1972." Verso Books, November 4, 2016. https://www.versobooks.com/blogs/2317-i-have-to-turn-this-prize-against-itself-john-berger-on-accepting-the-booker-prize-for-fiction-23-november-1972.

Blyden, Edward W. 1994. *Christianity, Islam and the Negro Race.* Baltimore: Black Classic Press.

Boehmer, Elleke. 2009. "Achebe and His Influence in Some Contemporary African Writing." *Interventions* 11, no. 2:141–53.

Bolter, Jay David, and Richard Grusin. 2000. *Remediation: Understanding New Media.* Cambridge: MIT Press.

Bourdieu, Pierre. 1993. *The Field of Cultural Production.* Oxford: Polity Press.

Bourrier, Karen, and Mike Thelwall. 2020. "The Social Lives of Books: Reading Victorian Literature on Goodreads." *Journal of Cultural Analytics* 5, no 1:1–34.

Boyd, Danah. 2010. "Privacy and Publicity in the Context of Big Data." April 29, 2010. https://www.danah.org/papers/talks/2010/WWW2010.html.

Brock, André. 2020. *Distributed Blackness: African American Cybercultures.* New York

University Press.

Brouillette, Sarah. 2007. *Postcolonial Writers in the Global Literary Marketplace*. London: Palgrave Macmillan UK.

———. 2023. "Wattpad, Platform Capitalism, and the Feminization of Publishing Work." *Book History* 26, no. 2:419–38.

Brown, Wendy. 1995. *States of Injury: Power and Freedom in Late Modernity*. Princeton: Princeton University Press.

Buruma, Ian. 2023."Doing the Work: The Protestant Ethic and the Spirit of Wokeness." *Harper's Magazine*, July 2023. https://harpers.org/archive/2023/07/protestant-ethic-and-the-spirit-of-wokeness/.

Butler, Judith. 2024. *Who's Afraid of Gender?* New York: Farrar Straus and Giroux.

Cammett, John M. 1967. *Antonio Gramsci and the Origins of Italian Communism*. Stanford: Stanford University Press.

Carotenuto, Matt. 2017. "Nobel Prizes and Politics in Kenya." Africa Is a Country, October 8, 2017. https://africasacountry.com/2017/10/nobel-prizes-and-politics-in-kenya.

Castells, Manuel. 2015. *Networks of Outrage and Hope: Social Movements in the Internet Age*. Hoboken: John Wiley & Sons.

Certeau, Michel de. 1984. *The Practice of Everyday Life*. Trans. Steven F. Rendall. Berkeley: University of California Press.

Chakrabarty, Dipesh. 2008. *Provincializing Europe: Postcolonial Thought and Historical Difference*. Princeton: Princeton University Press.

Chandler, James. 1999. *England in 1819: The Politics of Literary Culture and the Case of Romantic Historicism*. Chicago: University of Chicago Press.

Chinweizu, Onwuchekwa Jemie, and Ihechukwu Madubuike. 1985. *Toward the Decolonization of African Literature: African Fiction and Poetry and Their Critics*. London: KPI.

Cho, Alexander. 2018. "Default Publicness: Queer Youth of Color, Social Media, and Being Outed by the Machine." *New Media & Society* 20, no. 9:3183–3200.

Clark, Meredith. 2020. "Drag Them: A Brief Etymology of So-Called 'Cancel Culture.'" *Communication and the Public* 5, no. 3–4:92.

Code, Jillianne. 2013. "Agency and Identity in Social Media." In *Digital Identity and Social Media*, ed. S. Warburton and S. Hatzipanagos, 37–57. Hershey: Information Science Reference.

Coetzee, Carli. 2018. "Unsettling the Air-Conditioned Room: Journal Work as Ethical Labour." *Journal of the African Literature Association* 12, no. 2:101–15.

———. 2021. "Academic Fakes." *Journal of African Cultural Studies* 33, no. 3:272–75.

Coleridge, Samuel Taylor. 2014. *Biographia Literaria*. Edited by Adam Roberts. Edinburgh:

Edinburgh University Press.

Conrad, Joseph, and Norman Page. 1995. *Joseph Conrad: Three Novels;* Heart of Darkness, The Secret Agent *and* The Shadow-Line. Basingstoke: Macmillan Press.

Couldry, Nick, and Ulises A. Mejias. 2019. *The Costs of Connection: How Data Is Colonizing Human Life and Appropriating It for Capitalism*. Stanford: Stanford University Press.

Cronin, Richard. 2010. *Paper Pellets: British Literary Culture After Waterloo*. Oxford: Oxford University Press.

Dabiri, Emma. 2014. "Why I'm Not an Afropolitan." Africa Is a Country, October 2, 2014. http://africasacountry.com/2014/01/why-im-not-an-afropolitan/.

Dahir, Abdi Latif. 2021. "The New Magazines and Journals Shaping Africa's Literary Scene." *New York Times*, July 17, 2021. https://www.nytimes.com/2021/07/17/world/africa/lolwe-doek-africa-literary-magazines.html.

Davis, Caroline. 2021. *African Literature and the CIA: Networks of Authorship and Publishing*. Cambridge: Cambridge University Press.

Dean, Jodi. 2003. "Why the Net Is Not a Public Sphere." *Constellations* 10, no. 1:95–112.

———. 2009. *Democracy and Other Neoliberal Fantasies: Communicative Capitalism and Left Politics*. Durham: Duke University Press.

De Kosnik, Abigail. 2015. "'Fifty Shades' and the Archive of Women's Culture." *Cinema Journal* 54, no. 3:116–25.

Denby, David. 1996. *Great Books*. New York: Simon and Schuster.

During, Simon. 2010. *The Cultural Studies Reader*. London: Routledge.

Edoro, Ainehi. 2014a. "Achebe's Things Fall Apart Fan-Fiction Erotica: Thighs Fell Apart' by Kiru Taye, *Brittle Paper Exclusive*." *Brittle Paper*, February 14, 2014. https://brittlepaper.com/2014/02/thighs-fell-kiru-taye-fall-fan-fiction-erotica/.

———2014b. "African Fictional Characters in Bed—Okonkwo Is Less Talk, More Action." *Brittle Paper*, February 14, 2014. https://brittlepaper.com/2014/02/african-fictional-characters-bed-okonkwo/.

———. 2014c. "Drama Alert: 'Shine Your Fucking Eyes'; Read Binyavanga's 'Dear Caine Prize' Rant." *Brittle Paper*, October 11, 2014. https://brittlepaper.com/2014/10/binyavanga-dear-caine-prize-rant-1/.

———. 2014d. "Ikhide Versus Binyavanga: The Caine Prize Convo—Cainerversation—Continues." *Brittle Paper*, October 15, 2014. https://brittlepaper.com/2014/10/ikhide-ikheloa-binyavanga-caine-prize-cainerversation/.

———. 2015. "Wow . . . Adichie Gets VERY Candid." *Brittle Paper*, March 12, 2015. https://brittlepaper.com/2015/03/adichie-candid-elnathan-immoral/.

———. 2020. "Statement on the Departure of Brittle Paper's Former Deputy Editor." *Brittle*

Paper, April 15, 2020. https://brittlepaper.com/2020/04/statement-on-the-departure-of-brittle-papers-former-deputy-editor/.

Edoro-Glines, Ainehi. 2022. "Unruly Archives: Literary Form and the Social Media Imaginary." *ELH* 89, no. 2:523–46.

Eichhorn, Kate. 2019. *The End of Forgetting: Growing Up with Social Media.* Cambridge: Harvard University Press.

Ekeh, Peter P. 1975. "Colonialism and the Two Publics in Africa: A Theoretical Statement." *Comparative Studies in Society and History* 17, no. 1:91–112.

Ekotto, Frieda, and Kenneth W. Harrow. 2015. *Rethinking African Cultural Production.* Bloomington: Indiana University Press.

English, James F. 2005. *The Economy of Prestige: Prizes, Awards, and the Circulation of Cultural Value.* Cambridge: Harvard University Press.

English, James F., and John Frow. 2006. "Literary Authorship and Celebrity Culture." In *A Concise Companion to Contemporary British Fiction*, ed. James F. English, 39–57. Malden, MA: Blackwell.

Enkare Review Collective Team. 2018. "Statement on the Illegal Takeover of Enkare Review by Troy Onyango." *HapaKenya*, June 10, 2018. https://hapakenya.com/2018/06/10/statement-on-the-illegal-takeover-of-enkare-review-by-troy-onyango/.

Eze, Emmanuel Chukwudi. 1997. "The Color of Reason: The Idea of 'Race' in Kant's Anthropology." In *Postcolonial African Philosophy: A Reader*, ed. Emmanuel Chukwudi Eze, 103–40. Cambridge: Blackwell.

Fanon, Frantz. 1968. *The Wretched of the Earth.* New York: Grove Press.

Fear, William. 2023. "The Death of the Literary Feud: When Writers Become Fighters." *The Critic*, September 22, 2023. https://thecritic.co.uk/the-death-of-the-literary-feud/.

Fraser, Nancy. 1990. "Rethinking the Public Sphere: A Contribution to the Critique of Actually Existing Democracy." *Social Text* 25/26:56–80.

Frenkel, Ronit. 2008. "The Politics of Loss: Post-Colonial Pathos and Current Booker Prize-Nominated Texts from India and South Africa." *Scrutiny2: Issues in English Studies in Southern Africa* 13, no. 2:77–88.

Fyfe, Alexander. 2021. "'Reading and Writing . . . Loudly': Ikhide R. Ikheloa, Online Criticism, and African Literary Studies." *Social Dynamics* 47, no. 1:154–71.

Gadamer, Hans-Georg. 2004. *Truth and Method.* Trans. Joel Weinsheimer and Donald G Marshall. London: Continuum.

Gappah, Petina. 2023. "'We Are Daring to Invent the Future'—the Generation That Rewrote Africa's Story." *Financial Times*, March 9, 2023. https://www.ft.com/content/e1fad84a-903e-44ec-b7c5-920e88a91eac.

Gehrmann, Susanne. 2016. “Cosmopolitanism with African Roots: Afropolitanism’s Ambivalent Mobilities.” *Journal of African Cultural Studies* 28, no. 1:61–72.

Goldsmith, Meredith. 2016. “Of Publicity, Prizes, and Prestige: The Middle-Zone of the Marketplace in *Hudson River Bracketed.*” *American Literary Realism* 48, no. 3:232–50.

Goyal, Sana. 2020. “Playing with the Book: Namwali Serpell on the ‘Great Zambian Novel.’” *Wasafiri* 35, no. 1:42–47.

———. 2022. “Too Much Talking. We’ve Got Work To Do.” *Wasafiri*, March 12, 2022. https://www.wasafiri.org/article/too-much-talking-weve-got-work-to-do/.

Grady, Hugh, and Terence Hawkes. 2007. *Presentist Shakespeares*. London: Routledge.

Habila, Helon. 2013. “We Need New Names by NoViolet Bulawayo—Review.” *Guardian*, June 20, 2013. https://www.theguardian.com/books/2013/jun/20/need-new-names-bulawayo-review.

Harper’s Magazine. 2020. “A Letter on Justice and Open Debate. Harper’s Magazine.” July 7, 2020. https://harpers.org/a-letter-on-justice-and-open-debate/.

Herman, Edward S., and Noam Chomsky. 2002. *Manufacturing Consent the Political Economy of the Mass Media*. New York: Pantheon.

hooks, bell. 2014. “Beyoncé Is a Terrorist.” Genius, May 6, 2014. https://genius.com/Bell-hooks-beyonce-is-a-terrorist-annotated.

Hunt, Lynn. 2002. “Against Presentism.” *Perspectives on History*, May 1, 2002. https://www.historians.org/perspectives-article/against-presentism-may-2002/.

Huseyinzadegan, Dilek. 2018. “For What Can the Kantian Feminist Hope? Constructive Complicity in Appropriations of the Canon.” *Feminist Philosophy Quarterly* 4, no. 1.

Ibekwe, Nicholas. 2016. “Soyinka to Hold Private Funeral for Death of ‘Common Sense’ in Nigeria.” *Premium Times*, December 5, 2016. https://www.premiumtimesng.com/news/top-news/217112-soyinka-hold-private-funeral-death-common-sense-nigeria.

Iduma, Emmanuel. 2012. “Ikhide Ikheloa: People Take Me a Lot More Seriously Than I Am Willing to Take Myself.” *Bakwa*, August 18, 2012. https://bakwamagazine.com/2012/08/18/conversation-ikhide-ikheloa-people-take-me-a-lot-more-seriously-than-i-am-willing-to-take-myself/.

Ikheloa, Ikhide. 2011. “Walks with Julius: Teju Cole’s ‘Open City.’” Pa Ikhide, November 12, 2011. https://xokigbo.com/2011/11/12/walks-with-julius-teju-cole%E2%80%99s-%E2%80%98open-city%E2%80%99/.

———. 2012a. “Teju Cole, Palimpsests, and Sebald’s Ghost.” Pa Ikhide, September 23, 2012. https://xokigbo.com/2012/09/23/teju-cole-palimpsests-and-sebalds-ghost/.

———. 2012b. “The 2011 Caine Prize: How Not to Write about Africa.” Pa Ikhide, September 11, 2012. https://xokigbo.com/2012/03/11/

the-2011-caine-prize-how-not-to-write-about-africa/.

———. 2012c. "Walks with Julius: Teju Cole's 'Open City.'" Pa Ikhide, November 12, 2012, https://archive.ph/0atkY.

———. 2017. "El-Rufai Invites Writers to His Book Festival in July." Medium, June 11, 2017. https://medium.com/@ikhide/el-rufai-invites-writers-to-his-book-festival-in-july-of-oppressors-and-messiahs-the-distinction-c137729a8aa9.

Ipadeola, Tade. 2012. "Rotimi Babatunde's Bombay's Republic: Of Similitude and Verisimilitude." *African Writer Magazine*, August 1, 2012. https://www.africanwriter.com/rotimi-babatundes-bombays-republic-of-similitude-and-verisimilitude/.

Irele, Abiola. 1991. "The African Scholar." *Transition* 51:56–69.

Irewole, Eva. 2022. "Drama, Confusion as Oscars Academy Orders Nigerian Selection Committee to Revote." *Culture Newspaper*, October 15, 2022. https://www.theculturenewspaper.com/drama-confusion-as-oscars-academy-orders-nigerian-selection-committee-to-revote/.

Jaji, Tsitsi. 2020. "Our Readers Write: Mediating African Poetry's Audiences." *Research in African Literatures* 51, no. 1:70–93.

James Currey Society. 2022. "Ikhide R. Ikheloa to Receive James Currey Lifetime Achievement Award." https://jamescurreysociety.co.uk/blog/ikhide-r-ikheloa-to-receive-james-currey-lifetime-achievement-award-in-literary-criticism. Website no longer available.

Jamison, Anne. 2013. *Fic: Why Fanfiction Is Taking over the World.* Dallas: BenBella Books, Inc.

Jassanoff, Sheyla, ed. 2004. *States of Knowledge: The Co-Production of Science and Social Order.* New York: Routledge.

Jenkins, Henry. 1992. *Textual Poachers: Television Fans and Participatory Culture.* New York: Routledge.

———. 2005. "Star Trek Rerun, Reread, Rewritten: Fan Writing as Textual Poaching." In *Popular Culture: A Reader*, ed. Raiford Guins and Omayra Zaragoza, 249–63. London: Sage Publications.

Jeyifo, Biodun. 2013. "First There Was a Country; Then There Wasn't: Reflections on Achebe's New Book." *Journal of Asian and African Studies* 48, no. 6:683–97.

———. 2018. "English Is an African Language—Ka Dupe! [for and against Ngũgĩ]." *Journal of African Cultural Studies* 30, no. 2:133–47.

John, Elnathan. 2013. "The Consequences of Loving Ngozi." Elnathan John—The Dark Corner, July 15, 2013. https://web.archive.org/web/20130720222425/https://elnathanjohn.blogspot.com/2013/07/the-consequences-of-loving-ngozi.html?m=0.

Jones, Bethan. 2014. "Fifty Shades of Exploitation: Fan Labor and Fifty Shades of Grey." *Transformative Works and Cultures* 15:115–23.

Jones, Rebecca. 2011. "Sir Kazuo Ishiguro Warns of Young Authors Self-Censoring out of 'Fear.'" *BBC News*, March 1, 2011. https://www.bbc.com/news/entertainment-arts-56208347.

Kakanda, Gimba. 2017. "The KABAFEST Dilemma." Medium, July 5, 2017. https://medium.com/@gimbakakanda_37996/the-kabafest-dilemma-7303bcef1799.

Kant, Immanuel, and Robert B. Louden. 2009. *Anthropology from a Pragmatic Point of View.* Cambridge: Cambridge University Press.

Karppi, Tero, Lotta Kähkönen, Mona Mannevuo, Mari Pajala, and Tanja Sihvonen. 2016. "Affective Capitalism." *Ephemera: Theory and Politics in Organization* 16, no. 4:1–13.

Kemoli, Arthur, and David K. Mulwa. 1969. "The European Image of Africa and the African." *Busara* 2, no. 2:51–53.

Kiguru, Doseline. 2016a. "Literary Prizes, Writers' Organisations and Canon Formation in Africa." *African Studies* 75, no. 2:202–14.

———. 2016b. "Prizing African Literature: Creating a Literary Taste." *Social Dynamics* 42, no. 1:161–74.

———. 2022. "Scandals, Controversies and African Literary Prizes: Between Intertextuality and Plagiarism." In *Routledge Handbook of African Popular Culture*, ed. Grace Musila, 132–51. New York: Routledge.

Klein, Ezra. 2021. "Shame, Safety and Moving Beyond Cancel Culture." *The Ezra Klein Show*, podcast, April 27, 2021. https://www.nytimes.com/2021/04/27/opinion/ezra-klein-podcast-cancel-culture.html.

Kolbas, E. Dean. 2001. *Critical Theory and the Literary Canon*. Boulder: Westview.

Krishnan, Madhu. 2014. *Contemporary African Literature in English: Global Locations, Postcolonial Identifications*. Basingstoke: Palgrave Macmillan.

———. 2019. *Contingent Canons: African Literature and the Politics of Location*. Cambridge: Cambridge University Press.

Kukoyi, OluTimehin. 2021. "Your Power Ends Where Mine Begins: The Redeeming Freedom of Queerness." *Republic*, August 18, 2021. https://republic.com.ng/august-september-2021/redeeming-freedom-queerness/.

Kuntsman, Adi. 2012. "Introduction: Affective Fabrics of Digital Cultures." In *Digital Cultures and the Politics of Emotion*, ed. Athina Karatzogianni and Adi Kuntsman, 1–17. London: Palgrave Macmillan.

Kushner, Scott. 2015. "Comparative Non-Literature and Everyday Digital Textuality." The 2014–2015 Report on the State of the Discipline of Comparative Literature. https://stateofthediscipline.acla.org/entry/comparative-non-literature-and-everyday-digital-textuality-0.

Kuti Fela. 1972. "Roforofo Fight." *Roforofo Fight*. Jofabro.

Larkin, Brian. 2008. *Signal and Noise: Media, Infrastructure, and Urban Culture in Nigeria*. Durham: Duke University Press.

Lewis, Diane. 2004. "Understanding The Power of Fan Fiction for Young Authors." *Kliatt*, March 1, 2004.

Lewis, Rebecca, and Angèle Christin. 2022. "Platform Drama: Cancel Culture, Celebrity, and the Struggle for Accountability on YouTube." *New Media & Society* 24, no. 7:1632–1656.

Livingstone, Sonia. 2005. *Audience and Publics: When Cultural Engagement Matters for the Public Sphere*. Bristol: Intellect Books.

Long, Maebh. 2020. "Being Obotunde Ijimere and M. Lovori: Mapping Ulli Beier's Intercultural Hoaxes from Nigeria to Papua New Guinea." *Journal of Commonwealth Literature* 58, no. 2:293–307.

Macharia, Keguro. 2018. "Enkare, Patriarchal Power, Friends with Roses." *New Inquiry*, June 11, 2018. https://thenewinquiry.com/blog/enkare-patriarchal-power-friends-with-roses/.

———. 2019. *Frottage: Frictions of Intimacy across the Black Diaspora*. New York: New York University Press.

Marquez, Gabriel. 2016. "The Specter of the Nobel Prize." Trans. Z. Mahboob. *Ergo Magazine*, October 31, 2016. https://ergodotorg.wordpress.com/2016/10/31/the-spectre-of-the-nobel-prize/.

Marwick, Alice E., and Danah Boyd. 2011. "I Tweet Honestly I Tweet Passionately: Twitter Users Context Collapse and the Imagined Audience." *New Media & Society* 13, no. 1:114–33.

Massumi, Brian. 1995. "The Autonomy of Affect." *Cultural Critique* 31:83–109.

Matz, Jesse. 2017. *Lasting Impressions: The Legacies of Impressionism in Contemporary Culture*. New York: Columbia University Press.

May, Nikki. 2022. *Wahala: A Novel*. New York: Custom House.

Mazrui, Ali A. 2000. "Dr. Jekyll and Mr. Soyinka: The Strange Case of Nobel Schizophrenia." *West Africa Review* 1, no. 2.

Mbembe, Achille. 2001. *On the Postcolony*. Oakland: University of California Press.

Mbembe, Achille, and Bregtje van der Haak. 2015. "The Internet Is Afropolitan." *Chimurenga Chronic New Cartographies*, March 17, 2015. https://chimurengachronic.co.za/the-internet-is-afropolitan/.

Meyrowitz, Joshua. 1986. *No Sense of Place: The Impact of Electronic Media on Social Behavior*. Oxford: Oxford University Press.

Mignolo, Walter D. 2000. "The Many Faces of Cosmopolis: Border Thinking and Critical Cosmopolitanism." *Public Culture* 12, no. 3:721–48.

Mill, John Stuart. 1972. *Utilitarianism, on Liberty, Considerations on Representative Government*. London: Everyman.

Mills, Charles W. 2014. *The Racial Contract*. Ithaca: Cornell University Press.

Mittelman, James H. 2014. "A Better Intellectual Community Is Possible: Dialogues with Ali A. Mazrui." *African Studies Review* 57, no. 1:153–70.

Mogami, Gaamangwe Joy. 2018. "A Brief History of Enkare Review: A Dialogue with Carey Baraka." *Africa in Dialogue*, May 7, 2018. https://africaindialogue.com/2018/05/07/a-brief-history-of-enkare-review-a-dialogue-with-carey-baraka/.

Moretti, Franco. 2005. *Signs Taken for Wonders: On the Sociology of Literary Forms*. London: Verso.

Mosseri, Adam. 2021. "Shedding More Light on How Instagram Works." Instagram. https://about.instagram.com/blog/announcements/shedding-more-light-on-how-instagram-works.

Mouffe, Chantal, 2005. *On the Political*. New York: Routledge.

Mudimbe, V. Y. 2013. "Reading There Was a Country: A Personal History of Biafra." *Journal of Asian and African Studies* 48, no. 6:671–82.

Mühlhoff, Rainer. 2020. "Human-Aided Artificial Intelligence: Or, How to Run Large Computations in Human Brains? Toward a Media Sociology of Machine Learning." *New Media & Society* 22, no. 10:1868–84.

Murphy, Peter T. 1992. "Impersonation and Authorship in Romantic Britain." *ELH* 59, no. 3:625–49.

Murray, Simone. 2018. *The Digital Literary Sphere: Reading, Writing and Selling Books in the Internet Era*. Baltimore: Johns Hopkins University Press.

Musila, Grace A. 2012. "Writing History's Silences: Interview with Parselelo Kantai." *Kunapipi* 34, no. 1:71–80.

———. 2014. "Archives of the Present in Parselelo Kantai's Writing." In *Popular Culture in Africa: The Episteme of the Everyday*, ed. Stephanie Newell and Onookome Okome, 244–65. New York: Routledge.

———. 2015. *A Death Retold in Truth and Rumour: Kenya Britain and the Julie Ward Murder*. Suffolk: James Currey.

———. 2016a. "Lot's Wife Syndrome and Double Publics in South Africa." *PMLA* 131 no. 5:1452–61.

———. 2016b. "Part-Time Africans Europolitans and 'Africa Lite.'" *Journal of African Cultural Studies* 28, no. 1:109–13.

———. 2018. "Chimamanda Adichie: The Daughter of Postcolonial Theory." *Aljazeera*, February 4, 2018. https://www.aljazeera.com/opinions/2018/2/4/chimamanda-adichie-the-daughter-of-postcolonial-theory.

Nechushtai, Efrat, and Seth C. Lewis. 2019. "What Kind of News Gatekeepers Do We Want

Machines to Be? Filter Bubbles Fragmentation and the Normative Dimensions of Algorithmic Recommendations." *Computers in Human Behavior* 90 (January): 298–307.

Nesbitt-Ahmed, Zahrah. 2017. "Reclaiming African Literature in the Digital Age: An Exploration of Online Literary Platforms." *Critical African Studies* 9, no. 3:377–90.

Newell, Stephanie. 2001. "'Paracolonial' Networks: Some Speculations on Local Readerships in Colonial West Africa." *Interventions* 3, no. 3:336–54.

Newell, Stephanie, and Onookome Okome. 2014. "Introduction: Popular Culture in Africa; The Episteme of the Everyday." In *Popular Culture in Africa: The Episteme of the Everyday*, ed. Stephanie Newell and Onookome Okome, 1–23. New York: Routledge.

Nichols, Thomas M. 2017. *The Death of Expertise: The Campaign against Established Knowledge and Why It Matters.* New York: Oxford University Press.

Nikuze, Jean Pierre. 2019. "The Reading Habits of Ngũgĩ wa Thiong'o." Africa Is a Country, October 15, 2019. https://africasacountry.com/2019/10/the-reading-habits-of-ngugi-wa-thiongo.

Nnodim, Rita. 2002. "Ewi-Yoruba Neotraditional Media Poetry: The Poetics of a Genre." PhD diss., University of Birmingham.

Noble, Safiya Umoja. 2018. *Algorithms of Oppression: How Search Engines Reinforce Racism.* New York: New York University Press.

Norris, Pippa. 2020. "Closed Minds? Is a 'Cancel Culture' Stifling Academic Freedom and Intellectual Debate in Political Science?" HKS Working Paper. No. RWP20-025. https://ssrn.com/abstract=3671026.

Norton, Anne. 1995. "Heart of Darkness: Africa and African Americans in the Writings of Hannah Arendt." In *Feminist Interpretations of Hannah Arendt*, ed. Bonnie Honig, 247–61. University Park: Pennsylvania State University Press.

Nussbaum, Martha C. 2003. *Upheavals of Thought: The Intelligence of Emotions.* Cambridge: Cambridge University Press.

———. 2016. *Anger and Forgiveness: Resentment, Generosity, Justice.* Oxford: Oxford University Press.

Obadare, Ebenezer. 2016. *Humor, Silence, and Civil Society in Nigeria.* Rochester: Boydell & Brewer.

———. 2022. *Pastoral Power, Clerical State.* Notre Dame: University of Notre Dame Press.

Obi-Young, Otosirieze. 2018. "Brittle Paper Position." *Brittle Paper*, June 10, 2018. https://brittlepaper.com/2018/06/regarding-erasure-and-enkare-review/.

———. 2019. "Enkare Review Faces Backlash Over Graphic Short Story Comparing Pedophilia to Queerness." *Brittle Paper*, January 30, 2019. https://brittlepaper.com/2019/01/enkare-review-faces-backlash-over-graphic-short-story-comparing-paedophilia-to-queerness/.

Ochiagha, Terry. 2015. *Achebe and Friends at Umuahia: The Making of a Literary Elite*. Rochester: Boydell & Brewer.

Ochonu, Moses. 2011. "Dealing with The El-Rufai Nuisance by Moses Ochonu." *Sahara Reporters*, August, 17, 2011. https://saharareporters.com/2011/08/17/dealing-el-rufai-nuisance-moses-ochonu.

Odell, Jenny. 2020. *How to Do Nothing: Resisting the Attention Economy*. Brooklyn: Melville House.

Odhiambo, Tom. 2012. "*Kwani?* and the Imaginations around Re-invention of Art and Culture in Kenya." In *Rethinking East African Literary and Intellectual Landscapes*, ed. James Ogude, Grace A. Musila, and Dina Ligaga, 23–37. Trenton: Africa World Press.

Okome, Onookome. 2007. "Nollywood: Spectatorship, Audience and the Sites of Consumption." *Postcolonial Text* 3, no. 2:1–21.

Okot Bitek, Otoniya J. 2022. *A Is for Acholi*. Hamilton: Buckrider.

Okri, Ben. 2012. Introduction to *Weep Not Child*, by Ngũgĩ Wa Thiong'o, ix–xv. New York: Penguin Books.

Olaniyan, Tejumola. 2016. "ALA 2014 Presidential Address. Johannesburg, South Africa." *Journal of the African Literature Association* 10, no. 1:3–8.

O'Neil, Cathy. 2022. *The Shame Machine: Who Profits in the New Age of Humiliation*. New York: Crown.

Osborn, J. R., and Neil Jordan. 2023. "Special Issue on Marechera: Neil Jordan on Dambudzo Marechera." Special issue, *Hong Kong Review of Books*, August 3, 2023. https://hkrbooks.com/2023/08/03/special-issue-on-marechera-neil-jordan-on-dambudzo-marechera/.

Osofisan, Femi. 2008. "Wounded Eros and Cantillating Cupids." In *Outliers: Theorizing (Homo) Eroticism in Africa; A Collection of Essays and Creative Work on Sexuality in Africa*, 64–78. New York: IRN-Africa.

Ouma, Christopher, and Madhu Krishnan. 2021. "Small Magazines in Africa: Ecologies and Genealogies." *Social Dynamics* 47, no. 2:193–209.

Özkırımlı, Umut. 2023. *Canceled: The Left Way Back from Woke*. Cambridge: Polity Press.

Pahl, Miriam. 2016. "Afropolitanism as Critical Consciousness: Chimamanda Ngozi Adichie's and Teju Cole's Internet Presence." *Journal of African Cultural Studies* 28, no.1: 73–87.

Palmer, Eustace. 1972. *An Introduction to the African Novel*. New York: Africana.

Papacharissi, Zizi. 2015. *Affective Publics*. New York: Oxford University Press.

Parkes, Frank Kobina. 1965. *Songs from the Wilderness*. London: University of London Press.

Pasquale, Frank. 2015. *The Black Box Society: The Secret Algorithms That Control Money and Information*. Cambridge: Harvard University Press.

Phillips, Caryl. 2003. "Out of Africa." *Guardian*, February 22, 2003. https://www.theguardian.

com/books/2003/feb/22/classics.chinuaachebe.

Prensky, Marc. 2001. “Digital Natives, Digital Immigrants Part 1.” *On the Horizon* 9, no. 5:1–6.

Pucherová, Dobrota. 2012. “‘A Continent Learns to Tell Its Story at Last’: Notes on the Caine Prize.” *Journal of Postcolonial Writing* 48, no. 1:13–25.

Quayson, Ato. 2003. *Calibrations: Reading for the Social.* Minneapolis: University of Minnesota Press.

———. 2007. *Aesthetic Nervousness: Disability and the Crisis of Representation.* New York: Columbia University Press.

———. 2013. “I Can, Therefore I Shall: Identifications from the Novel to Facebook.” *Arcade*, December 3, 2013. https://shc.stanford.edu/arcade/interventions/i-can-therefore-i-shall-identifications-novel-facebook.

Quijano, Aníbal. 2000. “Coloniality of Power and Eurocentrism in Latin America.” *International Sociology* 15, no. 2:215–32.

Rabinbach, Anson. 1992. *The Human Motor: Energy, Fatigue, and the Origins of Modernity.* Oakland: University of California Press.

Rauch, Jonathan. 2021. *The Constitution of Knowledge: A Defense of Truth.* Washington, D.C.: Brookings Institution Press.

Rorty, Richard. 1984. “The Historiography of Philosophy: Four Genres.” *Philosophy in History* 67:266.

Ross, Loretta. 2019. “I’m a Black Feminist. I Think Call-Out Culture Is Toxic.” *New York Times*, August 17, 2019. https://www.nytimes.com/2019/08/17/opinion/sunday/cancel-culture-call-out.html.

Ross, Stephen. 2004. *Conrad and Empire.* Columbia: University of Missouri Press.

Sacks, Susanna. 2024. *Networked Poetics: African Poetry’s Digital Turn.* Amherst: University of Massachusetts.

Sacks, Susanna, and Sara Brouillette. 2023. “Introduction: Reading with Algorithms.” *Post45*, December 8, 2023. https://post45.org/2023/12/introduction-reading-with-algorithms.

Said, Edward W. 1993. *Culture and Imperialism.* New York: Knopf.

———. 2002. “The Public Role of Writers and Intellectuals.” In *The Public Intellectual*, ed. Helen Small, 19–39. Oxford: Blackwell Publishers.

Santana, Stephanie Bosch. 2013. “Exorcizing Afropolitanism: Binyavanga Wainaina Explains Why ‘I Am a Pan-Africanist, Not an Afropolitan’ at ASAUK 2012.” Africa in Words, February 8, 2013. http://africainwords.com/2013/02/08/exorcizing-afropolitanism-binyavanga-wainaina-explains-why-i-am-a-pan-africanist-not-an-afropolitan-at-asauk-2012/.

———. 2018. “From Nation to Network: Blog and Facebook Fiction from Southern Africa.”

Research in African Literatures 49, no. 1:187–208.

———. 2019. "The Story Club: African Literary Networks Offline." In *Routledge Handbook of African Literature*, ed. Moradewun Adejunmobi and Carli Coetzee, 385–98. Abingdon: Routledge.

Sarr, Mohamed Mbougar, and Lara Vergnaud. 2023. *The Most Secret Memory of Men*. New York: Other Press.

Seaver, Nick. 2022. *Computing Taste: Algorithms and the Makers of Music Recommendation*. Chicago: University of Chicago Press.

Serpell, Namwali. 2015. "Zambian Writer Namwali Serpell to Share Caine Prize Money." *BBC News*, July 7, 2015. https://www.bbc.com/news/world-africa-33424103.

Shringarpure, Bhakti. 2021. "But, First We'll Take This W." Africa Is a Country, October 8, 2021. https://africasacountry.com/2021/10/but-first-well-take-this-w.

Siles, Ignacio. 2023. *Living with Algorithms: Agency and User Culture in Costa Rica*. Cambridge: MIT Press.

Singh, Frances B. 1978. "The Colonialistic Bias of Heart of Darkness." *Conradiana* 10, no. 1:52.

Smith, Linda Tuhiwai. 1999. *Decolonizing Methodologies: Research and Indigenous Peoples*. Dunedin: University of Otago Press.

Snorton, C. Riley. 2020. "Black Studies at UChicago: An Interview." Department of English Language and Literature, University of Chicago, https://english.uchicago.edu/black-studies-uchicago-interview.

Snyder, Emile. 1984. "Strength and Growing Pains in the Life of a Young Association." *ALA Bulletin* 10, no. 4:11.

Soyinka, Wole. 1996. *The Open Sore of a Continent: A Personal Narrative of the Nigerian Crisis*. New York: Oxford University Press.

———. 2000. "The Problem with You, Ali Mazrui! Response to Ali's Millennial Conclusion." *West Africa Review* 1, no. 2.

———. 2006. *You Must Set Forth at Dawn: A Memoir*. New York: Random House.

———. 2020. "For Me, It Is Humanity First—Wole Soyinka." *TheNEWS Magazine*, December 29, 2020. https://thenewsnigeria.com.ng/2020/12/29/for-me-it-is-humanity-first-a-conversation-with-wole-soyinka/.

Srnicek, Nick. 2020. *Platform Capitalism*. Cambridge: Polity Press.

Stern, Alexander. 2021. "Opinion Fetishism: Can We Escape the Reductio Ad Tweetum?" *Hedgehog Review: Critical Reflections on Contemporary Culture*. https://hedgehogreview.com/web-features/thr/posts/opinion-fetishism.

Stern, Kristen. 2019. "Plagiarism, Intertextuality, and the Same Old Story: The Caine Prize Controversy Is Not Original." Africa in Words, October 28, 2019. https://africainwords.

com/2019/10/28/plagiarism-intertextuality-and-the-same-old-story-the-caine-prize-controversy-is-not-original/.

Strauhs, Doreen. 2013. *African Literary NGOs: Power Politics and Participation*. New York: Palgrave Macmillan.

Suhr-Sytsma, Nathan. 2018. "The Geography of Prestige: Prizes, Nigerian Writers, and World Literature." *ELH* 85, no. 4:1093–122.

———. 2021. "Reading for Lyric in the African Digital Litmag." *Social Dynamics* 47, no. 2:243–63.

Táíwò, Olúfẹ́mi. 2010. *How Colonialism Preempted Modernity in Africa*. Bloomington: Indiana University Press.

———. 2022. *Against Decolonisation: Taking African Agency Seriously*. London: Hurst & Company.

Thomas, Angela. 2006. "Fan Fiction Online: Engagement, Critical Response and Affective Play through Writing." *Australian Journal of Language and Literacy* 29, no.3:226–39.

Thomas, Dominic. 2002. *Nation-Building, Propaganda, and Literature in Francophone Africa*. Bloomington: Indiana University Press.

Tshuma, Novuyo. 2013. "Adichie and the Great Brouhaha—a Fine Line Between the Legitimacy of Hurt and Its Responsibility." *Saraba*, July 20, 2013, http://www.sarabamag.com/adichie-and-the-great-brouhaha-a-fine-line-between-the-legitimacy-of-hurt-and-its-responsibility/.

Tsika, Noah. 2016. *Pink 2.0: Encoding Queer Cinema on the Internet*. Bloomington: Indiana University Press.

Tsioulcas, Anastasia. 2021. "Chimamanda Ngozi Adichie Directs Fiery Essay at Former Student—and Cancel Culture." NPR, June 17, 2021. https://www.npr.org/2021/06/17/1007350665/chimamanda-ngozi-adichie-directs-fiery-essay-at-former-student-and-cancel-culture.

Tuck, Eve, and Wayne Yang. 2012. "Decolonization Is Not a Metaphor." *Decolonization: Indigeneity, Education and Society* 1:1–40.

Ubani, Alexander Thandi. 2018. "Brunel Shortlist 2018 Controversy: The Politics of Being Too Black." *Information Nigeria*, March 17, 2018. https://www.informationng.com/2018/03/brunel-shortlist-2018-controversy-the-politics-of-being-too-black.html.

Uimonen, Paula. 2020. "Decolonising Cosmopolitanism: An Anthropological Reading of Immanuel Kant and Kwame Nkrumah on the World as One." *Critique of Anthropology* 40, no. 1:81–101.

Umezurike, Uchechukwu Peter. 2020. "Self-Publishing in the Era of Military Rule in Nigeria, 1985–1999." *Journal of African Cultural Studies* 32, no. 2:212–30.

Utor, Florence. 2017. "KABAFEST 2017 . . . Taking Book Festival Train to Kaduna." *Guardian*, July 2, 2017. https://guardian.ng.

Verissimo, Jumoke. 2012. "Chinua Achebe Reflects on Biafra, but for Whom." Africa Is A Country, October 8, 2012. https://africasacountry.com/2012/10/chinua-achebe-reflects-on-biafra-but-for-whom.

Wainaina, Binyavanga. 2003. "Editorial." In *Kwani? 01*, ed. Binyavanga Wainaina. Nairobi: Kwani Trust.

———. 2011. *How to Write about Africa*. Nairobi: Kwani Trust.

Wallis, Kate. 2018. "Exchanges in Nairobi and Lagos: Mapping Literary Networks and World Literary Space." *Research in African Literatures* 49, no. 1:163–86.

wa Ngũgĩ, Mũkoma. 2018. *The Rise of the African Novel: Politics of Language Identity and Ownership*. Ann Arbor: University of Michigan Press.

Warzel, Charlie. 2021. "'It's Not Cancel Culture—It's a Platform Failure.' Adventures in Context Collapse." Galaxy Brain. https://warzel.substack.com/p/its-not-cancel-culture-its-a-platform.

wa Thiong'o, Ngũgĩ. 1986. *Decolonizing the Mind: The Politics of Language in African Literature*. Rochester: Boydell & Brewer.

———. 2012. *Globalectics: Theory and the Politics of Knowing*. New York: Columbia University Press.

Watts, Cedric. 1983. "'A Bloody Racist': About Achebe's View of Conrad." *The Yearbook of English Studies* 13:196–209.

Wheatley, Kim. 2016. *Romantic Feuds: Transcending the 'Age of Personality.'* London: Routledge.

Williams, Raymond. 1978. *Marxism and Literature*. Oxford: Oxford University Press.

Wiredu, Kwasi. 2002. "Conceptual Decolonization as an Imperative in Contemporary African Philosophy: Some Personal Reflections." *Rue Descartes* 2:53–64.

Wolff, Robert Paul, Barrington Moore Jr., and Herbert Marcuse. 1969. *Repressive Tolerance: A Critique of Pure Tolerance*. Boston: Beacon Press.

Yékú, James. 2020. "Deference to Paper: Textuality, Materiality, and Literary Digital Humanities in Africa." *Digital Studies / Le Champ Numérique* 10, no. 1:1–28.

———. 2021. "In Praise of Ostentation: Social Class in Lagos and the Aesthetics of Nollywood's Owambe Genres." *African Studies* 80, no. 3–4:434–50.

———. 2022a. *Cultural Netizenship: Social Media, Popular Culture, and Performance in Nigeria*. Bloomington: Indiana University Press.

———. 2022b. "Digital African Literatures and the Coloniality of Data." *Cambridge Journal of Postcolonial Literary Inquiry* 9, no. 3:381–98.

Zabus, Chantal. 2021. "Outing Africa: On Sexualities, Gender, and Transgender in African

Literatures." In *A Companion to African Literatures*, ed. Olakunle George, 381–98. Hoboken: John Wiley.

Zvomuya, Percy. 2012. "The Tough Alchemy of Ben Okri." *Mail and Guardian*, September 21–27, 2012. https://mg.co.za/article/2012-09-21-the-tough-alchemy-of-ben-okri.

Index